Critical Reflections on China's Belt & Road Initiative

Alan Chong • Quang Minh Pham
Editors

Critical Reflections on China's Belt & Road Initiative

palgrave
macmillan

Editors
Alan Chong
Centre for Multilateralism Studies
S. Rajaratnam School of
International Studies
Nanyang Technological University
Singapore, Singapore

Quang Minh Pham
University of Social Sciences
and Humanities
Vietnam National University, Hanoi
Hanoi, Vietnam

ISBN 978-981-13-2097-2   ISBN 978-981-13-2098-9   (eBook)
https://doi.org/10.1007/978-981-13-2098-9

Cover illustration: © Tahreer Photography / Getty Images

This Palgrave Macmillan imprint is published by the registered company Springer Nature
Singapore Pte Ltd.
The registered company address is: 152 Beach Road, #21-01/04 Gateway East, Singapore
189721, Singapore

ACKNOWLEDGEMENTS

China's Belt and Road Initiative (BRI) might potentially prove to be the truly defining development of the 'Pacific Century'. Like the Cold War and the rise of the East Asian 'tiger economies' before it, this vision has the potential to displace power as well as potentially generate new forms of Asian community and development. This book's purpose originated with the late L. H. M. (Lily) Ling's energy and drive to rethink the Belt and Road as pathways for Asians to reconnect the way they did in distant centuries, before the advent of colonialism and modern industrial ideologies. The very diverse interventions in this volume reflect a rainbow of opinions ranging across several spectrums straddling discussions of philosophical harmony, to economic development, to hegemony and intra-Global South cooperation.

In this endeavour, the contributions of the following people and their organizations, where appropriate, have had a crucial input in bringing about the birth of this book.

Peter M. Girke, the country representative of the Konrad Adenauer Stiftung (KAS) in Vietnam and his team (especially Nguyen Minh Tuyen and Pham To Hang), were instrumental in providing funding for the participation of non-Vietnam-based professors in the October 2017 conference;

Nguyen Thi Thuy Trang and Pham Thu Huyen of the Faculty of International Studies, University of Social Sciences and Humanities, VNU-Hanoi, for their active organizational support during the conference;

Daniel Milton Garcia of the 2017–2018 Master of Science in Strategic Studies class in the S. Rajaratnam School of International Studies, Singapore, for research assistance in supplying up to date news reports from around the world in aid of the preparation of both Introduction and Conclusion;

Benjamin Low Quan Hui for his unstinting 'second pair of eyes' in scrutinizing the authors' edits of three additional chapters;

Anugya Chitransh for her meticulous 'third pair of eyes' in scrutinizing the authors' edits of three chapters in the middle sections;

Damien Yeo, currently a student at the University of Melbourne, for his energy in producing the first draft of the Index at short notice.

Last but not least, this volume is dedicated to the memory of our late friend, L. H. M. (Lily) Ling, whose inspiration to be curious about pan-Asian thought will always remain with us.

Singapore   Alan Chong
Hanoi   Quang Minh Pham
December 2019

CONTENTS

Notes on Contributors

Nguyen Thi Lan Anh is former Deputy Director General of the Institute for East Sea (South China Sea) Studies, and Associate Professor and Vice Dean of the International Law Faculty of the Diplomatic Academy of Vietnam. She is responsible for analyzing the legal aspects of the South China Sea disputes as well as other issues related to ocean law and policy. She frequently participates in and leads Vietnamese delegations to Track 2 and 1.5 conferences and workshops in Asia.

Alan Chong is Associate Professor and Acting Head, Centre for Multilateralism Studies, at the S. Rajaratnam School of International Studies (RSIS) in Singapore. He has published widely on the notion of soft power and the role of ideas in constructing Asian international relations. He has published widely in journals such as *Contemporary Southeast Asia, Review of International Studies,* and *Cambridge Review of International Affairs.*

Manochehr Dorraj is Professor of International Affairs in the Department of Political Science, Texas Christian University. He is the author, coauthor, editor, or coeditor of seven books and more than 100 refereed journal articles and book chapters. The translation of his publications has appeared in 16 languages. During 2015, he was a visiting professor at Shanghai International Studies University, and in the 2017–2018 academic year, he was a visiting scholar at Fudan University's Development Institute in Shanghai, China.

Le Hoang Giang is a research assistant at the University of Social Sciences and Humanities (USSH), Vietnam National University, Hanoi, where he graduated with a BA in International Studies in 2017. He is an MSc student of International Relations Theory at the London School of Economics and Political Science.

Mai Ngan Ha is a former research fellow of the Institute for East Sea (South China Sea) Studies of the Diplomatic Academy of Vietnam and officer of the Department of International Organizations, Ministry of Foreign Affairs of Vietnam. She majors in international law with a special focus on Law of the Sea and is engaged in analyzing legal aspects of issues pertaining to the South China Sea disputes.

Pham Thi Thu Huyen holds a PhD in Political Science and Master of Law from the University of Social Sciences and Humanities (USSH), Vietnam National University in Hanoi. At the USSH, she teaches undergraduate courses and implements research projects. She is the author of more than 25 research papers and a book.

L. H. M. (Lily) Ling was Professor of International Affairs, Julien J. Studley Programmes in International Affairs, at The New School in New York, USA. Sadly, she passed away before this book was published and hence her chapter in this volume stands as a posthumous symbol of her scholarship in a number of hybrid fields such as Asian Studies and International Relations (IR). She is widely remembered as a pioneer of post-colonial and feminist approaches to IR, fields that have gained rapid momentum over the last decade.

Quang Minh Pham is Professor of History and Politics at the University of Social Sciences and Humanities (USSH), Vietnam National University, Hanoi. After receiving his PhD in Southeast Asian Studies from Humboldt University in Berlin, Germany in 2002, he became Deputy Dean, and then Dean of International Studies Faculty. He is Rector of USSH, VNU-Hanoi. He has published widely in Asian humanities and politics journals.

Toshiaki Tamaki is Professor in the Faculty of Economics, Kyoto Sangyo University, Japan. His major is economic history of early modern Europe. His interest has been shifting to European maritime expansion to Asia including the current issue of Asian world systems. He has published 16 books in Japanese and many articles in Japanese and English.

Ngo Tuan Thang is a lecturer at the Faculty of International Studies, University of Social Sciences and Humanities, Vietnam National University. His major is International Relations. His research interests include asymmetric international relationships, foreign policy of China, and China's relations with Southeast Asia.

Carlyle A. Thayer is Emeritus Professor, School of Humanities and Social Sciences, The University of New South Wales at the Australian Defence Force Academy, Canberra and Director of Thayer Consultancy, a registered small business in Australia that provides political analysis of current regional security issues and other research support to selected clients. He is a Southeast Asia regional specialist with a research focus on Vietnamese domestic politics and foreign policy.

Nguyen Thi Thanh Thuy is Associate Professor of Political Science and International Relations at the University of Social Sciences and Humanities in Hanoi. Thuy's academic activities consist of teaching undergraduate and graduate courses, implementing research projects, attending academic conferences and workshops, writing dozens of research papers, two books, and three book chapters. All of her academic work and publications focus on US foreign policy.

Nguyen Thi Thuy Trang is Lecturer in International Studies and the Vice Dean of the Faculty of International Studies in the University of Social Sciences and Humanities (USSH), Vietnam National University. She earned her master's degree in International Relations from Waseda University in Tokyo and holds a doctoral degree from USSH in Hanoi. Much of her work focuses on non-traditional security in Southeast Asia and international relations in the Asia-Pacific.

Trinh Van Dinh is the Deputy Director (Office for Research Affairs), at the University of Social Sciences and Humanities, Vietnam National University (VNU), and an expert on Vietnamese Studies, Chinese Studies, and scholarship on the Belt and Road Initiative. He is completing a research project on *Rationales and Practices for Evaluating the Role, Goals and Impacts of China's 21st-Century Silk Road System (2017–2019)*.

Shang-su Wu is a research fellow at the Regional Security Architecture Programme of the S. Rajaratnam School of International Studies (RSIS) in Singapore. His research interests cover military modernization, the

Taiwan Strait, and the railways of international relations. He has published in *The Pacific Review, Asian Survey, Contemporary Southeast Asia* and other journals. He has served as a volunteer in the Australian Railway Historical Society in Sydney and the Railway Cultural Society in Taiwan.

CHAPTER 1

Critical Perspectives from Outside China on the Belt and Road Initiative: An Introduction

Alan Chong and Quang Minh Pham

China's vision of invoking the ancient Silk Road to frame its inter-regional Belt and Road Initiative (BRI) opens up intellectual and political spaces for debating twenty-first century international order in Asia. However, what has emerged from President Xi Jinping's most elaborate articulation of the BRI is a top down process and one that envisions a distinct position for Chinese strategic leadership. Two large portions of Xi's speech at the

The authors wish to thank Daniel Milton Garcia of the 2017–2018 Master of Science in Strategic Studies class in the S. Rajaratnam School of International Studies, Singapore, for outstanding research assistance in preparing this chapter.

A. Chong (✉)
Centre for Multilateralism Studies, S. Rajaratnam School of International Studies, Nanyang Technological University, Singapore, Singapore
e-mail: iscschong@ntu.edu.sg

Q. M. Pham
University of Social Sciences and Humanities,
Vietnam National University, Hanoi, Hanoi, Vietnam
e-mail: minhpq@ussh.edu.vn

Belt and Road Forum for International Cooperation on 14 May 2017 bear this out. This first part establishes a less than subtle China-centred discourse on what the BRI means:

> In the autumn of 2013, respectively in Kazakhstan and Indonesia, I proposed the building of the Silk Road Economic Belt and the 21st Century Maritime Silk Road, which I call the Belt and Road Initiative. As a Chinese saying goes, "Peaches and plums do not speak, but they are so attractive that a path is formed below the trees." Four years on, over 100 countries and international organizations have supported and got involved in this initiative. Important resolutions passed by the UN General Assembly and Security Council contain reference to it. Thanks to our efforts, the vision of the Belt and Road Initiative is becoming a reality and bearing rich fruit.
>
> These [past] four years have seen deepened policy connectivity. I have said on many occasions that the pursuit of the Belt and Road Initiative is not meant to reinvent the wheel. Rather, it aims to complement the development strategies of countries involved by leveraging their comparative strengths. We have enhanced coordination with the policy initiatives of relevant countries, such as the Eurasian Economic Union of Russia, the Master Plan on ASEAN Connectivity, the Bright Road initiative of Kazakhstan, the Middle Corridor initiative of Turkey, the Development Road initiative of Mongolia, the Two Corridors, One Economic Circle initiative of Viet Nam, the Northern Powerhouse initiative of the UK and the Amber Road initiative of Poland. We are also promoting complementarity between China's development plan and those of Laos, Cambodia, Myanmar, Hungary and other countries. (Xi Jinping 2017)

Yet in the preamble of this speech, Xi honoured the memory of ancient Silk Road travellers such as Du Huan of China, Marco Polo of Italy and Ibn Battuta of Morocco. He neglected to note that these were independent individuals and in many cases, spiritually motivated ones. Moreover, sovereign states had not existed at that time. Xi then lauded the ancient Silk Road as manifesting the virtues of peace and cooperation, mutual learning, openness and inclusiveness and other win-win outcomes. This is a certainly positive note and a nod to 'history [as] our best teacher' (Xi Jinping 2017). In subsequent paragraphs, Xi went against this current by elaborating on people-to-people exchanges as an appendage of state-led efforts at forging harmonious relations on the BRI:

> These [past] four years have seen strengthened people-to-people connectivity. Friendship, which derives from close contact between the people, holds the key to sound state-to-state relations. Guided by the Silk Road spirit, we

the Belt and Road Initiative participating countries have pulled our efforts to build the educational Silk Road and the health Silk Road, and carried out cooperation in science, education, culture, health and people-to-people exchange. Such cooperation has helped lay a solid popular and social foundation for pursuing the Belt and Road Initiative. Every year, the Chinese government provides 10,000 government scholarships to the relevant countries. China's local governments have also set up special Silk Road scholarships to encourage international cultural and educational exchanges. Projects of people-to-people cooperation such as Silk Road culture year, tourism year, art festival, film and TV project, seminar and think tank dialogue are flourishing. These interactions have brought our people increasingly closer.

These fruitful outcomes show that the Belt and Road Initiative responds to the trend of the times, conforms to the law of development, and meets the people's interests. It surely has broad prospects. (Xi Jinping 2017)

There is a built-in irony to all this. People-to-people relations should ideally be unforced and even spontaneous. But the state—specifically the Chinese state—has to count the quality of social interactions in terms of the volume of scholarships, numbers of exchanges, tourism events, 'culture year' and art festivals, and so forth. In short, this is bureaucratic framing of the twenty-first century Silk Road that detracts from the latter's historical precedent.

Understandably, the discourse of the BRI today needs to accommodate significant aspects of modernity thriving amongst the states and societies partaking in the BRI. Modern and modernizing states tend to be jealous of preserving their own sovereign powers and institutionalizing the domestic rule of law. Many Asian states have also yet to fully build nations that are inclusive of all ethnicities and accepting of a social contract between the ruler and the ruled. Additionally, many Asian states, including democratic ones, officially practice a national ideology that guides development and national stability. This is an inevitable offshoot of modernization. But this road to modernization is fraught with uneven accomplishments and reversals (Apter 1965; Diamond et al. 1987). State-society relations may occasionally be tense over matters such as economic distress, the gap between rich and poor, environmental disasters and ethnic representation in government. Connecting all these conditions along the geographical expanse of the BRI will prove extremely challenging.

Hence, in this book we contribute to scholarship on China's BRI by examining the many possibilities that the BRI is about adjusting paradigms and frameworks of cooperation between peoples, economies and states, as well as occasionally philosophizing about what connectivity can holistically mean in the twenty-first century. We are not being critical of China's BRI as an agent of possible displacement and initiator of a new Asian international order from an ideological standpoint. As President Xi's remarks have rightly alluded, the BRI is an unprecedented strategic vision but it also needs to be examined in terms of which obstacles it might encounter. Additionally, the BRI has upped the ante at a moment of intellectual efflo-rescence in the study of international relations: The inquiry into forms of non-western 'IR' that posit fluidity, plurality and harmony between peoples as much as states (Ling 2014; Chong 2012). More comprehensively, we have asked the authors of the various chapters to probe at the implications of what BRI means for inclusiveness or exclusiveness of development on national, regional and international scales.

NORMATIVE CONCERNS AND THE SHADOW OF GEOPOLITICAL CENSORSHIP

In prefacing the variety of critical chapters to this volume, we are mindful of carefully justifying the selection of authors on the understanding that most grand projects conceptualized by empires of the past, as well as more recent great powers, carry with them their particular inward oriented jus-tifications. The scholarship of Harold Innis, Marshall McLuhan and Ronald Deibert have persistently argued that territorial projects are often accompanied by biases in these powers' communication policies and tech-nologies. In studying the ancient Greek civilizational empire for instance, Innis came to the conclusion that despite the odd example of Sparta, most of the factionalized Greek city states never approximated the absolutist empires of Asia at the time. In Innis' view, 'the powerful oral tradition of the Greeks and the flexibility of the alphabet enabled them to resist the tendencies of empire in the East towards absolute monarchism and theoc-racy' (Innis 2007, p. 104). Likewise, when one scrutinizes the enunciation of the BRI in relation to the governing conditions within the People's Republic of China, one quickly realizes that Beijing is controlling the dis-course of promoting the BRI very tightly. As internal official documents have elaborated it, the Xi government has announced that critical attitudes towards China articulated under the influence of liberal openness or from western sources are collectively a national security threat (Buckley 2013; Myers and Cheng, 68 things, 2017). This extends likewise to discussions of the BRI. On the other hand, Beijing sees no contradiction between restricting critical thought and promoting pro-China propaganda through Chinese language courses, Confucius Institutes and even online adult education courses. The entire climate of corporate and journalism-driven financial news reporting has come under a cloud of censorship (Hernandez 2015; Tsang 2015). Beijing makes no apologies for sanitizing the Internet of content deemed inimical to China's national security (Myers and Wee, China feels vindicated, 2017).

More disturbingly, the idea of academic and civil society freedom to improve government by supplying constructive criticism has retreated significantly since the era of reforms initiated by Deng Xiaoping. In the latest study on the subject of Chinese civil society, a China-born sociologist argued that when dramatic social calamities such as the 2008 Sichuan earthquake occurred, spontaneous social 'self-help' efforts mounted by citizens were approved *post facto* by the government under labels such as 'nationalism' and acts of 'citizenship' (Xu 2017, pp. 8–28). The Chinese authorities were in fact slow to respond on the ground, prompting local citizens to take matters into their own hands since they were equipped with 'prior experience of providing social services' such as purchasing, delivering and distributing food and water; updating rescue information and donation notices online; cooking for survivors; babysitting; and so on (Xu 2017, p. 43). In a clear sign of defensiveness, the official *People's Daily* published an editorial two days after the earthquake that compared the relief operations to a 'great battle' that ought to occupy the attention of all levels of the Chinese Communist Party. The editorial stressed that disaster relief was 'first and foremost a political task' (Xu 2017, p. 44). Once this call to mobilization was explained, saving people's lives became top priority and the government could be seen to be compassionate to earthquake victims and survivors alike. This is obviously symptomatic of an insecure great power.

In March 2017, a report issued jointly by the Centre for International Media Assistance and the National Endowment for Democracy argued that China has transcended a defensive position associated with its censorship of all domestic media and the formidable Great Internet Firewall. The report noted that 'without much fanfare, it [China] has turned its focus outward, seeking to take its influence over the information environment global. Through a combination of market-oriented mechanisms, propaganda pressure tactics, and action in international arenas, China is attempting to harness the global information ecosystem in unprecedented ways' (Kalathil 2017, p. 1). The report highlighted three prongs of this new information manipulation strategy. Firstly, influencing foreign media reporting through Press releases, briefings and other cultivation; secondly, articulating the need for Internet sovereignty at the United Nations (UN) and other world forums; and thirdly, influencing 'global culture' into becoming more pro-China through funding and shaping cultural festivals, sports events and engaging Hollywood's film narratives through instruments of financing, market access and personal influence with film makers (Kalathil 2017, pp. 3, 32). True to expectations, the widely respected journal *China Quarterly*, published by Cambridge University Press was initially forced in August 2017 by China to excise 315 published papers from its online database hosted in the country. A massive outcry by academics worldwide forced Cambridge University Press to stage a U-turn within days of complying with Beijing's demands. The Press decided that it was more palatable to defy Chinese censorship than to sacrifice the spirit of academic inquiry. Less successful in resisting Chinese pressure is the Australian publisher Allen and Unwin whose author, Professor Clive Hamilton, alleged in a book ominously titled *Silent Invasion* that China's proxies had sought to influence Australia's democratically elected parliament and political parties through bribes and other illicit measures (Westcott 2017). In June 2019, the so-called 'extradition law protests' in Hong Kong revealed that even the foreign business community based in the territory stayed silent on the issues that vexed ordinary Hongkongers out of fear of Beijing's retaliation against their operations both in Hong Kong and on the mainland. Many speculated that the territory might lose its status as a 'middle ground' between China and the business world (Stevenson 2019). This volume studying the BRI echoes the concerns of media theorists, civil society quarters, businesses and academic publishers caught up in the daunting campaign of censorship and silence surrounding Chinese foreign policy ventures abroad.

On the contrary, the ancient Silk Road was a mostly ungoverned and spontaneous transmission belt of knowledge in both eastward and westward directions (Elisseef 2000). Whenever war in eastern Europe and the Mediterranean sought to close off trade with Asian centres between the 1000s and 1200s, itinerant Europeans like the Polo brothers, pilgrims like Ibn Battuta and numerous adventurous Arab merchants pioneered their own pathways to the East. Historian Peter Frankopan noted that until the era of Marco Polo's sojourn in Mongol-controlled China, the latter's knowledge of the outside world had been 'distinctly sketchy and limited'

(Frankopan 2015, p. 185). Subsequently, the famed naval expeditions of the early 1400s led by Admiral Zheng He and his compatriots during the Ming Dynasty represented a high point of ancient Chinese attempts to actively reach out to the rest of the world. Thereafter, it was a return by Chinese dynasties to the comfort of passivity and relative isolation vis-à-vis foreign contact. Therefore, a critical study of the BRI ought to probe at the geopolitical, economic and ideological significance of what the ancient Silk Road meant. In fact, as Frankopan and others have trenchantly argued, there were many Silk Roads on land and via the sea (Frankopan 2015, pp. 1–26). The majority of chapters collected in this volume tout the idea of plurality in ideas, governance, economic intercourse, social adaptation and toleration as characteristics of the original Silk Road. The more reflective chapters inquire into how travellers on the ancient Silk Roads found answers to the eternal question of cohabiting with human differences in beliefs and customs. Ling's chapter is also boldly counter-intuitive by asking if intra-Asian international frictions could be overcome through the paradigmatic change offered by the creative pathways embedded in the BRI. Trade, infrastructure and twinning civilizations all go together in restoring intra-Asian amity in the spirit of the pre-sovereign, ancient Silk Roads. As Chong's chapter puts it too, both the metaphor and reality of the ancient Roads still challenge us today. If the ancient Persian and Greek alike viewed the roads as pathways to empire, others perceived the Roads as civilization builders. Non-state pilgrims also generated their own paradigm for the religious Roads in seeking Providence through revelation (Dawson 1966). These were then proverbial and literal roads to faith. Can these not be reprised today given the rich repositories of Islamic, Buddhist, Zoroastrian and Christian artefacts preserved all along today's asphalt, rail and waterborne Roads?

CRITICAL GEOPOLITICS

Another significant theme that arises from scanning President Xi's remarks on the BRI is that of the geopolitics of political reputation, national identity and the nature of the development process itself. This is evident in the two quotes earlier from Xi containing conflated references to state-driven development, people-to-people connectivity and the desire to connect development processes that were designed through the lenses of national sovereignties. One is tempted to simply dismiss Xi's elaboration of the BRI as stock Chinese propaganda about development. Instead, the prospect of reviving the ancient Silk Road connects directly with the popular field of study known as critical geopolitics. As John Agnew and Stuart Corbridge, two of the foremost proponents of this perspective, put it, the reading of geopolitics 'must not be confined to a reading of a world ordered geographically into a more or less fixed hierarchy of states, cores and peripheries, spheres of influence, flashpoints, buffer zones and strategic relations' (Agnew and Corbridge 1995, p. 5). Agnew and Corbridge go on to argue that the dominance of the Westphalian territorial state is 'not a trans-historical given', and therefore that economic transactions across sovereign borders cannot be assumed to be linear, inexorable and unchanging once implementation has commenced (Agnew and Corbridge 1995, pp. 5–6). The interactions between politics and economics are diachronic rather than synchronic in nature. Agnew and Corbridge argue that critical geopolitics liberate political economy from confinement to physical parts of the globe. They boldly posit that 'success or failure' of different localities in the world capitalist economy 'is due to their historical accumulation of assets and liabilities and their ability to adapt to changing circumstances, and not the result of "natural" resource endowments' (Agnew and Corbridge 1995, p. 6). In this regard, international political economy today is as much concerned with flows of labour, goods and services, as with spaces of representation of those flows. A critical geopolitics therefore refers 'not only to the material spatial practices through which the international political economy is constituted, but also to the ways in which it is represented and contested' (Agnew and Corbridge 1995, p. 7).

At least three of the contributions to this book offer insights along the lines of critical geopolitics. The chapter by Pham and Giang, for instance, scrutinizes the BRI in terms of four dilemmas for China's place in development with respect to the BRI, the world vis-à-vis the BRI, Asia vis-à-vis the BRI, and of course, their native Vietnam vis-à-vis the BRI. Hanoi, the capital of Vietnam, is where the conference that mooted this volume was hosted, and from which the chapters for this volume were drawn. This was done with good reason. The ancient landed and maritime Silk Roads all connected this territory into the transcontinental circulation of goods, spices and ideas. Vietnam too witnessed the arrival of colonialism from both the land and the sea, hence it is the perfect Southeast Asian location to reflect on the BRI. Moreover, the prestige of being hosted by the country's premier university, the Vietnam National University, was symbolically important for those of us scholars from the so-called 'First World' research institutions who wished to ensure that globalization should facilitate collaborations outside our respective intellectual comfort zones. This is done with a view towards making sure that neo-liberal globalization should not reproduce a rigid western intellectual hegemony. This book in effect offers critical perspectives from diverse locations in time, in space and even from diverse points within Asia and the Middle East.

Another exceptional chapter in the mode of critical geopolitics by Trinh van Dinh compares the scale and thrust of the BRI to China's dynastic practices of pursuing grand infrastructural projects by *diktat*. Dinh ventures provocatively that there are parallels between the BRI and ancient dynasties' plans to master space and populations through infrastructural improvement. Wu Shang-su's chapter on railway developments in the BRI, while not strictly about critical geopolitics, adheres to the spirit of the latter by analysing how China's railway extensions of the Silk Road recreate a potential 'hegemony' of connectivity to its north, west and south to varying degrees of success. By building the lines that connect its neighbours and distant partners, Beijing and its proxies assert significant technological domination over how its BRI partners conduct their economic activities. Additionally, building or aligning railways are commensurate with enlarging great power influences far beyond their physical borders since connectivity requires technical conformity so that goods and the vehicles that carry them can obtain efficient and safe passage.

Although these three chapters are highlighted as squarely in the realm of critical geopolitics, in reality the vast majority of the contributions on the political economy front also take on board critical geopolitics in the way they analyse fresh international trade and investment connections in a mostly 'South-South' configuration that seem to have been in hiatus for as long as colonial and decolonization processes have predetermined patterns of development.

The Rest of Asia: Satellites, Free Riders or Equal Partners?

On the political economy front, scrutiny of the BRI necessarily takes on a policy-oriented direction. These are critical perspectives in the sense that in every bilateral or multilateral partnership the questions of equality of status and empathy towards the respective national interests arise. Although Xi's statements articulate the desire for the BRI to accommodate assorted national development plans, the existing scholarship on Chinese aid and investment policies towards the Global South and Asia do not provide adequate reassurance for the participants in the BRI.

Firstly, some scholars have floated the idea that Chinese development imperatives overseas are a little more than the substitution of the familiar western policy template of neo-imperialism and 'development of underdevelopment'. A case study of Chinese investment in Angola since the early 2000s has argued that they have mostly propped up an authoritarian nationalist regime by delivering mass-produced housing and infrastructure in the name of a vaguely understood notion of inclusive progress (De Morais 2011). Not only have Chinese construction proven shoddy and delayed, the Chinese companies appear to have only minimally engaged local Angolan labourers. Worse, Chinese government-to-government agreements with the government in Luanda have merely opened the way for Chinese private and state-owned corporations to dominate the contracts in Angola at the expense of local labourers and companies. Additionally, the government in Luanda has been accused of turning a blind eye to criminal resource expropriation rackets run by the expatriate Chinese community in the country. Incidents of anti-Chinese vigilantism by Angolan citizens angry and fearful of Chinese economic penetration have become quite common as a result (De Morais 2011, pp. 73–74). Echoes of such lessons can be found in the on-going Sino-Japanese geo-economic competition for high speed rail projects across Southeast Asia and South Asia. China is often perceived to be outbidding Japan because of the collusion between Chinese foreign policy goals and the ability to compel Chinese rail firms to competitively offer price and political 'discounts' to seal the deal (Kesavan 2017; Larmer 2017; Wu and Chong 2018).

Secondly, another theme can be identified in recent scholarship: The statist, top down implementation characteristic of Chinese aid and investment. This is both good and bad. It is positive in the sense that unlike democratic great power donors where aid packages have to be often debated and ratified in their domestic political arenas following government-to-government signature, China can guarantee that whatever is promised at the negotiating table and sealed with bilateral signatures will be delivered in large measure. This is Beijing's advantage as a one-party state that controls civil society and other forms of domestic dissent. But this also opens the way for a tremendous amount of bureaucratic politics between China's Ministries of Foreign Affairs, Commerce, Health, Science and Technology, Communications, Education and Agriculture, as well as the assorted state-owned enterprises and banks that actually deliver the aid on the ground

(Breslin 2013). According to Shaun Breslin, most analyses of China's aid and investment to the Global South will encounter trends of incoherence. More importantly, Breslin finds that 'the balance between challenge and opportunity largely depends on the existing political economy of the partner country' (Breslin 2013, p. 1287). This clearly implies that the BRI remains in a 'plasticine' stage. It is wide open to country-specific negotiation as to what suits the government of the day in the local partner territory (Bozzato 2017; Wu and Chong 2018; Hashmi 2019).

Yet, others lament that Chinese aid and investments may suffer implementation difficulties simply because Beijing is not learning from the earlier difficulties of the World Bank and Asian Development Bank in consulting local civil society and non-governmental organizations (NGOs) about the social, economic and environmental impacts of large-scale infrastructure projects. This has happened with China's African ventures and it is repeating itself in Beijing's partnerships in Indochina (Alden and Hughes 2009; Dosch and Hensengerth 2005; Hensengerth 2015). The blind spot of a top down approach to aid and investment lies in the neglect of the displacement effects of large-scale ground-breaking projects on people and their livelihoods, as well as on the ecological environment. Additionally, some political economists have pointed out that Chinese aid and investment guidelines enjoy wide political latitude that cannot be mapped in any sense to standards set by the Organisation for Economic Co-operation and Development (OECD), World Bank or G7 donor policies (Bräutigam 2011). China does not have a dedicated Ministry of Official Development Assistance, or its equivalent, and does not appear to have drawn up a standard, transparent suite of developmental loan policies. Hence it can price the interest rate on loans below prevailing market rates and supplement them with 'add on' concessionary grants or ancillary gifts to sweeten a bilateral aid package, as has happened in the early 2000s with 'special state loans' to Angola and the modernization plan for Nigerian railways (Bräutigam 2011, pp. 757–759). A converse reading of Beijing's wide political latitude to making loans is however also possible. Beijing's aid is exceptionally attractive to many Global South states simply because it is willing to be flexible and accommodative to local needs. The invocation of 'friendship' considerations, the presumed ideological solidarity of countries on the modern Silk Road focused on development and the avoidance of loan conditionality upon prevailing market rates and human rights standards, all act to enhance the appeal of China's BRI vision.

Indeed, the chapters authored by Manochehr Dorraj, Nguyen Thi Thuy Trang, Pham Thi Thu Huyen and Ngo Tuan Thang praise the attraction of China's blandishments regarding the BRI as being helpful for 'South-South Cooperation' as opposed to the conditionality and political strictures set by the G7 states. At the same time, chapters by Nguyen Thi Lanh Anh and Mai Ngan Ha, along with Carlyle Thayer's, point out that China's BRI aid potentially marginalizes existing international law and extends China's economic reach towards possible political domination in partner countries' domestic politics. The chapter by Toshiaki Tamaki also contributes to debate by raising the prospect that China may well be aspiring to displace the US' benevolent hegemony in international political economy through the BRI. This in turn may trigger negative counter-reactions by Japan and others who have benefitted from the US-led post-1945 liberal economic order. Understandably, the chapter by Nguyen Thi Thanh Thuy explains why the United States under President Donald Trump has been vacillating towards the BRI while preferring that China continues adapting to the current liberal economic order.

IMAGINING THE SILK ROADS THROUGH PHILOSOPHY AND HISTORY

Like a multifaceted venture in medical examination, the first two substantive chapters of the book comprises contributions that critically re-evaluate the timelessness of the Silk Roads and how this quality enables it to carry metaphors and lessons across history. L. H. M. (Lily) Ling's chapter titled 'Squaring the Circle: China's "Belt and Road Initiative" (BRI) and the Ancient Silk Roads' takes seriously the assumption that Theory is very important in framing how one sees the world. The 'China threat' thesis, for instance, arises out of western fears. Moreover, US/western views dominate via discursive acts of 'epistemicide' that fix real world problems via analyses of threats to western dominance. In Asia, daily life and politics are about fluid problem solving. Time, space, knowledge and identity need to be problematized. Armed with this spirit, Ling invites her readers to treat the BRI (or its earlier moniker 'One Belt One Road') as a creative open political space. She begins with the premise that *both* the Silk Road spirit and BRI hegemony operate simultaneously. Furthermore, this apparent contradiction can produce measures not only to evaluate the BRI but also check it. These measures apply to the Chinese government as much as BRI-recipients. Her methodology draws on Buddhism's five-rank protocol for non-duality *with* duality (To have the former without the latter, Buddhism points out, would simply reinstate another duality!). Here, the concept of Interbeing (相即, *tiep hien*, attributed to philosopher Thich Nhat Hanh) figures crucially as a means of demonstrating and achieving non-duality with duality. Ling boldly predicts that the BRI will eventuate in the vision of 'Asian Capitalism 5.0' in the current millennium whereby the BRI seeks to integrate contemporary capitalist globalization with the inclusive spirit of the ancient Silk Roads.

Taking the trans-Asia relational turn further is Alan Chong's chapter titled 'Mercantile Harmony: The Ancient Silk Roads as Intercultural Meeting Points amongst Monks, Pilgrims and Merchants'. In it, he argues that the international and intercultural relations of Asia are frequently misperceived and predicted to be ripe for conflict. His chapter takes inspiration from political philosophy by posing a counter-question by reading the stories and recollections of pilgrims that have travelled the Middle East, Persia, Central Asia, the Straits of Malacca and the Indian Ocean towards Arabia: Have the different faiths of pilgrims and the rival ideologies of merchants stoked inevitable conflict in southern Asia's pre-modern past? Based on a philosophical reading of assorted texts by Ibn Battuta, Fa-Hsien, Tomé Pires and Marco Polo, his chapter ventures the answer that ancient Asians and Europeans have developed a unique sense of circulating and integrating difference into hybrid amalgamations that have generated a culture of toleration that co-evolved with prosperous trading relations all along the maritime Silk Road. This profile of openness ought to be sustained today when one articulates the BRI.

CRITICAL GEOGRAPHIES ON THE ROAD

Critical geographies of the Belt and Road begin with dilemmatic thinking. The chapter by Quang Minh Pham and Le Hoang Giang expound this dilemma on three levels. They boldly suggest that China itself is in a dilemma because the BRI fits the template of an internal propaganda ploy to consolidate President Xi's power base by constructing a grand vision of China's future development. The current enthusiastic embrace of the BRI equals uncertainty about its fate post-Xi. Likewise for the United States and Asia, it is objectively correct to praise the BRI for scripting China into a constructive mode of global development. The Initiative is a veritable front door invitation to China to invest, build advanced economies among its trade partners and collaborate with local populations in win-win projects. On the other hand, it facilitates Chinese diplomatic and economic penetration into the host countries. The latter potentially both envy and fear China's political weight right in the midst of local politics and economic spaces. For Vietnam in particular, China's investment heft brings jobs and spreads income growth but it could equally introduce zero-sum competition for Vietnamese products when Chinese manufactures enter common local markets across Asia and in Vietnam itself. Additionally, embracing the BRI ought not to mean the dilution of Hanoi's sovereign claims to parts of the South China Sea.

Trinh van Dinh's chapter 'Infrastructure Construction as Empire Consolidation in Chinese History' appraises the BRI through the historical treatment of the idea of 'connectivity' in China's ancient history. The nature of the 'connectivity' can also be understood in its mechanical aspects: Interconnection, complementation to perfect the existing, build on the basis of the existing routes or even initiate renewal. But the new story that has emerged with the Belt and Road Initiative is that it presents a way of survival and development for the State and its corresponding society, a theme repeated in many of China's strategic projects. The BRI transforms individual works into a massive, unified body that creates a new look, generates productivity and imparts new vitality to a future Chinese power. Hence, President Xi Jinping might be regarded as the latest strongman in the long train of great builders among Chinese 'emperors'.

Rounding up the section on critical geography, we have the chapter by Wu Shang-su titled 'Rail Developments under the BRI'. Since land transportation occupies a great deal of the Belt and Road Initiative (BRI), the railway plays an indispensable role. After a few years of development, BRI rail projects have connected China and its various neighbours. Through those rail lines, the second largest economy in the world is likely to affect the neighbouring countries and consequently reshape the geopolitical landscape. However, different rail gauges and the presence of rival great powers, namely Russia and India, as well as other external technology providers, constrain China's rail expansion in Mongolia and Central Asia. In Southeast Asia, Beijing faces more favourable conditions. There are few great powers to obstruct Beijing in the subregion, and there is demand for separated rail systems of the standard gauge variety. However, the centrepiece of rail planning in Southeast Asia, the Singapore-Kunming Rail Link (SKRL), has not progressed well, probably due to the reasons of costs, affordability and low public dependence on rail. Although the BRI rail projects may not consistently be a game changer for China's geopolitical ambitions, they have inspired other regional countries, especially the landlocked ones, to develop strategic connections, whether with Chinese involvement or not.

CRITICAL POLITICAL ECONOMY ON THE ROAD

In this penultimate section, the chapters take on a more policy-oriented, but still critical tone. These chapters study the big trends and policy leanings originating from the signals and indices issued by the various nation-state players in the BRI. Heading this list is Manochehr Dorraj's chapter: 'The Belt and Road Initiative and China's Relations with Iran and Saudi Arabia: A Delicate Balancing Act'. In this chapter, Dorraj discusses China's bilateral energy, trade, political and security ties with arguably, the two more important regional powers in the Middle East, namely, Iran and Saudi Arabia. Dorraj also briefly analyses China's delicate balancing act between these two rivals. This has enabled it to have cordial relations with both. He concludes by speculating on the future directions of China's relations with these two countries and how it may impact the success of the BRI, the larger Chinese policy towards the region and beyond.

Carlyle A. Thayer's chapter titled 'Australia and China's Belt and Road Initiative: Economic Opportunities and Geo-Strategic Concerns' sounds an even deeper alarm at China's political economy approach to an unusual partner in the BRI—Australia. Thayer's chapter explains Australia's reluctance to join the BRI and the current downturn in its bilateral relations with China. His chapter is divided into five parts. Part 1 provides a broad overview of Australia-China relations. Part 2 explores the opportunities for cooperation. Part 3 examines the domestic debate over the pros and cons of joining the BRI. Part 4 discusses the major geo-strategic obstacles to Australia's formal participation in the BRI. Part 5 offers some concluding observations suggesting a mixed picture. In general, Australia is pushing back through toughened domestic policing against foreign subversion. But it also faces a dilemma in pushing China too far away. The prospect of a successful BRI in Asia looms amidst a quickening US decline and leadership in the global economy. Moreover, China's Asian Infrastructure Investment Bank (AIIB) looks increasingly to be a serious rival to the Washington-dominated World Bank. Nonetheless, BRI might yet prove to be an overly optimistic plan given on-going hiccups in its implementation.

Interestingly, Nguyen Thi Lanh Anh and Mai Ngan Ha's chapter on the 'Legal Challenges to the Belt and Road Initiative' continues with a focus on the quandaries posed for the rule of law, both domestic and international, by the BRI. Anh and Ha's main argument is that many aspects of the BRI are showing signs of inconsistency with respect to the current international framework. Their chapter discusses the legal challenges to the Initiative under four branches of international law. Firstly, it analyses the current international legal framework on human rights and compares it with China's BRI practices. Secondly, it broaches the development of international environmental law and queries how China may be falling short of their obligations under it. Thirdly, the chapter examines China's perspective on the applicability of current dispute settlement mechanisms for BRI projects and ventures a proposal for a new means of dispute resolution handcrafted for the Initiative. Finally, their chapter raises the oft-debated issue of transparency of the entire BRI. Transparency is of course the key to reassuring Beijing's partners that their involvement will eventuate in a win-win relationship. It remains to be seen if Beijing fully understands this dimension.

Next, Toshiaki Tamaki's chapter provocatively asks 'Is the Economic Hegemony moving from the US to China? A Historical Perspective'. Taking on a historical interpretation of hegemonic economic orders, this chapter queries whether China's BRI policy will really be efficacious. Some researchers may be sceptical towards the possibility of the realization of President Xi's aim because it is a challenging enterprise. Can Eurasia really become an economic and trading zone similar to the Atlantic one in terms of the size and amount of money invested? Is economic hegemony moving from the United States to China? Can China overcome the issues of wage gaps and environmental pollution while referring to One Belt One Road (OBOR)? Tamaki's chapter aims to discuss and reveal the meaning of BRI/OBOR from the perspective of economic history. Interestingly, Tamaki dissects the meaning of the BRI from a critical retrospective reading of the economic history of the Dutch and English predecessors of the current American-led liberal economic order. He concludes that the Chinese are still not inventing a new system through which huge money can automatically be poured into consolidating a Hegemonic State. Chinese policy is still following too closely the liberal order jointly upheld by the United States and Europe.

Nguyen Thi Thuy Trang's chapter titled 'China's Belt and Road Initiative: China's Motivations and Its Impacts on Developing Countries' rounds up this political economy section of the book with some projections regarding the risks and fortunes of developing countries under the BRI. Based on multilevel analysis, the chapter argues that China has masked strategic, economic and political calculations and motivations behind their leaders' rhetorical statement. For developing countries, along with the benefits they could receive, they would also be faced with a number of risks and challenges in economic, political and security terms. Trang raises a number of troubling concerns vis-à-vis Chinese protectionism in the implementation of the BRI. There is for instance the fear that BRI contracts will be awarded mostly to Chinese firms that employ Chinese workers and China-made technology. This reprises the fear articulated by scholars of China's experiences in Africa that the local developmental partner is a necessarily subservient one (De Morais 2011). Compounding this is equally the worry that Chinese firms and managers will treat BRI partner territories as 'dumping grounds' and testing grounds for low quality and trial technologies. Equally worrying from a developmental perspective is that Chinese aid might well turn out to have burdensome repayment terms creating long term debt relationships with BRI partner countries. Therefore, Beijing's developing country partners will likely be cautious about how 'mutual benefits' will be realized when the BRI is implemented in their respective local contexts.

CRITICAL NATIONAL PERSPECTIVES

National perspectives of states and societies outside a grand strategic vision initiated by a great power, such as the BRI, are always a helpful counterbalance against over-optimism. Moreover, if there are kinks in the original plan, it is often the view from outside that provides the ideal mirror of the problems at hand. Nguyen Thi Thanh Thuy's study of 'US Attitudes and Reactions towards China's "Belt and Road" Initiative' proposes to read US attitudes and reactions, through the lenses of the US federal and local governments, as well as of the business and scholarly communities, towards the BRI. Interestingly, her conclusion suggests there is a deep bifurcation among the various opinion makers. US officialdom and scholars are highly suspicious of China's strategic motives in launching the BRI especially vis-à-vis the position of the US-dominated liberal economic order. On the other hand, the US business community have become instant converts to the positive prospects of the BRI since it brings jobs, investments and rents for the US economy.

Following closely upon the US case is the chapter by Pham Thi Thu Huyen and Ngo Tuan Thang titled 'China's Belt and Road Initiative (BRI): Challenges and Opportunities for Vietnam'. The authors posit that while Vietnam welcomes the funding that the BRI will inject from China to improve infrastructure and boost trade and tourism, suspicions on the foreign policy and security front remain. The BRI may eventually provide China with political and economic leverage over Vietnam's position in the South China Sea dispute notwithstanding diplomatic confidence building measures already in place bilaterally. Additionally, China can use the development card to play Vietnam's neighbours in Indochina against Hanoi's interests. Echoing a theme mentioned in the section on the philosophy and history of the Silk Road, Vietnam worries that China may politicize history, memory and archaeology along the Silk Roads to assert political domination over Southeast Asia in the name of development.

Given the broad range of perspectives covered in this book, the BRI ought to be treated as the entrée for deeper policy-oriented and intellectual conversations about either a pan-Asian or trans-Pacific developmental order. Already, Japan and the United States, in tandem with India, have stirred controversy against the BRI by pushing the idea of a 'Free and Open Indo-Pacific' (FOIP) vision that privileges national autonomy in decisions about development over the construction of mega-projects. The pitting of the FOIP against the BRI has stirred unprecedented debate across Asia. Some of this debate is merely geographical, but increasingly much of it is going the way of geopolitics and resistance to Beijing (Varghese 2019). It is therefore not surprising that the range of chapters captured here range from pure academic treatises to policy commentaries and advocacy pieces.

That said, the BRI is unlikely to be a neo-realist order defined by sheer military measures of power, nor simply of monopolistic economic power. If there is one consistent refrain throughout this open ended volume, it is one that decries political and economic hegemony. Leadership and vision are universally welcome, not the dictatorial imperative of hegemony. Compassion and consideration for the weak and underdeveloped have been equally a universal echo through these diverse chapters. Equally striking was the need to rediscover the spirit of spontaneity, friendship, spirituality, empathy and intellectual curiosity that characterized the ancient Silk Roads. There is a great deal of humane consideration animating these chapters and their critiques. It is thus our hope in this volume that the BRI is not simply an open and shut project file for building infrastructure. It is about shaping an inclusive world order of peoples, economies as well as sovereignties.

REFERENCES

Agnew, J., and S. Corbridge. 1995. *Mastering Space: Hegemony, Territory and International Political Economy*. London: Routledge.

Alden, C.J., and C.R. Hughes. 2009. Harmony and Discord in China's Africa Strategy: Some Implications for Foreign Policy. *The China Quarterly 199*: 563–584.

Apter, D.E. 1965. *The Politics of Modernization*. Chicago, IL: University of Chicago Press.

Bozzato, F. 2017. Gifts that Bind: China's Aid to the Pacific Island Nations. *Asia Japan Journal 12*: 17–36.

Bräutigam, D. 2011. Aid 'With Chinese Characteristics': Chinese Foreign Aid and Development Finance Meet the OECD-DAC Aid Regime. *Journal of International Development 23* (5): 752–764.

Breslin, S. 2013. China and the South: Objectives, Actors and Interactions. *Development and Change 44* (6): 1273–1294.

Buckley, C. 2013. China Memo Reveals Fears of Western Influence. *International Herald Tribune*, August 21, pp. 1, 3.

Chong, A. 2012. Premodern Southeast Asia as a Guide to International Relations between Peoples: Prowess and Prestige in "Intersocietal Relations" in the Sejarah Melayu. *Alternatives: Global, Local, Political 37* (2): 87–105.

Dawson, C., ed. 1966. *Mission to Asia: Narratives and Letters of the Franciscan Missionaries in Mongolia and China in the Thirteenth and Fourteenth Centuries*. 2nd ed., Trans. A.N. Abbey. New York: Harper Torchbooks – The Cathedral Library.

De Morais, R.M. 2011. The New Imperialism: China in Angola. *World Affairs 173* (6): 67–74.

Diamond, L., S.M. Lipset, and J. Linz. 1987. Building and Sustaining Democratic Government in Developing Countries: Some Tentative Findings. *World Affairs 150* (1): 5–19.

Dosch, J., and O. Hensengerth. 2005. Sub-Regional Cooperation in Southeast Asia: The Mekong Basin. *European Journal of East Asian Studies 4* (2): 263–285.

Elisseef, V., ed. 2000. *The Silk Roads: Highways of Culture and Commerce*. New York: Berghahn Books and UNESCO Publishing.

Frankopan, P. 2015. *The Silk Roads: A New History of the World*. London: Bloomsbury Publishing.

Hashmi, S. 2019. *Making Sense of Five Years of China's Belt and Road Initiative*. Future Directions International – Independent Strategic Analysis of Australia's Global Interests. Nedlands, Western Australia: Future Directions International.

Hensengerth, O. 2015. Global Norms in Domestic Politics: Environmental Norm Contestation in Cambodia's Hydropower Sector. *The Pacific Review 28* (4): 505–528.

Hernandez, J.C. 2015. Enlisting Mao in a Soft Power Mission. *International New York Times*, October 21, pp. 1, 4.

Innis, H.A. 2007. *Empire and Communications*. Toronto: Dundurn Press.

Kalathil, S. 2017. *Beyond the Great Firewall: How China Became a Global Information Power*. CIMA and NED. Washington, DC: Centre for International Media Assistance and National Endowment for Democracy.

Kesavan, K. 2017, November 16. *Emerging Sino-Japanese Rivalry on High Speed Railway Projects in Asia*. Available at India Writes: http://www.indiawrites. org/emerging-sino-japanese-rivalry-on-high-speed-railway-projects-in-asia/. Accessed 16 Nov 2017.

Larmer, B. 2017. Is China the World's New Colonial Power? *New York Times International Edition*, May 2. https://www.nytimes.com/2017/05/02/magazine/is-china-the-worlds-new-colonial-power.html. Accessed 10 June 2019.

Ling, L.H. 2014. *The Dao of World Politics: Towards a Post-Westphalian, Worldist International Relations*. Abingdon: Routledge.

Myers, S.L., and A. Cheng. 2017. 68 Things You Can't Say on the Web in China. *New York Times International Edition*, September 18, pp. 1, 8.

Myers, S.L., and S.-L. Wee. 2017. China Feels Vindicated in Its Control over Internet. *New York Times International Edition*, October 18, pp. 3, 7.

Stevenson, A. 2019. Deep Concern in Hong Kong. *New York Times International Edition*, June 13, p. 5.

Tsang, A. 2015. Reporter's Shaming Signals Shift in China. *International New York Times*, September 7, pp. 1, 17.

Varghese, P. 2019. *The Indo-Pacific and Its Strategic Challenges: An Australian Perspective*. Singapore: ISEAS-Yusof Ishak Institute.

Westcott, B. 2017, November 13. *Professor Says Publisher Dumped His Book Because It Was Scared of China*. Available at CNN Money: http://money.cnn. com/2017/11/13/news/china-australia-book-publisher-censorship-allegations/index.html. Accessed 14 Nov 2017.

Wu, S.-s., and A. Chong. 2018. Developmental Railpolitics: The Political Economy of China's High-Speed Rail Projects in Thailand and Indonesia. *Contemporary Southeast Asia 40* (3): 503–526.

Xi Jinping. 2017, May 14. *Work Together to Build the Silk Road Economic Belt and The 21st Century Maritime Silk Road. Speech by His Excellency, President Xi Jinping of the People's Republic of China*. Full text of President Xi's speech at opening of Belt and Road forum – Xinhuanet: http://news.xinhuanet.com/english/2017-05/14/c_136282982.htm. Accessed 9 Nov 2017.

Xu, B. 2017. *The Politics of Compassion: The Sichuan Earthquake and Civic Engagement in China*. Stanford, CA: Stanford University Press.

PART I

Imagining the Silk Roads Through Philosophy and History

Squaring the Circle: China's "Belt and Road Initiative" (BRI) and the Ancient Silk Roads

L. H. M. (Lily) Ling

INTRODUCTION

Will the "Belt and Road Initiative" (BRI) turn China into the world's next "colonial power"? Two recent articles from the *New York Times* make this charge (Larmer 2017a, b).[1] Through the BRI, the author claims, China will bestride continents as a developmental behemoth, inflicting environmental damage, imposing extractive capitalism, depriving localities of not just jobs but also skills, saddling them with heavy debt, exhibiting cultural arrogance, and—most disturbingly—training their militaries.[2] The author concludes with this observation regarding all Chinese overseas, whether they are members of a diaspora or agents of the People's Republic:

L. H. M. (Lily) Ling was deceased at the time of publication.

[1] Clearly, more outlets than the *New York Times* make this charge. See, for example, *The Straits Times* (Goh 2017) and *The Guardian* (2017). Nonetheless, I focus on this one source to represent what many consider a "liberal," even "progressive," voice in the Western-led "international" media.

[2] For a fuller discussion of these charges and my critique of them, see Ling (2017a).

L. H. M. (Lily) Ling (Deceased)

© The Author(s) 2020
A. Chong, Q. M. Pham (eds.), *Critical Reflections on China's Belt & Road Initiative*, https://doi.org/10.1007/978-981-13-2098-9_2

What binds these individuals together is an abiding belief that their presence overseas is making China better and stronger. This shared conviction, as much as the state that has nurtured it, is what makes China a colossus, a nation that can be seen by others, in the same instant, as a blessing and a curse.

China presents the BRI very differently. It's a "win-win" (*gongying*, 共赢) partnership, President Xi Jinping declares since announcing the initiative in 2013 (Xi 2017). The BRI, he stresses, will follow the four core principles of the ancient Silk Roads (2 BCE–15 CE): "peace and cooperation" (*heping hezuo*, 和平合作), "openness and inclusiveness" (*kaifang baorong*, 开放包容), "mutual learning" (*huxue hujian*, 互学互鉴), and "mutual benefit" (*huli gongying*, 互利共赢). These constitute a "Silk Road spirit" that will, among other things, facilitate "civilizational connections" with local partners whereby "exchange will replace estrangement (*gehe*, 隔阂), mutual learning will replace clashes (*chongtu*, 冲突), and coexistence (*gongcun*, 共存) will replace a sense of superiority (*youyue*, 优越)" (Xi 2017).[3]

How does one judge? More disturbingly, what if *both* scenarios pertain? Is it possible to have a Silk-Road spirit *and* BRI hegemony? And if so, what then?

This chapter conducts a thought experiment. It tackles the latter questions to answer the first. That is, it begins with the premise that *both* the Silk-Road spirit and BRI hegemony operate simultaneously; furthermore, this apparent contradiction can produce measures not only to evaluate the BRI but also to check it. These measures apply to the Chinese government as much as BRI recipients. My method draws on Buddhism's five-rank protocol for non-duality *with* duality (To have the former without the latter, Buddhism points out, would simply reinstate another duality!). Here, the concept of Interbeing (Thich 1988) figures crucially as a means of demonstrating and achieving non-duality with duality. I conclude with the implications of this analysis for world politics, as a domain of practice, and International Relations (IR), as a field of study.

I begin with Daoism's (道學) *yin/yang* (陰陽) theory.

---

[3] Elsewhere, I expand this socio-historical phenomenon into an epistemic one called the Silk-Road Ethos (Ling and Perrigoue 2018).

RECONCILING OPPOSITES

Yin/Yang's Non-duality with Duality

Daoist *yin/yang* theory begins with a dyad of opposite equals: that is, *yin* versus *yang* (see Fig. 2.1). *Yin*, the female principle, represents all that is soft, dark, warm, and nurturing; *yang*, the male principle, all that is hard, bright, cold, and punishing. Neither supersedes the other. Laozi, the mythical founder of Daoism, did not discriminate between *yin* and *yang*. "The meekest in the world," teaches the *Daodejing* (*Classic of the Way*, c. 4 BCE), "[can] [p]enetrat[e] the strongest in the world. ... Nothing in the world can match it" (Laozi quoted in Thompson 2000, p. 17) Accordingly, each *yin* and *yang* has its own time, significance, utility, and power; it depends on the circumstance.[4]

Internal intimacies emerge: that is, *yin*-within-*yang* and *yang*-within-*yin*.[5] The ontological parity between *yin* and *yang* necessarily generates a presence of each within the other; otherwise, nothing could "hook" *yin*

Fig. 2.1 Daoist *yin/yang* relations

---

[4] For instance, flowing water (*yin*) in summer has as much value in preserving life as hardened ice (*yang*) in winter.

[5] In this way, *yin/yang* theory turns Hegel's master-slave dialectic inside-out. Daoism insists that a part of the master exists inside the slave just as a part of the slave exists inside the master (Brincat and Ling 2014).

and *yang* together as a sustainable pair.[6] They might as well be random particles, bouncing against each other like billiard balls or one consuming the other thereby destroying the pairing. Daoism's classic graph of *yin* and *yang* conveys these relations visually through color: an S-like curve or "border" separates *yin* from *yang* but inside the black sphere of *yin*, a white spot of *yang* exists; correspondingly, inside the white sphere of *yang*, a black spot of *yin* exists. With this co-created "three-ness" (Ling 2019), *yin* and *yang* connect and comply with each other *as much as* they conflict and mutually contradict. The Way or *dao* thus lies in balancing the two as the best means of securing a healthy, happy, and durable future. Herein lies the value of non-duality with duality.

Buddhism's five-rank protocol takes place in the third domain of internal intimacies. It offers the most dynamic, creative arena of pushing *yin* and *yang* beyond their initial, static opposition. The protocol's first two ranks—(1) "the relative [*yin*] within the absolute [*yang*]" and (2) "the absolute [*yang*] within the relative [*yin*]"—caution, in effect, that appearances can be deceiving. Things may seem different on the surface (*yin* vs. *yang*) but they share a common condition or essence underneath (*yin*-within-*yang* and *yang*-within-*yin*). Even so, the commonality between different things does not negate each entity's unique qualities (*yin* remains the female principle; *yang*, the male). From these two ranks, comes the third—(3) "coming [*yin*] from within the absolute [*yang*]." "No longer in the abstract, the whole universe becomes your very life itself, and, inevitably, compassion arises" (Loori 2009, p. xxvii). A fourth rank—(4) "arriving at mutual integration"—urges action based on this insight. "At this stage, the absolute and relative are integrated, but they're still two things" (Loori 2009, p. xxvii). Accordingly, the fifth rank—(5) "unity attained"— affirms "[t]here is no more duality. [The entity] is one thing—neither absolute nor relative, up nor down, profane nor holy, good nor bad, male nor female" (Loori 2009, p. xxvii).

What happens when we apply this protocol to the Silk Road-*yin* and the BRI-*yang*?

Let's see.

---

[6] Loori (2009, xxvii) notes: "'Catching the self,' 'catching the hook,' 'being caught by the hook,' 'being caught by the Way,' are all expressions of the interplay of opposites." See Ling (2002) for a discussion of "discursive hooks" in IR.

THE FIVE-RANK PROTOCOL

Integrating Silk Road-yin with BRI-yang

We proceed with each rank as identified above.

Ranks 1 and 2: Recognizing "Relative [yin] within Absolute [yang]" and "Absolute [yang] within Relative [yin]"
Interestingly, Xi anticipates Rank 1 (Xi has a history of favoring Buddhism and Daoism [Johnson 2017]). By infusing the BRI with the Silk-Road spirit of "peace and cooperation," "openness and inclusiveness," "mutual learning," and "mutual benefit," Xi aims to allay skeptics and critics. No one needs to fear the BRI, Xi intimates, for it derives inspiration from the beloved Silk Roads! Xi's purpose may not be to achieve non-duality with duality; nonetheless, he satisfies the first condition of this Buddhist protocol.

But Xi overlooks Rank 2 (In this sense, Xi's understanding of the Buddhist/Daoist approach remains underdeveloped). To complete the dyad, we must substantiate the BRI *yang*-within-Silk Road-*yin*. Only then could we have engagement between Silk Road-*yin* and BRI-*yang*. Toward this end, I draw on Silk-Road history but metaphorically. Clearly, a massive, state-directed investment scheme like the contemporary BRI did not occur at any time during the ancient Silk Roads. Nonetheless, those who lived in the era of the Silk Roads perfectly understood what it meant to have strangers in one's midst, whether they were merchants, monks, or warriors.

For this reason, I turn to al-Ghazali's rules of hospitality. In his celebrated work, *The Revival of the Religious Sciences*, al-Ghazali (450–505 AH/1058-1111), one of Islam's great thinkers from the twelfth-century, sought to enshrine the norms and principles of Silk-Road hospitality in daily life. I focus on his chapter titled, "On the Manners Relating to Eating" (Book XI). Note these four instructions (Garden, 2014, pp. 14–42):

1. Do not Impose. A host should not impose. Invitations should go only to those who can accept and with happiness.
2. Consider One's Own. To prevent feelings of resentment, the host should reserve portions of the dinner for his household before the guest arrives.

3. Gladden the Heart of the Other. A guest should not focus exclusively on gratifying the stomach. The guest should also "gladden" the host's heart by not making extra demands. Conversely, the guest could suggest but only if it would please the host.
4. Dine with Ease. For both host and guest, being comfortable at the table is more important than increasing the meal by two dishes.

These instructions inform Rank 3. They remind us of what Rank 2—the BRI-within-the Silk Roads—could consist of and bring to its engagement with Rank 1—the Silk Roads-within-BRI. This interaction highlights *common* guidelines for integration.

Rank 3: "Coming [yin] from within the Absolute [yang]"
In Rank 3, we discover the following:

1. Avoid Hegemonic Acts: "Peace and Cooperation" + "Non-Imposition." Xi Jinping defines the Silk-Road spirit's first principle, "peace and cooperation," as a type of interaction devoid of "warships, guns or swords" (*jianchuan he lipao*, 坚船和利炮); instead, it entails "camel caravans" (*tuo dui*, 驼队) with lots of "good will" (*shan yi*, 善意). "Generation after generation," Xi (2017) notes, "the silk route travelers have built a bridge for peace and East-West cooperation." When integrated with al-Ghazali's principle of "non-imposition" for both hosts and guests, a general policy emerges: avoid hegemonic acts. This means not imposing the Self's agenda (e.g., "infrastructure-building") onto Others that are unwilling or ill-prepared to accept, thereby producing undesirable outcomes (e.g., unpayable debts) that defeat the original, positive intention (e.g., economic development). With this guideline, the BRI could take structural asymmetries into account and try to curtail them as much as possible. This means not just protecting investor claims but also the rights and interests of the recipient. The latter, moreover, means more than just the state or its ruling elites. The concept includes the entire national "household" and its members.
2. Consider the National Household: "Openness and Inclusiveness" + "Consider One's Own." The Silk-Road spirit's second principle, "openness and inclusiveness," refers to the search for "commonality amid difference" (*qiutong cunyi*, 求同存异). Xi adds: "These routes

enabled people of various civilizations, religions and races to interact with and embrace each other with [an] open mind. In the course of exchange, they fostered a spirit of mutual respect and were engaged in a common endeavor to pursue prosperity."[7] With al-Ghazali's emphasis on consideration for one's own household when inviting outsiders to one's house, a second guideline emerges: consideration of one's national household. This means leaders need to protect the welfare of their own populace before inviting Others—like China's BRI—into their midst. Otherwise, a sense of injustice will simply swell until, one day, it implodes the entire house. Correspondingly, the Chinese Communist Party (CCP) needs to ensure that China's domestic economy, infrastructures, and general development can *sustain* the BRI. And the CCP has an obligation to the national household to make these criteria and their fulfillment transparent.

3. Consider the Whole Community: "Mutual Benefit" + "Gladden the Heart of the Other." Here, I match the Silk-Road spirit's fourth principle, "mutual benefit," with al-Ghazali's third instruction, "gladden the heart of the other." The ancient Silk Roads, Xi points out, created an area of great, common prosperity. "The ancient prosperous cities of Alma-Ata (阿拉木图), Samarkand (撒马尔罕) and Chang'an (长安) and ports of Sur (苏尔港) and Guangzhou (广州) thrived, so did the Roman Empire (*luoma*, 罗马) as well as Parthia (*anxi*, 安息) and Kushan (*guishuang*, 贵霜) Kingdoms" (Xi 2017). Likewise, a dinner party succeeds only when all those in attendance, both guest and host, gladden one another's hearts. In terms of political economy, this means neither power nor profits can decide everything. Leaders have a responsibility to ask: how *else* would the national household—the *whole* community—benefit? If no benefit accrues, then the plan or project or investment needs to be reconceived. This principle applies to the Chinese government as much as BRI recipients.

4. Beyond Instrumentality: "Mutual Learning" + "Dining at Ease." The fourth Silk-Road principle involves "mutual learning." The ancient Silk Roads did not just convey commerce and trade. They also facilitated learning and adaptations. Just as astronomy, calendars,

---

[7] The original text is more lyrical: "They wrote together (*bingjian shuxie*, 并肩书写), respecting one another's 'grand poetry' (*zhuangli shipian*, 壮丽诗篇), and painted together on the 'beautiful canvas' of common development" (携手绘就共同发展的美好画卷) (Xi 2017).

and medicines entered China through Buddhist, Islamic, and Arabic sources so did China's "four major inventions" (*sida faming*, 四大发明) (Xi 2017).[8] Similarly, al-Ghazali inveighed upon his readers that diners should experience "ease": the quality of comfort far exceeds in importance to the quantity of food. In relation to the BRI, adding extra material incentives (an extra "dish" or two) cannot substitute for a feeling of trust between investor and recipient, regardless of who is host or guest, who is dominant or subordinate. Incentives may entice the present but ease in relations assures the future. Hence, BRI negotiations cannot focus on instrumental, material exchanges only. These must consider, also, how investors and recipients, whether they are national governments or transnational corporate investors, *relate* to local communities. This stipulation echoes the first principle of non-imposition.

Rank 3 sparks a converging sensibility. Compassion and enlightenment begin to rise. Nevertheless, the absolute and relative "are still two things." We need Rank 4 to formalize the integration.

Rank 4: "Arriving at Mutual Integration"
Rank 4 focuses on a program of action. Transplanted to the BRI, this means fieldwork. It will help us verify what is happening on the ground as well as identify pockets of change and/or resistance. However, we cannot resort to typical, social-scientific methods. Ethnography, surveys, and other methods of standard fieldwork can still apply but these must align with the dualist/non-dualist philosophy that frames this research. Otherwise, our methods would undermine our methodology.

For this reason, I draw on Thich Nhat Hanh's (1988) articulation of Interbeing (*tiep hien* in Vietnamese). It updates the Buddhist tenet of co-dependent arising (*pratītyasamutpaāda* in Sanskrit), expressed most commonly as: "you are in me and I in you" (*ni zhong you wo, wo zhong you ni* in Mandarin Chinese). Because Interbeing involves a process—that is, one *becomes* through others—it necessarily guides action with a set of spiritually minded and analytically rigorous rules of practice.

Thich Nhat Hanh distills them into the following:

---

[8] These were: the compass, gunpowder, papermaking, and printing.

1. Nonattachment from views: ... the first aim of the practice is to be free of all attachments, especially [dogmas, prejudices, habits, and what we consider to be the Truth] ....
2. Direct-experimentation: ... Direct practice-realization, not intellectual research, brings about insight ....
3. Appropriateness: ... [U]nderstanding and compassion ... must reflect the needs of people and the realities of societies ....
4. Skillful means (*upaya*): ... [S]how the Buddha's Way and guide people in their efforts to practice the Way and guide people in their efforts to practice the Way in their own particular circumstances .... (Thich Nhat Hanh 1988, p. 8).

These injunctions help to formulate the following research questions:

1. Nonattachment to Knowledge. Is there transference of knowledge (e.g., skills, technology, jobs, and capital) between the local and global, domestic and international? Even if one party tends to monopolize these features currently, do opportunities exist for a shift to occur in the future? If not, how can we enhance these opportunities and reduce the resistances? Equally important, how is what I'm learning transforming *me*, the researcher? That is, how does this research experience alter my knowledge of the world as well as my relationship to it (Banerjee 2018)?
2. Direct-Experimentation with Our Subjects. The principle of direct-experimentation will help us stay alert to the habit of distancing ourselves from our "subjects" of study. We must ask: What does the BRI look and feel like from the perspective of the Locality, the Recipient, and the Subaltern (however defined)? The reverse applies as well: What does BRI look and feel like from the perspective of the Globality, the Investor, and the Hegemon? Is there any reciprocity between Center and Periphery (wherever located) or does one always dominate the other? If so, where do opportunities exist to "release" reciprocities between the Center and the Periphery?
3. Appropriateness in Power Relations: Center-Periphery Relations. Do BRI contracts stay true to the four core principles of the Silk-Road spirit? Or do they continue the developmental priorities of neoliberal globalization? Do BRI recipients have any formal or informal means of voicing their "needs" and "realities"? If not, where and how can our research help?

4. *Upaya* through Intersubjectivity. Do opportunities exist to shift from the current state of identity marked by geopolitical, geoeconomic competition (e.g., "Kazakh" vs. "Chinese") to a more civilizational one based on Interbeing (e.g., "Kazakh" + "Chinese" = "Hybrid")? If so, how, when, who, and where?

Rank 5: "Unity Attained"

Interbeing instantiates Rank 5: "unity attained." It helps to determine whether the two principals—Silk Road-*yin* and BRI-*yang*—can *embark* upon the journey to "true mind," never expecting or caring about the destination. Just moving toward the Way suffices.

Thich Nhat Hanh (1988, p. 3) further elaborates on what Interbeing means in daily life:

> The word *tiep* means "being in touch with" and "continuing." *Hien* means "realizing" and "making it here and now." ... What are we to be in touch with? The answer is reality, the reality of the world and the reality of the [true] mind. ... Getting in touch with true mind is like digging deep in the soil and reaching a hidden source that fills our well with fresh water. When we discover our true mind, we are filled with understanding and compassion, which nourishes us and those around us as well.

A critical reader could shrug: Nice scheme but too pie-in-the-sky. How do we know it works outside of Zen monasteries?

NON-DUALITY WITH DUALITY

Historical Record

Integrating contending realities, I submit, has been going on for millennia. Our personal, daily lives revolve around it as much as the global political economy (Ling 2014). We recognize such integrations as an *episteme* only now due to the "epistemic violence" (Spivak 1988) and "epistemicide" (Santos 2014) that the global North has committed against the global South for the past six centuries. Consequently, formal education tends to erase the knowledge of the colonized as "quaint," at best, or "nonsense," at worst; in contrast, it privileges the colonizer's *episteme* as the "best," "legitimate," or "civilized."[9] Yet ordinary peoples retain a sense of Self-within-the-Other despite centuries of attempted annihilation by colonizers. For this reason, Andean activist Humberto Cholango could declare in a letter to Pope Benedict XVI in 2007 that "We are still here" (Cholango quoted in Cadena 2010, p. 335). He added: "[We] have always been here and will continue to be here. ... Our religions NEVER DIED [because] we learned how to merge our beliefs and symbols with the ones of the invaders and oppressors" (Cholango quoted in Cadena 2010, p. 334, original emphasis).

Indeed, the social sciences are beginning to decolonize (Kataneksza et al. 2018). Decolonial scholars note sites of subaltern resilience in languages, cities, and borderlands, even under different structures of power like patriarchy and other hegemonic orders in a global context (Soja 1996; Charusheela and Zein-Elbadin 2004; Ashcroft et al. 2006; Anievas et al. 2015; Pham and Shilliam 2016). In each case, they find subaltern resilience through "hybridities," "creolization," "thirdspace," or what I specify here: non-duality with duality.

A more recent example comes from Asian Capitalism. Since the end of World War II to the present, Asian Capitalism has integrated collectively across time (past-present-future) and space (Confucian and Westphalian world orders) (Ling 1987) to culminate into its latest, fifth-generation version: China's BRI.

Asian Capitalisms 1.0–5.0
I list Asian Capitalism in reverse order. Each generation learns from the successes *and* failures of the previous ones:

- Asian Capitalism 5.0 (2000s). The BRI seeks to integrate contemporary capitalist globalization with the ancient Silk Roads. This ambitious program recognizes the benefits of neoliberal globalization (e.g., a more efficient, capital-accumulating economy) but also its detriments (e.g., increasing gap in identity, not just wealth, between China's "cosmopolitan" eastern seaboard and its vast interior). This sensibility stems from China's own concerns, of course, but it also accords with the experiences of regional neighbors that have undertaken similar capitalist reforms.

[9] See, for example, Nandy (1988b) and Masuzawa (2005).

- Asian Capitalism 4.0 (1990s). India turns to neoliberal reform in 1991. In *The Beautiful and the Damned*, Deb (2011) details the seeming contradictions that confound a neoliberalizing India. But the country's economic reforms borrow greatly from China's previous—and highly successful[10]—experiment with capitalism.
- Asian Capitalism 3.0 (1980s). China crosses socialism with capitalism to produce "socialism with Chinese characteristics." At the same time, Chinese leaders and institutions learn as a precedent from their regional, capitalist rivals: "the four little dragons."
- Asian Capitalism 2.0 (1970s). Hong Kong, Singapore, South Korea, and Taiwan adopt and adapt Japan's model of the developmental states. They also aim to avoid imperial Japan's mistake by shifting competition with the West from the battlefield to the marketplace.
- Asian Capitalism 1.0 (1960s). Postwar Japan surges into the world's second largest economy. Its success, however, draws much from Japan's prewar foundations. Meiji Japan merged Confucian/Shinto traditions with Westphalian capitalist-colonialism primarily to avoid China's mistake: that is, refusing to learn from the West, thereby provoking the Opium Wars (1840–1842 and 1856–1860) that shattered the Confucian world order. Meiji leaders did not want Japan to suffer a similar fate.

Non-Interbeing in World Politics

Still, Asian Capitalism has not attained or even aspired for Interbeing. Indeed, previous attempts to reframe world politics in post-Westphalian terms have failed miserably.[11] Two notable examples include the Kyoto School in the 1930s and the Third World Non-Aligned Movement (NAM) announced in Bandung in 1955. The Kyoto School introduced Buddhist concepts like "emptiness" (*mu*) and "inbetweeness" (*aidagara*) for world politics but these devolved into Japan's imperialist project of the Greater East Asia Co-Prosperity Sphere (Shimizu 2011). NAM also seemed to herald a new era in world politics, especially from the perspective of the global South, but two key members—India and China—declared war over a border dispute just seven years later (Ling et al. 2016).

---

[10] The World Bank (2017) reports that China averaged 10% growth per annum for the past three decades and has lifted 800 million out of poverty.

[11] Although thinkers from and in Asia are experiencing an intellectual resurgence along these lines. See Ling and Chen (2018) and Pham and Shilliam (2016).

Evidence explains why. As decolonial scholars have amply shown, our supposed Liberal World Order, with its rules-based, open, and fair system for all,[12] reincarnates its past three centuries of racialized-genderized colonial hegemony (Amin 2009; Hobson 2012; Vitalis 2015; Ling 2017c).[13] At most, the Liberal World Order can admit the co-presence of Others in the company of the Western-led, Westphalian Self but not coexistence and certainly not co-leadership (Odysseos 2007). Given this overarching hegemony, neither Asian Capitalism nor any other post-Westphalian effort can reach Interbeing—until now. Precisely because the BRI enacts Asian Capitalism 5.0, the region is ready to face Westphalia eye-to-eye. This means not just another way of doing and relating but also, more profoundly, thinking and being (Ling 2016).

Please note: I am not setting up another duality of "East" versus "West," Buddhism/Daoism versus Westphalianism. The Asian Capitalisms listed above should underscore how these dichotomies have no purchase. Asian Capitalism does not indicate one system (Westphalian colonial-capitalism) consuming another (Confucian patriarchal-agrarianism). Rather, the two have been entwining through internal intimacies since the nineteenth century; otherwise, Asian Capitalism would not have posed a periodic challenge to Westphalian hegemony since the nineteenth century. Here, Bhabha's (1994) concept of postcolonial mimicry argues the case half-way. While Bhabha rightly points out that the fawning Other's mimicry of the hegemonic Self may seem to reinforce the status quo but, really, disturbs its assumptions about colonial distance and superiority, he fails to recognize what happens when mimicry succeeds in substance, not just performance (Ling 2002b). When substantive mimicry takes place, as in Asian capitalism, integrations of non-duality with duality pry open

---

[12] For renditions of this approach, see Ikenberry and Slaughter (2006) and Ikenberry (2008).

[13] I call it Hypermasculine Eurocentric Whiteness (HEW) (Ling 2017b, c). *Hypermasculinity* refers to an ideology that denigrates anything smacking of the feminine: for example, welfare, intellection, and compassion (Nandy 1988a). Imperial England used it to colonize India and other parts of the world. *Eurocentrism* regards all things European—people, customs, languages, institutions, philosophies, even fashions, and lifestyles—as definitive of "civilization" (Gong 1984; Anghie 2005; Aydin 2007; Bowden 2009; Suzuki 2009). And *whiteness* constructs a racialized order of privilege and entitlement derived from all of the above (Baldwin 1984; Biss 2015). An ideology more than biology, HEW can enthrall "third-world states" as much as the "white states" of North America, Western Europe, Australia, and New Zealand (Higgott 1998). By the same token, HEW can repel its key constituency—the so-called white males—as much as decolonized Others who seek a more emancipated world politics.

cognitive, emotional, and practical space to elude hegemony by transforming it.

Elsewhere (Ling 2014), I formalize the integrative possibilities between "East" and "West," Buddhism/Daoism and Westphalianism in a model that I call worldist dialogics. I refrain from repeating that discussion here since my main purpose is to outline a social-scientific application for Buddhism's five-rank protocol for non-duality with duality.

CONCLUSION

Entanglements entwining entanglements is the buddhas and ancestors interpenetrating buddhas and ancestors. Eihei Dōgen (道元禅師), thirteenth-century Japanese Zen monk, quoted in Loori (2009, p. xxix)

With Buddhism's five-rank protocol as aid, the BRI can transform into more than its original intent. Not only could localities wield greater agency in negotiating with the BRI but this protocol also explains *why* those with structural power (*yang*) should listen to those without (*yin*). Entanglements through internal intimacies (*yin*-within-*yang* and *yang*-within-*yin*) invariably ensue and ultimately will decide the future. Neither the dominant nor the subordinate can avoid it.

Perhaps the best analogy comes from the *bodhisattva* Guanyin. She dispenses mercy to the world's needy with a "thousand arms and eyes" yet they all operate from the same celestial body. Still, as the Zen master Wansong[14] instructs, "[the *bodhisattva's*] hands and eyes are not something attached to her body, which would make them separate entities, but rather the totality of her being" (Loori 2009, p. xxxiii).

The critical reader could dismiss this paper's approach as Buddhist/Daoist only. It lacks "universality." I hasten to point out, however, that transcending non-duality with duality through Interbeing resonates with other pre-Westphalian worldviews as well: e.g., Hinduism's *darśana* ("auspicious sight"); Confucianism's *ren* ("mutual sociality"); ancient Greece's *poiesis* ("poetic inspiration"); Nguni Bantu's *ubuntu* ("human kindness"); the Lakota's cosmology of "hoop" or circle ("all is related"); and Andeanism's *pachamama* ("earth/time mother"), just to name a few.

---

[14] Buddhist monk, Wansong Xingxiu (萬松行秀; 1166–1246), lived under the Jin Dynasty and the Mongol Empire.

Indeed, this approach represents most philosophies and worldviews; Westphalianism, in contrast, only a small sliver.

It's about time for a shift. No longer should we allow Westphalianism to dominate, turning world politics into all *yang* and no *yin*, not to mention any mutual impact or reciprocities. More inclusive concerns need to guide the global agenda. These foreground ordinary people leading ordinary lives but with extraordinary outcomes. Interbeing as methodology and norm will help. With it, we can square the circle—not as a finality but a first step in the right direction.

REFERENCES

Amin, Samir. 2009. *Eurocentrism*. 2nd ed. New York: Monthly Review Press.

Anghie, Anthony. 2005. *Imperialism, Sovereignty, and the Making of International Law*. Cambridge: Cambridge University Press.

Anievas, Alexander, Nivi Manchanda, and Robbie Shilliam. 2015. *Race and Racism in International Relations: Confronting the Global Colour Line*. London: Routledge.

Ashcroft, Bill, Gareth Griffiths, and Helen Tiffin, eds. 2006. *The Postcolonial Studies Reader*. 2nd ed. New York: Routledge.

Aydin, Cemil. 2007. *The Politics of Anti-Westernism in Asia: Visions of World Order in Pan-Islamic and Pan-Asian Thought*. New York: Columbia University Press.

Baldwin, James. 1984. On Being White...And Other Lies. http://www.cwsworkshop.org/pdfs/CARC/Family_Herstories/2_On_Being_White.PDF. Accessed 31 Dec 2015.

Banerjee, Payal. 2018. The Wisdom of the Road: Research and Pedagogy on India-China and the Silk Road Ethos. *Asian Journal of Comparative Politics* 3 (3): 269–282.

Bhabha, Homi K. 1994. Remembering Fanon: Self, Psyche and the Colonial Condition. In *Colonial Discourse and Post-Colonial Theory: A Reader*, ed. R.J. Patrick Williams and Laura Chrisman, 112–123. New York: Columbia University Press.

Biss, Eula. 2015. Debt: Reckoning with What Is Owed – And What Can Never Be Paid. *New York Times Magazine*, December 6, pp. 50–51, 83.

Bowden, Brett. 2009. *The Empire of Civilization: The Evolution of an Imperial Idea*. Chicago: The University of Chicago Press.

Brincat, Shannon, and L.H.M. Ling. 2014. Dialectics for IR: Hegel and the *Dao*. *Globalizations* 11 (3): 1–27.

Cadena, Marisol de la. 2010. Indigenous Cosmopolitics in the Andes: Conceptual Reflections beyond 'Politics'. *Cultural Anthropology* 25 (2): 334–370.

Charusheela, S., and Eiman Zein-Elbadin, eds. 2004. *Postcolonialism Meets Economics*. London: Routledge.

Deb, Siddhartha. 2011. *The Beautiful and the Damned: A Portrait of the New India*. New York: Farrar, Straus, and Giroux.

Garden, Kenneth. 2014. *The First Islamic Reviver: Abu Hamid al-Ghazali and His Revival of the Religious Sciences*. New York: Oxford University Press.

Goh, Sui Noi. 2017. 19th Party Congress: Xi Jinping's Name Written into Chinese Communist Party Charter. *The Straits Times*, October 24. http://www.straitstimes.com/asia/east-asia/19th-party-congress-xi-jinpings-name-written-into-chinese-communist-party-charter. Accessed 24 Oct 2017.

Gong, Gerrit W. 1984. *The Standard of "Civilization" in International Society*. Oxford: Clarendon Press.

Guardian, The. 2017, October 18. Xi Jinping Heralds 'New Era' of Chinese Power at Communist Party Congress. https://www.theguardian.com/world/2017/oct/18/xi-jinping-speech-new-era-chinese-power-party-congress. Accessed 24 Oct 2017.

Higgott, Richard. 1998. The Asian Economic Crisis: A Study in the Politics of Resentment. *New Political Economy* 3 (3): 333–356.

Hobson, John M. 2012. *The Eurocentric Conception of World Politics: Western International Relations Theory, 1760–2010*. Cambridge: Cambridge University Press.

Ikenberry, G. John. 2008. The Rise of China and the Future of the West: Can the Liberal System Survive? *Foreign Affairs*, January/February. https://www.foreignaffairs.com/articles/asia/2008-01-01/rise-china-and-future-west. Accessed 30 Dec 2015.

Ikenberry, G. John, and Anne-Marie Slaughter, Co-Directors. 2006. *Forging a World of Liberty Under Law: US National Security in the 21st Century*. Final Report of the Princeton Project on National Security. Princeton: Woodrow Wilson School of Public and International Affairs. http://www.princeton.edu/~ppns/report.html. Accessed 13 Sep 2009.

Johnson, Ian. 2017. What a Buddhist Monk Taught Xi Jinping. *New York Times*, March 24. https://www.nytimes.com/2017/03/24/opinion/sunday/chinas-communists-embrace-religion.html. Accessed 26 Oct 2017.

Kataneksza, Jacquelin, L.H.M. Ling, and Sara Shroff. 2018. Decoloniality: (Re)Making Worlds. In *International Organization and Global Governance*, ed. Thomas G. Weiss and Rorden Wilkinson, 2nd ed., 205–217. London: Routledge.

Larmer, Brook. 2017a. Is China the World's New Colonial Power? *New York Times Magazine*, May 2. https://www.nytimes.com/2017/05/02/magazine/is-china-the-worlds-new-colonial-power.html. Accessed 24 Oct 2017.

———. 2017b. What the World's Emptiest International Airport Says About China's Influence. *New York Times Magazine*, September 13. https://www.

nytimes.com/2017/09/13/magazine/what-the-worlds-emptiest-international-airport-says-about-chinas-influence.html. Accessed 24 Oct 2017.

Ling, L.H.M. 1987. *Institutional Learning*. Ph.D. dissertation, Department of Political Science, Massachusetts Institute of Technology.

———. 2002a. Cultural Chauvinism and the Liberal International Order: 'West versus Rest' in Asia's Financial Crisis. In *Power, Postcolonialism, and International Relations: Reading Race, Gender, Class*, ed. Geeta Chowdhry and Sheila Nair, 115–141. London: Routledge.

———. 2002b. *Postcolonial International Relations: Conquest and Desire between Asia and the West*. London: Palgrave Macmillan.

———. 2014. *The Dao of World Politics: Towards a Post-Westphalian, Worldist International Relations*. London: Routledge.

———. 2016. Postcolonial-Feminism: Transformative Possibilities in Thought and Action, Heart and Soul. *Postcolonial Studies* 19 (4): 478–480.

———. 2017a. *China's OBOR: 21st-Century Power Politics or New World in the Making?* Paper delivered at a workshop on "Cultural Interests and Values," University of Edinburgh, 14–15 June.

———. 2017b. Don't Flatter Yourself: World Politics as We Know It Is Changing and So Must Disciplinary IR. In *What Is the Point of IR?* ed. Synne L. Dyvik, Jan Selby, and Rorden Wilkinson, 135–146. London: Routledge.

———. 2017c. World Politics in Colour. *Millennium: Journal of International Studies* 45 (3): 473–491.

———. 2019. Three-Ness: Healing World Politics with Epistemic Compassion. *Politics* 39(1): 35–49. https://doi.org/10.1177/0263395718783351.

Ling, L.H.M., and Boyu Chen. 2018. IR and the Rise of Asia: A New Moral Imagination for World Politics? In *The Sage Handbook of History, Philosophy and Sociology of International Relations*, ed. Andreas Gofas, Inana Hamati-Ataya, and Nicholas Onuf. London: Sage Publications.

Ling, L.H.M., and Alisha C. Perrigoue. 2018. OBOR and the Silk Road Ethos: An Ancient Template for Contemporary World Politics. For a special issue on "The Silk Roads: Globalization before Neoliberalization", *Asian Journal of Comparative Politics*.

Ling, L.H.M., Adriana Abdenur, Payal Banerjee, Nimmi Kurian, Mahendra P. Lama, and Li Bo. 2016. *India China: Rethinking Borders and Security*. Ann Arbor: University of Michigan Press.

Loori, John Daido. 2009. *The True Dharma Eye: Zen Master Dōgen's Three Hundred Kōans*. Trans. Kazuaki Tanahashi and John Daido Loori. Boston: Shambhala.

Masuzawa, Tomoko. 2005. *The Invention of World Religions: Or, How European Universalism Was Preserved in the Language of Pluralism*. Chicago: University of Chicago Press.

Nandy, Ashis. 1988a. *The Intimate Enemy: The Psychology of Colonialism*. New Delhi: Oxford University Press.

————, ed. 1988b. *Science, Hegemony, and Violence: A Requiem for Modernity.* Tokyo: United Nations University.

Odysseos, Louiza. 2007. *The Subject of Co-Existence: Otherness in International Relations.* Minneapolis: University of Minnesota Press.

Pham, Quỳnh N., and Robbie Shilliam. 2016. *Meanings of Bandung: Postcolonial Orders and Decolonial Visions.* London: Rowman & Littlefield.

Santos, Boaventura de Sousa. 2014. *Epistemologies of the South: Justice Against Epistemicide.* New York: Routledge.

Shimizu, Kosuke. 2011. Nishida Kitaro and Japan's Interwar Foreign Policy: War Involvement and Culturalist Political Discourse. *International Relations of the Asia-Pacific* 11 (1): 157–183.

Soja, Edward W. 1996. *Thirdspace: Journeys to Los Angeles and Other Real-and-Imagined Places.* Malden, MA: Blackwell Publishing.

Spivak, Gayatri Chakravorty. 1988. Can the Subaltern Speak? In *Marxism and the Interpretation of Culture*, ed. Cary Nelson and Lawrence Grossberg, 271–316. Champaign-Urbana: University of Illinois Press.

Suzuki, Shogo. 2009. *Civilization and Empire: China and Japan's Encounter with European International Society.* New York: Routledge.

Thich, Nhat Hanh. 1988. *Interbeing.* 3rd ed. Berkeley: Parallax Press.

Thompson, Paul. 2000. On the Formal Treatment of Textual Testimony. In *The Guodian Laozi: Proceedings of the International Conference, Dartmouth College, May 1998*, ed. Sarah Allan and Crispin Williams, 89–106. Berkeley: Society for the Study of Early China and the Institute of East Asian Studies, University of California, Berkeley.

Vitalis, Robert. 2015. *White World Order, Black Power Politics: The Birth of American International Relations.* Ithaca: Cornell University Press.

World Bank. 2017, March 28. *Country Report for China.* http://www.financialexpress.com/world-news/china-lifting-800-million-people-out-of-poverty-is-historic-world-bank/892459/. Accessed 16 Oct 2017.

Xi Jinping. 2017, May 14. *Work Together to Build the Silk Road Economic Belt and the 21st Century Maritime Silk Road.* Speech at the opening ceremony of "The Belt and Road Forum for International Cooperation". http://www.tianfateng.cn/5707.html. Accessed 22 May 2017.

CHAPTER 3

Mercantile Harmony: The Ancient Silk Roads as Intercultural Meeting Points Amongst Monks, Pilgrims and Merchants

Alan Chong

The critical study of China's Belt and Road initiative is often framed synonymously as the exploration of what the original, ancient Silk Road meant (Bradsher 2015; Blyth 2017; Elisseef 2000; Xinhua News Agency 2016). In embarking on this research angle, I was struck by how historians have preferred to re-describe the Silk Road in plural terms (Frankopan 2015). In reading up the primary travellers' texts that form the heart of this chapter, it occurred to me that much of modern Asia can enrich its development by learning from its past. This is a past that offers many overlapping roads towards the improvement of human conduct and intercultural tolerance. In particular, this chapter grapples with the question of how travellers on the ancient Silk Roads found answers to the eternal question of cohabiting with human differences in beliefs and customs.

I argue that the overlapping ethics of tolerance amongst the multiple Silk Roads alluded to in this chapter amount to what I label 'mercantile

A. Chong (✉)
Centre for Multilateralism Studies, S. Rajaratnam School of International Studies, Nanyang Technological University, Singapore, Singapore
e-mail: iscschong@ntu.edu.sg

© The Author(s) 2020
A. Chong, Q. M. Pham (eds.), *Critical Reflections on China's Belt & Road Initiative*, https://doi.org/10.1007/978-981-13-2098-9_3

41

harmony'. This concept captures the idea of harmony between peoples and individual elite rulers rather than states. Moreover, this is a harmony based on empathy and the happenstance of spiritual revelation. On a third level, this harmony is 'mercantile', or trade-like and merchant-like, in the sense that interlocutors exchange ideas and admiration on the basis of perceived relative advantages. In a fourth sense, mercantile harmony is the solidarity forged among fellow travellers on the road. They could be pilgrims, traders, religious persons, owners of hospitality premises, itinerant workers or diplomats. To varying degrees of distinctions, all travellers need to brave the capricious weather, the prospect of drought, shortage of food, attacks by wild animals and bandits and the possibility of being treated as belligerents amidst warring conditions. Enlightened travellers develop a healthy reciprocal relationship with the political authorities controlling cities, towns, monasteries and agricultural lands straddling the Silk Roads. As is to be deduced, mercantile harmony leaves its mark on physical and cultural geography by creating a particular reputation about a place and its ability to transform lives, fortunes and physical well-being.

To clarify the concept of mercantile harmony, the metaphor of the road needs some further elaboration. In the narrative of Peter Frankopan, it was both the Persian empire *and* Alexander the Great's succeeding empire dominating the Middle East that realized the need for a road network to consolidate political, social and economic gains (Frankopan 2015, pp. 2–6). In an argument reminiscent of what the social sciences term medium theory today, both Darius III of Persia and Alexander of Greece after him found the road network a vital artery for the efficiency of governing the empire. Persia had flourished in both political reputation and economic prowess because she was easily connected internally (Frankopan 2015, p. 2). This was a civilization envied by Alexander of Macedon who consequently kept most of Persia's infrastructure intact while energetically pushing the frontiers of his empire into present-day Afghanistan. This is known because cities were named after him such as Herat (Alexandria in Aria), Kandahar (Alexandria in Arachosia) and Bagram (Alexandria ad Caucasum) (Frankopan 2015, p. 5). These cities were constructed for the simultaneous purpose of holding territory and consolidating the road network. Travellers would frequent the roads if they led towards the attainment of safety and wealth in cities, while garrisons based in the latter would patrol the roads to ensure that brigands and foreign enemies would be kept at bay for peaceful passage. This was ostensibly a strategic foil against the 'barbarians' of the steppes who raided settled communities for a living and lived off the land. In the imperial and architectural visions of both the Persian and the Greek, roads thus consolidated an ongoing campaign pushing back at the impromptu and destructive qualities of nomadic lifestyles.

My approach in this chapter takes after the idea of roads as civilization builders. Taking in the golden age of the ancient Silk Roads between A.D. 399 and A.D. 1515, mercantile harmony can even be derived as a political philosophy. Religion was a significant motivation for travel. Both the proverbial and literal roads stretching into the distant horizons served simultaneously as the test of faith and a quest for fulfilment of spiritual camaraderie as the records of Fa-Hsien and Ibn Battuta reveal. Likewise, Marco Polo conveniently mixed a thinly disguised Christian worldview with pure wanderlust, along with a little profit. Put differently, the Silk Roads lured the precursor of the modern packaged tourist and the 'lonely planet-inspired' backpacker, but with significantly more intellect and cultural sensitivity (Elisseef 2000; Frankopan 2015). Additionally, both the tourist and the pilgrim share the quest for noble spiritual existence expressed not unreasonably in worldly expressions of names and places.

Finally, by reading the last and most imperial of the four texts, the *Suma Oriental* by the Portuguese Tomé Pires, we return to ponder the question of empire raised by the Persians and Greeks: how can the mastery of the Silk Roads engender an evergreen empire? In Tomé Pires' account, this question was refracted through the maritime dimension. The Portuguese were consciously seeking to comprehend the rise and fall of prosperous and well-armed port cities, and their corresponding sea control, with the aim of wealth acquisition. Tomé Pires' journey to the east produced a sub-text for which his political masters wanted answers to: what would make Lisbon's imperial control in Asia endure even if he did not recognize at the time that he was possibly traversing a fluid, non-exclusive maritime Silk Road?

Therefore, this chapter is itself a *journey* of rediscovering peaceful coexistence amongst the human diversity of beliefs through ancient travel reports that shed light on what roads of discovery connecting Asia and Europe can enlighten us in twenty-first century modernity. Arguably, within reasonable limits, these four texts may be likened to the paths trodden by Alexis de Tocqueville's *Democracy in America* or the Gospels of the *New Testament* of the Christian Bible in their fusion of geographical inquiry with philosophical teaching. Using the lamp of the wisdom of the ancients, one can tweak the cruel excesses of modern politics to improve social relations peacefully in a globalizing world. One can also read the ancient travellers' search for roads to enlightenment to uncover the forgotten pre-modern threads of what 'IR' outside the west started from, with a view towards re-evaluating humane standards for a rising Asia (Drakard 1999; Acharya 2001; Shilliam 2011; Ling 2014; Buzan and Zhang 2014; Chong 2017).

The record of Fa-Hsien (337–422) is chronologically the earliest of the four books read here. As James Legge, the missionary turned historian, notes, Fa-Hsien was an authentic representative of the blend of Buddhism, Daoism and Confucianism that existed in much of ancient China. The latter two could not be comprehended, nor adhered to, without an admixture of beliefs from the former even if many ordinary Chinese, as perceived by James Legge in the 1880s, appeared to proclaim adherence to Confucianism as a primary belief system, over Buddhism and Daoism (Legge 1886, pp. 7–8). Not much is known about Fa-Hsien but Legge's scholarship reading ancient sources indicated that he was independent-minded from a young age. Having lost his father early on, Fa-Hsien had resolved to take up residence in the monastery in order 'to be far from the dust and vulgar ways of life' (Legge 1886, p. 1). His uncle apparently approved of his unusually spiritually oriented nephew and did not press him to quit the monastery to care for his mother, who herself ultimately became reconciled to her son's gifted nature. Legge recounts a story whereby Fa-Hsien encountered thieves in the rice fields near the monastery where he was carrying out a harvest. Instead of fleeing like his fellow monks, Fa-Hsien lectured the thieves on their unprincipled neglect of charity in precipitating their current state of misery and destitution. He argued that if the thieves did not mend their ways, their thievery would lead to compounded poverty and distress later on (Legge 1886, p. 2). The thieves fled in shame without taking their loot and Fa-Hsien was acclaimed as virtuous and full of courage amongst his peers. Upon completing his tenure as the novice monk, he assumed the 'obligations of the full Buddhist orders' and embarked on a highly anticipated quest to scour India for key Buddhist texts in order to further his and his fellow monks' spiritual training (Legge 1886, p. 2). Although Legge warns the readers of Fa-Hsien's work that some of his accounts of Buddhist miracles were exaggerated and grotesque, Fa-Hsien could be counted upon to record most of his impressions and factual observations accurately (Legge 1886, p. 5). This is why one must read Fa-Hsien for insights into the humanistic value of sojourning along the ancient Silk Roads.

Travelling a longer stretch of the landed Silk Road some eight and a half centuries later, Marco Polo (1254–1324) the Venetian offered his readers insights into the cultural distances and human geography straddling Europe and Asia as well as the spaces in between. Indeed, in the space of two return journeys from Venice to Cathay (China), including a 17 year long stay at Khubilai Khan's court, Polo was in awe of how common humanity operated under very different ideological socializations. He was intrepid in communicating with the Other and mostly open minded in observing sociological and anthropological diversities. Despite his text being treated as an open ended travelogue of assorted musings and sketches, I will read it as a philosophically inspired travelogue. Polo's Christian worldview comes through but he rarely imposes on the reader. Some Christian frames operate in his literary and political depictions but it soon becomes evident that there is a larger humanity involved in his observations about life and politics on the landed Silk Road. Polo hailed from an itinerant trading family and this might have accounted for his open minded approach to social diversity (Cliff 2015). As I have argued, with Polo's example in mind, prosperous and continuous trading requires a commensurate level of respect for one's interlocutors.

Ibn Battuta (1304–1377) was the Arab equivalent of both Fa-Hsien and Marco Polo. He travelled from Arab North Africa through the Arab and Persian lands, thence on to India and China for ostensibly religious reasons. He had originally wanted to make the pilgrimage to Mecca and its associated holy cities in Arabia. But chance encounters with 'saints', fellow Muslim legal scholars and assorted rulers persuaded him that he needed to follow his friends' recommendations that he visit their Islamic fraternity residing in India and China to establish solidarity with the faithful. Most interestingly, he did not couch his travelogue in thick Islamic discourse (Mackintosh-Smith 2003). He was always grateful for the kindnesses shown to travelling pilgrims regardless of skin colour and creed, but devoted significant attention to the vanities of men and women, and the bounty of nature that they manipulated for worldly ends. Trade and its delivery of material abundance to the most inland of cities fascinated him even if he was not a merchant himself. For an observer schooled in Islamic jurisprudence, Battuta's observations were remarkable for their balance and openness, even if some of his contemporaries suspected him of exaggeration in some parts (Mackintosh-Smith 2003).

Chronologically, in fourth position, we can place Tomé Pires' (1465–1540) *Suma Oriental: an account of the East, from the Red Sea to Japan, written in Malacca and India in 1512–1515* as a work describing globalizing Asia along the maritime Silk Road with a few qualifications. Firstly, Pires wrote in the service of Portuguese imperialism, albeit from the position of earnestly seeking enlightenment about the customs and politics of Asia. This might be construed by some as a tainted text, authored from the position of a would-be exploiter and a temporal victor in the opening chapter of the western colonization of Asia. Secondly, Pires wrote as an ethnic 'outsider' to Asia, hence his work is little more than depicting Asia through western eyes. *But these issues matter less intellectually, and culturally, if we revalue the critical roles played by otherness in both producing and reproducing globalization.* The other can be advantageous in both interpreting and connecting the political geography of early globalizing Asia in the sense that, like Battuta and Polo, he is connecting the proverbial dots into a grand thematic design where few have perceived before.

Pires ranged over a wide swath of maritime Asia which few have recorded before in such extensive depth prior to 1515. Armando Cortesão's introduction to his translation of the *Suma* acknowledges that while little is known of Pires' background, he found enough fragmentary evidence through the private letters written by Pires to his family and various officials that he trained a watchful eye over the state of Portuguese colonies in Asia stemming from his duties as a responsible apothecary both at the India and Malacca stations he had occasion to visit. It was also known that he departed for Asia under the initial patronage of Jorge de Vasconcelos, the director or purveyor of the *Casa de Mina e India*, the Portuguese equivalent of a Ministry for Colonial Affairs; and of a Dr Diogo Lopes, 'perhaps the chief royal physician, with whom Pires might have been connected after his service as apothecary to Prince Afonso', a son of Portuguese monarch John II (1455–1495) (Cortesão 1944). Subsequently, his painstaking reports of his travels had certainly earned him sufficient royal favour to have been appointed Portugal's first ambassador to the kingdom of China. Pires' work should therefore be considered as a work of colonial intelligence-gathering, covering an Asia awaiting its turn as a regional theatre for western penetration. Moreover, the mix of moderated observation, and the occasionally normative orientation, in the tone of the *Suma* supports its value as a text worth its intellectual weight amongst many rival contributions to our understanding of an early globalizing Asia that was already presenting global discourse with an unstated pattern of mercantile civilization.

The Spirit of Sacrifice as Place Marker:
The Travels of Buddhism

The Silk Road as a metaphor for political and other branches of philosophy is strongly articulated in Fa-Hsien's account of Buddhistic Kingdoms. His third person narrative is perhaps peculiar amongst travelogues, but his was a journey in search of texts and narratives that enlighten the purpose of life. Fa-Hsien's tone deliberately marginalizes the ego and decentres the storyteller. In true Buddhist fashion, the purpose of travel is to listen and watch for inspiration with the 'mind's eye' as it were. Fa-Hsien quotes a large number of aphorisms that reveal the nature of what he and his fellow Buddhist travellers were scouring the landscape of India and Southeast Asia for. On the banks of the northern Ganges, near the city of Kanyakubja, Fa-Hsien noted that this site was important for being the place where Buddha laid down the Law to his disciples: "'The bitterness and vanity of life as impermanent and uncertain", and that "The body is as a bubble or foam on the water'" (Fa-Hsien 1886, p. 54). This injunction was commemorated for all time by believers erecting a *stupa* ('tope') permanently on the site.

Fa-Hsien and his fellow Buddhist travellers treated the journey of faith across much of what we call India very seriously. This was the 'Middle Kingdom' in his imagination and not China. The early 'roads' were not paved and travelling was aggravated by the uninhabited lands in between religiously signified locations. Most of the journeys could only be completed by stopping over in kingdoms that recognized 'our Law' of Buddha. Hospitality to the faithful as well as to other travelling strangers mattered to Fa-Hsien's records. No place merited description unless it offered hospitality, or conversely, demonstrated the neglect of it. Fa-Hsien's narrative blatantly denigrated the acquisition of worldly goods, and likewise praised all monks who quit worldly lives and became 'all students of Indian books and the Indian language' (Fa-Hsien 1886, p. 14). India and Indians were treated synonymously as the sacred 'land of Buddha' and Buddhism. Fa-Hsien has left us with many descriptions like the following which implied that politics and proto-international relations revolved around the example of Buddha's sacrifice of flesh for the greater happiness and harmony of nature and the peoples of the world:

> Going on further for two days to the east, they came to the place where the Bodhisattva [i.e. the revered moniker for Lord Buddha] threw down his body to feed a starving tigress. In these two places also large topes [i.e. *stupas*] have been built, both adorned with layers of all the precious

substances. The kings, ministers, and peoples of the kingdoms around vie with one another in making offerings at them. The trains [of worshippers] of those who come to scatter flowers and light lamps at them never cease. The nations of those quarters call those (and the other two mentioned before) 'the four great topes'. (Fa-Hsien 1886, p. 32)

Throughout the text, Fa-Hsien juxtaposed the meritable preservation of bone relics of Lord Buddha set within temples called *viharas* as the greatest acts of reverence for the teaching of Buddhism. Kings who ritualized their admiration for these relics were admired for their internalization of Buddha's call for asceticism rather than their fine attire or ornate palaces. Where kings should display their accumulation of treasury on were the altars where Buddha's relics sat, or where *stupas* needed to be built to commemorate meritorious deeds.

Moreover, asceticism meant that all religious places needed to be kept neat and tidy. In the odd instance where human beings failed to maintain the *stupas* and *viharas* in good order, nature—or what modern environmental politics would call 'Gaia'—set an example of vigilant rectitude and worship. In one location, where a king's ambition was converted towards self-abnegation, where 'the ground all about became overgrown with vegetation, and there was nobody to sprinkle and sweep (about the tope); ... a herd of elephants came regularly, which brought water with their trunks to water the ground, and various kinds of flowers and incense, which they presented at the tope.' Nature's example shamed one devotee who came to worship at the tope so much that he vowed to assume the role of a Shaman and founded a monastery on the spot. From henceforth, the monks of the monastery would take over from nature in keeping the spirit of the religious site alive (Fa-Hsien 1886, p. 69). In the rare instances where Fa-Hsien condescended to describe merchants and commerce, he tended to describe their activities to be in conformity to the times and centrality of rituals ordered around the main monastery in a city. Prayer time was regulated and orderly, a pattern to be mirrored in worldly life.

Interestingly, Fa-Hsien ended his annals by recording the story of how his maritime journey back to China endured tempestuous seas in the vicinity of Java by seeking Buddha's intervention through meditation and prayer. In contrast, the 'Brahmans' and merchants on board acted in panic by throwing overboard their bulky goods and other belongings to lighten their ship in the hope that she would stay afloat in the raging waters. The only thing Fa-Hsien resisted discarding were the scrolls and religious images he had collected from India for his temples in China. Travelling the seas were hazardous in those times with knowledge of tides and ocean life undeveloped, hence 'the merchants [and Brahmans] were full of terror, not knowing where they were going' (Fa-Hsien 1886, p. 112). At one point, they suspected Fa-Hsien to be the jinx that ought to be disembarked at the nearest land. Fa-Hsien remained steadfast in his spiritual communion with Buddha and the ship safely found sanctuary in a harbour, albeit slightly short of their destination of Kwang-Chow. Thereupon, they chanced upon disciples of Buddha who verified Fa-Hsien's reputation to his fellow travellers and conducted them all safely to their destinations. Fa-Hsien's Silk Road was the one paved by markers of faith and otherworldly orientations. His was a text addressing mostly human solidarity and divinity at the deliberate expense of material acquisition.

TOLERATION, ORDER AND NEO-CHRISTIAN VIRTUE

Marco Polo's *The Travels*, by contrast, contained an embedded sense of toleration and openness towards appreciating foreign cultures. But this is always on the basis of reciprocal civility and basic human decency. The lands to the east of Constantinople in the mid-1200s were mostly *terra incognita* to the populations of Europe who lived under the myriad successors to the Roman Empire. In fact, most regarded the east with dread since the Mongols had terrorized eastern Europe and laid waste most of the populations of Armenia, Georgia, Russia and Hungary and were poised to sack Vienna in 1242, when news of the death of Genghis Khan's son Ögedei halted their advance. Before the Mongols, there were the Muslim armies that threatened Europe through armed proselytization and forcible occupation all along the Mediterranean coasts. Nonetheless, the Catholic Church, secured in its Papal seat in Rome, sent a series of envoys in the direction of the Mongol rulers to explore the possibilities of converting them and ultimately rendering them more peaceful towards Europe. The Pope was encouraged by stories that the Mongol Khans who conquered and ruled what we call Central Asia today spared Catholic Christians and the other schismatic Christian branches that constituted the Greek Church, the Nestorians and the Miaphysites (Cliff 2015, pp. xix–xx). All these rebels against the Roman Church nonetheless offered sincere hospitality and guidance to all Christian travellers who trekked the overland Silk Road towards Asia. The Polos' first unrecorded overland trip to Cathay apparently contributed to these impressions.

It was within this context that the male members of the itinerant trading family of Niccolò Polo and his brother Maffeo, together with Niccolò's son, Marco Polo, set out along the overland Silk Road for a second time following a trading errand from Venice to Constantinople (Cliff 2015, pp. xx–xxi). Restless in Constantinople, the Polos tried changing their fortunes by shifting their trading activities to the Crimean port of Sudak across the Black Sea. This apparently was the regular practice amongst traders at the time. From Sudak, the Polos heard of the cosmopolitan reputation of Berke Khan of the 'Golden Horde' of Mongols. Berke was rumoured to have converted to Islam and welcomed traders into his realm. Around 1258, Berke and his rivals were engaged in fratricidal struggles. The Polos made their way to Bukhara, deeper in Persia, and were trapped there by the fighting in the surrounding country. By 1260, the Polos caught the attention of a Mongol ambassador who transited Bukhara on his way to visit the court of the great Khubilai Khan, ruler of Cathay (China). The ambassador regarded the Polos as specimens of cultural curiosity and invited them to join him in his journey to Khubilai's court (Cliff 2015, p. xxi). This was where *The Travels* began.

While the Polos were said to be either following the trail of profit or indulging their curiosity with little overt religious motivation, *The Travels* suggest that Marco was a shrewd observer who superimposed his value frames upon his anecdotes and purported eyewitness accounts of the praiseworthy, Christian-like practices of monarchs, traders and residents along the landed Silk Road. Like Fa-Hsien before them, the Polos found the land journeys arduous, compounded in no small part by stretches of livestock-free, deserted landscapes and the ever-present dangers of being attacked by wayward human beings. Sample for instance the neo-biblical tones of Marco's description of the 'road to Cathay' after leaving the city of Balkh: 'When the traveller leaves this city that I have been telling you about, he rides for as many as twelve days towards the east-north-east without seeing a single dwelling, because the people have all fled to mountain fastnesses to escape the bandits and invaders who used to wreak havoc on them. There is plenty of water and game, and there are also some lions. No food is to be had during this twelve day journey, so anyone who passes this way has to carry food with them, both for themselves and for their horses' (Polo 2015, p. 47).

Against such bleak human and physical landscapes, Marco kept his eye out for hospitality to strangers and the associated practice of good governance. When the Polos arrived at Khubilai Khan's temporary capital of

Kaipingfu on this second of their three visits to Cathay (China), the Polos followed local custom in kneeling before the great Khan and rendered 'obeisance with utmost humility' (Polo 2015, p. 10). Far from being the arrogant, xenophobic host one might expect the Mongol overlord to be, the latter reciprocated the Polos' respect with tremendous hospitality. One might add that Khubilai was already enchanted with the whole idea of meeting 'Latins' for the first time to the extent that he was predisposed to treat the Polos with dignity. Perhaps one might regard this as an incipient globalization of social encounter since the Great Khan was desirous, in Marco's account, of meeting the Catholic Pope and learning about the monarchs and lords who ruled in the west. Khubilai took a special liking to Marco, the youthful son of Niccolò, in part because he quickly immersed himself in the learning of Tartar customs, language and arts, as well as demonstrating 'exceptional astuteness and foresight'. It probably also helped that Niccolò disarmed the Great Khan's reservations, if any, upon seeing the boy by introducing him as 'he is my son, and your servant. I have brought him at great risk and trouble from those faraway lands to present him to you as your slave' (Polo 2015, p. 11). Khubilai Khan set Marco the task of serving as his emissary to 'a country called Qarajang'. Marco carefully studied the precedents set by Khubilai's envoys and quietly strove to avoid their mistakes by positively exceeding his stated remit by recounting every novelty and remarkable sight he had encountered while on his diplomatic mission. This impressed the Great Khan sufficiently for the former to retain Marco Polo as his special envoy for distant missions for a purported seventeen years (Polo 2015, p. 12).

Marco Polo's detailed account of Khubilai Khan's attitude towards the destitute in his kingdom was also positively glowing:

> Let me also tell you that no one who goes to the emperor's court to ask for bread is turned away empty handed; all who apply are given a portion. And you should know that more than 30,000 supplicants turn up daily, and not a day goes by without the appointed officials doling out 20,000 bowls of rice, millet and panic free of charge. … For this astonishing and staggering munificence, all the people are so fond of him that they revere him as a god. (Polo 2015, p. 136)

Marco also devoted nearly 20 pages of *The Travels* extolling Khubilai's penchant for collecting precious metals and gems to enrich his treasury while paying fair prices to all subjects who brought them to him. Even merchants travelling to the capital Khanbaliq willingly exchanged their cargoes of precious gems for the Khan's promissory notes of credit which the merchants then used to buy other goods from Cathay to trade outside it. Even hunting game and female prostitution were regulated by the Great Khan (Polo 2015, pp. 120–125).

Marco also went out of his way to recount in great detail how a certain Saracen mercenary named Ahmad exceeded the trust placed in him by the Great Khan as a lesson in correcting corruption and nepotism in high places. Ahmad had won the Great Khan's favour through his apparent loyalty, shrewdness and determination. But the source of his influence over Khubilai lay in the arts of sorcery. He cast a spell on Khubilai so that the latter would delegate to him plenipotentiary powers to appoint and dismiss officials. This supernatural influence extended to the impunity with which Ahmad employed gangs of thugs to compel fathers to surrender their eligible beautiful daughters to him in exchange for government appointments. Ahmad acquired great wealth through his entrenched system of extortion and forced patronage to the point where the ordinary Cathayans were enraged beyond relief. Two military commanders of non-Tartar and non-Saracen stock plotted to have Ahmad assassinated in tandem with planned uprisings in several cities. Ahmad was indeed beheaded by an assassin's blade but his loyal lieutenant launched a successful rearguard action to stop the mass revolt. Khubilai Khan learnt of these events and resolved to punish the ringleaders of the revolt while also thoroughly investigating Ahmad's nefarious network. As a result, Ahmad's dead body was thrown to the dogs so that they would feast on it. Those of Ahmad's sons who had taken after their father's evil ways were flayed alive. Finally, the Saracens' reputation attracted the Great Khan's wrath since their evil, intolerant ways contributed to Ahmad's abuse of power. From then on, Saracens could not kill anyone accused of not sharing their faith and had their sexual liberties with women restricted (Polo 2015, pp. 105–108). In recounting this episode, Marco Polo appeared to be framing Khubilai Khan in the image of a virtuous king visiting divine fury upon the wicked.

In fact, tales of moral degeneration abound in *The Travels* as if Marco Polo wanted to instruct his readers to reform their governance as the means to make the landed Silk Road safe for travellers of all faiths and professions. Worldly, power hungry kings who manipulated young men to commit assassinations across Central Asia and what we now call the Arab world came to ruin, lost their lives and ultimately their kingdoms due to immoral conduct. Native populations in Kashmir and Tibet were depicted in a condemnatory tone as 'idolaters and are completely depraved. They deem it no sin to commit robberies and other crimes and are the greatest rascals and thieves in the world' (Polo 2015, pp. 51, 152). While Marco noted that idolaters also live off the land and breed cattle like so many settled communities, he was reluctant to devote space to celebrating their achievements in the way he described and approved of Khubilai Khan's exploits in ordering his empire and building ornate settlements (Polo 2015, pp. 153–154). Man should advance and improve himself through avoidance of the ways of the animal even if he has to consume nature for sustenance. At the end of the day, Marco Polo was writing *for* civilizing the Silk Road. In this regard, his Catholic Christian upbringing probably framed his admiration of well-ordered places along the Road. Embracing *any* religion, including local variants of civic religion, was an improvement in the human condition, while sorcery and idolatry were primitive and evil-lesser substitutes.

ISLAM, HOSPITALITY AND OTHER GOOD DEEDS

Ibn Battuta travelled roughly the same routes that Marco Polo took from 1325 onwards. Unlike Marco, and perhaps more like Fa-Hsien nine centuries before him, Battuta was a Moroccan-born Muslim in search of both worldly and spiritual knowledge, speeded on his way by a chance meeting with an Islamic saint, Burhan al-Din the Lame who requested Battuta to convey greetings to his religious brothers in Sind, India and China (Mackintosh-Smith 2003, p. xi). The year 1325 also represented a different context in relations between Asia and Europe, one that was far more amenable to travel than during Marco Polo's time. The Crusades by Catholic Christianity against the Muslim world were a distant memory and the settled postures of the Tartars, or Mongols, as described by Marco Polo, meant that a vast majority of Tartars adopted the main religion of the Asian lands they conquered. In the areas known today as the Middle East and Central Asia, Ibn Battuta could look forward to the comforting familiarity of being hosted by Islamic populations. Trade was important in defining the Silk Roads and Battuta carried some valuable credentials with him. He was schooled in *fiqh*, or Islamic jurisprudence, which came in handy at many royal courts that ruled the territories Battuta travelled through (Mackintosh-Smith 2003, pp. x–xi). He was a rare man of talent as well as one predisposed towards helping his hosts deepen their Islamic identity and interconnections with like-minded polities.

Echoing Fa-Hsien and Marco Polo, Battuta expended much writing space on the travails of travel and celebrated the occasions when affable local hosts provided comfort and balm. On one of his initial series of stops following his departure from Tangier in present-day Morocco, Battuta was forced to depend on the kindness of strangers at the town of Bijaya where he was attacked by a severe fever. Battuta was stubborn and resisted the entreaties of his fellow travellers to rest as long as necessary vowing 'if God decrees my death, then my death shall be on the road' (Battuta 2003, p. 4). Impressed by this affirmation of faith in Allah, one of his fellow travellers promised to lend him his animal ride and lighter tents in order that he can travel faster with them 'for fear of molestation by roving Arabs on the road'. As promised, Battuta and his friend made good speed to the next town and claimed that 'this was the first of the divine mercies which were manifested to me in the course of that journey to the Hijaz' (Battuta 2003, p. 4). The grace of Allah continued upon reaching the next town, Qusantinah, where heavy rains soaked Battuta's clothing. The governor of the town offered to wash his soiled clothes and lent him new ones, including a gift of a mantle of 'fine Ba'albek cloth, in one of whose corners he had tied two gold dinars', which was a sign of honour (Battuta 2003, p. 4). In Egypt, Battuta crossed the Nile and encountered the relentless attacks by hyenas during night encampment despite travelling in a large party. Battuta records that he was fortunate to have survived with only a sack of dates eaten by the hyenas. At the next town, Aidhab, the 'black-skinned' Bujah people supplied Battuta and his entourage with fish, milk, dates, grain and blankets (Battuta 2003, p. 23).

Likewise, when Battuta reached Damascus in present-day Syria, he chose to focus his impressions on multiple acts of mercy and forgiveness towards accidental damages caused by careless slaves and poor manual labourers. Battuta wrote: 'Anyone who is a stranger there living on charity is always protected from having to earn it at the expense of his self-respect, and carefully sheltered from anything that might injure his dignity' (Battuta 2003, pp. 40–41). Battuta too was in need of money for living expenses by this stage. Fortunately, his new friend, a certain Maliki Professor Nur al-Din as-Sakhawi, came to his rescue having counted Battuta as a close relative after breaking fast with him in his house during the nights of Ramadan. This open ended charity was explained away by Nur al-Din with these words: 'It [the travelling provisions] will come in useful for anything of importance that you may be in need of', to which Battuta exclaimed 'may God reward him well!' (Battuta 2003, p. 41)

Charity and magnanimity characterized much of the remainder of Battuta's reflections on religiously motivated hospitality on the Silk Road. In a special chapter dedicated to his religious sojourn in Mecca, Islam's holiest city, Battuta begins his narrative by noting that Mecca is isolated geographically in a valley and that this was in complete accord with the Q'uran's description of her as sitting 'in a valley bare of corn'. But the magnanimity of Allah responded to her every need 'so that every delicacy is brought to her' (Battuta 2003, p. 47). Battuta claims to have consumed in Mecca grapes, figs, peaches and fresh dates 'that have not their equal in the world' and 'the flesh meats in Mecca are fat and exceedingly delicious in taste' (Battuta 2003, p. 48). Is this not a description more fitting for a trading centre? Battuta does not pause to explain the incongruence between Mecca's religious image and its gastronomic bounty. He asserts that 'the citizens of Mecca are given to well-doing, of consummate generosity and good disposition, liberal to the poor and to those who have renounced the world, and kindly towards strangers' (Battuta 2003, p. 48). In other words, this is a virtuous hub of material plenty. Battuta comments approvingly that when Meccans conduct a feast, they first offer food to those 'poor brethren' who have devoted themselves to the religious life as well as those 'sojourning at the Sanctuary'. 'Courtesy, kindness and delicacy' must be the demeanour the donor of food must assume. It is therefore not uncommon that the destitute follow the rich Meccans to their homes when it is known that the former have ordered bread baked for themselves. Battuta notes that no destitute person ever leaves dissatisfied after following the rich man. Moreover, Meccans have developed a good habit of donating groceries to orphan children who beg for food with two baskets by their side. Ironically, Battuta observed that Meccans are 'elegant and clean in their dress ... use perfumes freely, paint their eyes with kohl, and are constantly polishing their teeth with twigs of green arak-wood' (Battuta 2003, p. 48). This implies that Meccans exhibit public vanity and some degree of outward opulence as well. Battuta's description of women is even more telling about Mecca as a city of wealth and fashion: 'Meccan women are of rare and surpassing beauty, pious and chaste. They too make much of perfumes, to such a degree that a woman will spend the night hungry and buy perfume with the price of her food' (Battuta 2003, p. 49). It is only after describing these worldly aspects that Battuta delves into colourful stories of 'blessed import', healing trances and observing the fast.

It is as if Battuta wished to make the point that the foundation of the pious good life and spiritual radiance is built upon material bounty. It is therefore likely that in this spirit, Battuta narrated the story of how the deceased religious poet Shaikh al-Sa'di's grave in the Persian city of Shiraz kept giving back to the underprivileged long after the good man was called back to heaven. His grave was attached to a hospice that was deliberately sited beside the poet's tomb. This hospice had a fine building and a resplendent garden, and it was known that the Shaikh had expressly built marble cisterns within the grounds to allow anyone to enter the grounds to wash their clothes. Anyone could also eat at the table beside his tomb after washing their clothes. Battuta interpreted this as the Shaikh continuously making merit in the sight of God long after he was gone from earth. Battuta performed the same ritual at the Shaikh's tomb in order to gain the latter's blessings (Battuta 2003, p. 74).

When Battuta visited China, he wrote about its population in a bifurcated manner. While he pointedly described the Chinese as 'infidels' who worship idols 'and burn their dead as the Indians do', he noted the respect Chinese people showed to the Muslims who had to live apart from them for religious reasons. He admired the abstemious dressing—like the 'tunic[s] of coarse cloth'—of the wealthy and approved of their hoarding of gold and silver objects (Battuta 2003, p. 262). He also attributed the market value of silk to Chinese merchants trading heavily in it. Additionally, the Chinese were artisans and skilled craftsmen without equal. They had mastered the art of painting foreigners and encouraged artists to practice the drawing of portraits as a sign of honour for their visit. Finally, Battuta praised China as the safest country for the traveller given its *funduq* system of offering the traveller a sense of security and monitoring their presence at a way station between cities. The director of the *funduq* could also act as a safekeeper of the traveller's funds when he turns in for the night, arrange a guide for the traveller's onward journey and even arranges concubines for travellers if they should so desire! (Battuta 2003, p. 264) The remit of the *funduq* system is that it is a highway inn, concierge and safe deposit box for the medieval traveller. Through all these observations, Battuta is saying to his readers that universal coexistence is possible between rival faiths and belief systems so long as basic human needs are met along the many roads of human encounter in this world. Materialism can be in the service of noble, godly ends.

SEARCHING FOR THE IDEAL GLOBAL PORT CITY

On its part, the world of Tomé Pires' *Suma* reduces maritime Asia, circa 1515, to trade and its ancillary effects as a source of socio-political legitimacy for the monarchies, port cities and other proto-state entities. While the logic of this frame of analysis can be contested intellectually and politically in the twenty-first century given the fluid polarities of 'globalizing politics' in the era of the Internet, let us go along with Pires' worldview of mercantile civilization as the primary heuristic container for interpreting Asia for the moment. Pires leaves his reader in little doubt that the progress of civilization is made possible on the basis of material exchange. One need only sample his lengthy prefacing note to the King of Portugal:

> [I]n this *Suma* I shall speak not only of the division of the parts, provinces, kingdoms and regions and their boundaries, but also of the dealings and trade that they have with one another, which trading in merchandise is so necessary that without it the world could not go on. It is this that ennobles kingdoms and makes their people great, that ennobles cities, that brings war and peace. In this world it is customary for merchandise to be clean—I do not speak of the dealings in it, which are held in esteem—for what can be better than that which is based on truth. Pope Paul II was originally a merchant and he was not ashamed of the time he spent in trade, and the scholars of Athens used to praise trade as a wonderful thing, and nowadays it is carried on throughout the world, and particularly in these parts it is held in such high esteem that the great lords here do not do anything else but trade. It is pleasant, necessary and convenient, although it brings reverses, which make it more esteemed. (Pires, Suma Oriental Volume I, 1944a, p. 4)

It is obvious that this could have been authored by a late twentieth century agent of globalization: an International Monetary Fund (IMF) or World Bank official, the scion of an Asian tycoon armed with Protestant ethics, or a trader in the murky borderlands of Indochina and south China, or in the Tumen River Delta economic zone straddling the Russian Far East, northern China and various Central Asian Republics. Conversely, this excerpt could be seized upon by anti-globalization non-state civil society lobbies to condemn the naked materialist exploitation embedded in the vision of a borderless world of unlimited consumption and production chains. But mercantile civilization, as I have derived it in interpretation of the central thrust of Tomé Pires' writings, is more than a vision of pure capitalism. As he describes them, multiple *cultures* of mercantile civilization exist in as varied a range as the kingdoms that straddle coastal Asia.

It is also possible that Tomé Pires was consciously projecting Portugal's formula of neo-Malthusian political economy onto his observations. Medieval Portugal was a highly stratified society in the 1500s (Subrahmanyam 2012, p. 55). Even within its compact territory, relative to its European neighbours, there were divisions between coast and interior, north versus south, Lisbon against the rest of the country, as well as differences between Catholic clergy, urban bourgeoisie and the nobility (who were themselves divided against one another). To diffuse these tensions, His Majesty Dom Duarte (1433–1438) created a system of entailed estates whereby grants of land were made out to the eldest sons of the nobility, and treated by law as inalienable in every aspect, thereby leaving a large number of younger sons in each family as a '"surplus" to be exported', in Sanjay Subrahmanyam's turn of phrase, as entrepreneurs, explorers and military commanders to North Africa and subsequently, Asia (Subrahmanyam 2012, p. 55). Urban bourgeoisie tended to support overseas ventures in Asia or elsewhere only if the royal approval awarded to them did not crimp their abilities to reap profits from these distant trading networks. Moreover, the 'service nobility', mainly those who worked in banking and finance, literally saw profit in participating in royally sanctioned trade overseas. And finally, the urban labouring classes who coincided with the largest population concentrations in the northern parts of the country saw maritime activity as a safety valve for their economic and social prospects (Subrahmanyam 2012, pp. 56–57). An Asian dimension to Portugal's burgeoning maritime empire thus offered tantalizing solutions to domestic socio-political pressures. The interplay of early civil society demands, economic interests and elite interests intersected to embolden men like Tomé Pires to dedicate themselves to empire building through commerce, military occupation or supplying intelligence according to their agenda. Although Pires formally divided the *Suma* into five books, covering the political geography of 'Arabia, Egypt, and Persia as far as Cambay'; 'Cambay to Bhatkal (Baticalla)'; 'Bhatkal to Bengal'; 'Bengal to China'; 'all the islands'; and with a sixth book devoted to Malacca itself, we will not be examining his text in that order. Instead, as promised in the introduction, we will frame the reading of the *Suma* according to the drift of my argument of mercantile harmony.

To Pires, intrinsic to the claim of being a port city or trading kingdom of good repute is the idea that the society that exists within it exhibits some markers of improvement and aspiration towards a better life, however defined. In the world of the early sixteenth century, one cannot quite impose the framework of modernization as the ideal analytical trajectory. Instead, the world of maritime Asia encountered by Pires tended to exhibit social progress through varying degrees of subjective piety at one extreme, and social and material indulgence at the other. In Pires' representation, the world of pre-Portuguese conquest Malacca exhibited the misalignment of piety and materialism amongst its ruling elite. The King of Malacca overreached himself in wanting to dispossess the first Portuguese merchants of their lives while acquiring their goods. Moreover, the King's interpretation of Islam was laced with deep xenophobia and a superficial puritanism—as Pires saw it. Pires' contrasting vision of Malacca after the Portuguese conquest predictably asserted that the new masters were now delivering 'greater truth and justice' than what was witnessed by both native Malays and the foreign trading community before Portuguese governance: 'A Solomon was needed to govern Malacca, and it deserves one' (Pires, Suma Oriental Volume II, 1944b, pp. 281–283). Malacca's reputation as a trading hub could only soar as assorted foreign merchants returned to a well-ordered port.

Likewise, Pires indicted the Sultan of Cairo for mismanaging interreligious and communitarian harmony in both the city and its adjacent territories, contributing steadily to the erosion of its trading reputation. Instead, the Sultan of Cairo had overindulged himself in the company of his large number of wives and the services of slaves behind the palace walls, at the expense of his subjects' needs. Pires juxtaposed the Sultan's worldly extravagance against his dwindling revenue collection, derived from the taxation of spices passing through the city and pilgrims en route to worship at the Holy Sepulchre (Pires, Suma Oriental Volume I, 1944a, pp. 10–11).

In contrast to Malacca and Cairo, Persia has exhibited both extremes of indulgence and piety. Trade and the attendant accumulation of wealth and leisure time have 'spoiled' them:

> The Persians are very fond of pleasure, very orderly in their dress, and use many perfumes. They anoint themselves with aloes and with costly scented unguents. They have many wives. They are served by eunuchs, and the eunuchs who have charge of the women rise to be great lords. The Moors in general are all jealous men, and thus for all their good looks most of them are sodomites, including the Persians and the people of Ormuz. And they do not consider this to be unsuitable to their condition, nor are they punished for it, and there are even public places where they practice this for

money. And those who suffer this are beardless and go about dressed like women, and the Moors laugh at us when we point out to them the turpitude of that sin. (Pires, Suma Oriental Volume I, 1944a, p. 23)

At the other extreme, wealth, trade and power encouraged Persian leaders to practice the cult of the Prophet which was derived from the tussle between Prophet Mohammed's son-in-law Ali and four companions in Mohammed's company—Othman, Abu Bakr, Omar and Hacabar—following the Prophet's passing. According to Pires' account, Ali made himself out to be a true prophet in his own right and discredited not only his father-in-law Mohammed, but also the original four companions: 'And he [Ali] commanded that from thenceforward they should name Ali in their prayers and not Mohammed, saying that he had won much land at the point of his lance, that the twelve signs of the heavens were with him and that they had come together at his birth to make him a knight and a great prophet' (Pires, Suma Oriental Volume I, 1944a, p. 25). From then on, Persian kings and nobles had to choose which Prophet they were devotees of, and on that basis they decided their alliances and enemies. It came to pass that Sheikh Ismail, a devotee of Prophet Ali came to power by avenging his father's death at the hands of the King of Shiraz (an important Persian city) who was a believer in Mohammed. Sheikh Ismail attempted to join the trading reputation of Shiraz, and the representation of a united Persia believing solely in Prophet Ali, with the projection of his diplomatic authority forged through sword and merchandise:

the ambassadors sent by this Sheikh are attended by many mounted men, well dressed people of good appearance, very sumptuous, with vessels of gold and silver, which show forth the greatness of the Sheikh. To all the Moorish kings he sends gifts and presents, and learned men so that they may follow his law. He says that he will not rest until he sees all the Moors made followers of Ali in his time, and after that will come that which he knows ought to come. The Moorish people are for this new Sheikh and are so much the more angry at Your Highness power [of deviating from belief in Prophet Ali]. (Pires, Suma Oriental Volume I, 1944a, p. 29)

Finally, Pires even recognizes that heathens who are neither Muslim nor Christian sought to dignify their wealth with a large measure of constructed piety, as in the case of the landowners in the trading centre of Goa in the Indian subcontinent:

There are a great many heathens in this kingdom of Goa, more than in the kingdom of the Deccan. Some of them are very honoured men with large fortunes; and almost the whole kingdom lies in their hands, because they are natives and possess the land and they pay the taxes. Some of them are noblemen with many followers and lands of their own, and are persons of great repute, and wealthy, and they live on their estates, which are very gay and fresh. The heathens of the kingdom of Goa surpass those of Cambay. They have beautiful temples of their own in this kingdom; they have priests or Brahmans of many kinds. There are some very honoured stocks among these Brahmans. Some of them will not eat anything which has contained blood or anything prepared by the hand of another. These Brahmans are greatly revered throughout the country, particularly among the heathen. Like those of Cambay, the poor ones serve to take merchandise and letters safely through the land, because the rich ones rank as great lords. They are clever, prudent, learned in their religion. A Brahman would not become a Mohammedan (even) if he were made a king. (Pires, Suma Oriental Volume I, 1944a, p. 59)

In these myriad ways, Pires was making the point that piety and indulgence were conjoined as forms of social control exercised upon the permanent and transient populations of great trading cities, even if their degrees of success varied inevitably across the different parts of Asia.

In the *Suma*, Pires has indirectly sketched for his readers an allusion to the geographically connected Asian global city in the course of his pronouncements upon those sites he praises as archetypes of the great trading centre. Let us turn to consider his description of the glory of the port of Aden:

This town has a great trade with the people of Cairo as well as with those of all India, and the people of India trade with it. There are many important merchants in the city with great riches, and many from other countries live there also. This city is a meeting place for merchants. It is one of the four great trading cities in the world, and it has dealings inside the straits with Jidda, to which it trades most of the spices and drugs in exchange for the said (merchandise). It trades cloth to Dahlak and receives seed pearls in exchange; it trades coarse cloths and various trifling things to Zeila and Berbera in exchange for gold, horses, slaves and ivory; it trades with Sokotra, sending cloth, straw of Mecca, Socotrine aloes, and dragon's-blood; it trades with Ormuz, whence it brings horses; and out of the goods from Cairo it trades gold, foodstuffs, wheat, and rice if there is any, spices, seed pearls, musk, silk and any other drugs; it trades with Cambay, taking there the merchandise from Cairo and opium, and returning large quantities of cloth, with which it trades in Arabia and the Islands, and seeds, glass beads, beads from Cambay, many carnelians of all colours, and chiefly spices and drugs from Malacca, cloves, nutmeg, mace, sandalwood, cubeb, seed pearls and things of that sort ... it traded the merchandise from Malacca also with Pegu in exchange for lac, benzoin, musk and precious stones, rice also from Bengal, rice from Siam, and merchandise from China which comes through Ayuthia. And in this way it has become great, prosperous and rich, and the king receives all his revenues from Aden alone, for all the rest is nothing. (Pires, Suma Oriental Volume I, 1944a, pp. 16–17)

What we see here is the visible shape of a junction of exchange. This junction is a hub for transfers of luxuries, wealth and practical goods to onward third and fourth destinations. There is a pluralism of tradable items concomitant with a pluralism of merchants transiting though and residing in Aden. This hub also conflates the near and the far, 'global' and 'local', and draws the produce of lesser sites into a network of transregional circulation. While the physical geography of a deep harbour and an enlightened leadership appreciative of fostering the traffic and residence of foreign traders matter in building connectivity, the availability of a climate of public safety, the ability to consume and produce unique spices and manufactures matter in establishing greatness.

Consequently, Pires is dismissive of other towns on the Arabian peninsula such as Tor, Jidda, Fartak, Zeila, Berbera and Sokotra as attractive trading sites. These places are mostly plagued by poor physical attributes such as shallow, rocky harbours, 'bare ground and no grass' and infested by 'nomad robbers' demanding a degree of military protection of merchants far in excess of what these towns are worth in terms of valuable local produce (Pires, Suma Oriental Volume I, 1944a, pp. 18–19). Other factors of decline for reigning trading hubs, as noted by Pires, include traits of treachery and slipshod handiwork by craftsmen (Bengal), and a royal disinclination towards trade, discouragement of seamanship and allowing proximate interlopers to manage trade exclusively from one's borders (Japan) (Pires, Suma Oriental Volume I, 1944a, pp. 93, 131).

Pires did however distinguish the immense trading potential of Canton as a collection point of produce from all of China and of foreign merchants from the rest of Asia, from the stifling xenophobic authoritarianism of the Chinese emperor and his officials. If Canton represented in Portuguese eyes the unlimited wealth that could be traded out of China, the Portuguese would ultimately despatch Pires himself as their first ambassador to convince the Chinese to open up. As much as we can discern from Armando Cortesão's thumbnail sketch of Pires' life, Pires' mission manifested ironically a clumsy combination of military prowess, piety and indulgence to the Chinese court, resulting unfortunately in the delegation's dismal end (Cortesão 1944, pp. xxxvi–l). If there is a lesson to be learned from Pires' demise, it is that his articulation of mercantile civilization was not universally shared even if he has left us with some measured observations about the ideal port city along the maritime Silk Road.

Conclusion: A Silk Road Ecumenism?

In this unusual reading of assorted ancient travelogues *as* political theory and political sociology, I have attempted to find some tentative answers to the question of how travellers on the ancient Silk Roads found answers to the eternal question of cohabiting with human differences in beliefs and customs.

One clear answer is the idea of travelling the Road itself. Roads are *both* cultural and religious metaphors. Fa-Hsien, Marco Polo and Ibn Battuta travelled in search of inner need. For the Buddhist and Islamic pilgrims, the Road functioned as the vehicle and trial of their faith. The search for enlightenment meant overcoming or braving physical and other physiological dangers materializing unexpectedly on the road. A chance encounter with the right person could unlock a whole refreshing spring of spiritual affirmation. Friendship is spiritual. To be hospitable is to attain the highest of human values. To fulfil the needs of the destitute and the harassed traveller is to literally manifest pious magnanimity. Even in Pires' highly political and materialistic travelogue, the traveller put into a port because of its reputation for hospitality.

The Silk Road was also the road to knowledge and appreciation of diversity. Diversity did not necessarily need realignment to suit one's preconceptions. Diversity could offer valuable yet humble lessons about the multiple paths to the proverbial good life on earth, as well as in the afterlife. Finally, knowledge of well-ordered and chaste societies could be found outside of the traveller's pre-existing worldviews. One's willingness to learn is at stake. Conversely, in the narratives of all four travellers, negative moral examples of governance are a test of one's inner virtue particularly in dealing with the temptation of choosing the road of serving power and materialism alone as the zenith of the human condition. It was very clear in the writings of Fa-Hsien, Polo and Battuta that they adopted a consequentialist rule to judge the effects of pursuing worldliness alone.

Tomé Pires was also consequentialist but angled his views to support harmony between piety and indulgence only in order to uphold mercantile empire.

Ultimately, all four travellers never comprehensively resolve the tension between piety and material indulgence. As Pires captured it in his sharp observations on how prosperous city-cum-trading-empires sustain themselves, good governance must contain elements of discipline and public order. At the same time, craftsmen must take pride in their work, and traders must pioneer their terms of exchange and the range of goods on offer. There ought to be worldly rewards for those who work hard for their livelihood. In this regard, some find satisfaction in the pleasures of gastronomy, personal vanity or the pleasures of the flesh. There are more than a few distant echoes of this in today's hyper connected global cities of commerce, leisure and information hubbing. *But* the voices of Fa-Hsien, Polo and Battuta helpfully counsel that trade and its effects must add to the richness of human life in its aspects of virtue and service to humanity. In this way, mercantile harmony, rather than simply mercantile civilization *a la* Pires, is accessible to all along the Silk Roads, open to easy transaction if one is willing to improve one's spiritual and material well-being in balanced formation.

REFERENCES

Acharya, A. 2001. *Constructing a Security Community in Southeast Asia: ASEAN and the Problem of Regional Order*. London: Routledge.

Battuta, I. 2003. *The Travels of Ibn Battuta*. Ed. T. Mackintosh-Smith. London: Picador an imprint of Pan Macmillan.

Blyth, N. 2017. Belt and Road Initiative – A Project Worth More Than the Sum of Its Parts. *The Business Times (Singapore)*, May 12, p. 25.

Bradsher, K. 2015. A New Silk Road? Partners Are Wary. *International New York Times*, December 26–27, pp. 1, 13.

Buzan, B., and Y. Zhang, eds. 2014. *Contesting International Society in East Asia*. Cambridge: Cambridge University Press.

Chong, A. 2017. Civilisations and Harm: The Politics of Civilising Processes between the West and the Non-West. *Review of International Studies 43* (4): 637–653.

Cliff, N. 2015. Introduction. In *The Travels*, ed. M. Polo, xi–xlii. London: Penguin Books.

Cortesão, A. 1944. Introduction: The Paris Codex. In *The Suma Oriental of Tome Pires, an Account of the East, from the Red Sea to Japan, Written in Malacca and India in 1512–1515*, ed. T. Pires and A. Cortesão, xiii–xcvi. London: The Hakluyt Society.

Drakard, J. 1999. *A Kingdom of Words: Language and Power in Sumatra*. Kuala Lumpur: Oxford University Press.

Elisseef, V., ed. 2000. *The Silk Roads: Highways of Culture and Commerce*. New York: Berghahn Books and UNESCO Publishing.

Fa-Hsien. 1886. *A Record of Buddhistic Kingdoms; Being an Account by the Chinese Monk Fa-Hien (Ha-Hsien) of His Travels in India and Ceylon, A.D.399–414, in Search of the Buddhist Books of Discipline*. Translated and Annotated with a Corean Recension of the Chinese Text. Trans. J. Legge. Oxford: Clarendon Press.

Frankopan, P. 2015. *The Silk Roads: A New History of the World*. London: Bloomsbury Publishing.

Legge, J. 1886. Introduction. In *A Record of Buddhistic Kingdoms; Being an Account by the Chinese Monk Fa-Hien (Ha-Hsien) of His Travels in India and Ceylon, A.D.399–414, in Search of the Buddhist Books of Discipline. Translated and Annotated with a Corean Recension of the Chinese Text*, ed. Fa-Hsien and J. Legge, 1–8. Oxford: Clarendon Press.

Ling, L.H. 2014. *The Dao of World Politics: Towards a Post-Westphalian, Worldist International Relations*. Abingdon: Routledge.

Mackintosh-Smith, T. 2003. Foreword. In *The Travels of Ibn Battuta*, vii–xviii. London: Picador an imprint of Pan Macmillan.

Pires, T. 1944a. *The Suma Oriental of Tomé Pires: An Account of the East, from the Red Sea to Japan, Written in Malacca and India in 1512–1515*. Vol. I, Ed. A. Cortesão and Trans. A. Cortesão. London: The Hakluyt Society.

———. 1944b. *The Suma Oriental of Tomé Pires: An Account of the East, from the Red Sea to Japan, Written in Malacca and India in 1512–1515*. Vol. II, Ed. A. Cortesão and Trans. A. Cortesao. London: The Hakluyt Society.

Polo, M. 2015. *The Travels*. London: Penguin Books.

Shilliam, R., ed. 2011. *International Relations and Non-western Thought: Imperialism, Colonialism, and Investigations of Global Modernity*. Abingdon: Routledge.

Subrahmanyam, S. 2012. *The Portuguese Empire in Asia, 1500–1700: A Political and Economic History*. 2nd ed. Chichester: Wiley-Blackwell.

Xinhua News Agency. 2016, May 27. *Better Coordination Called for China-Indochina Peninsula Economic Corridor Construction*. Available at Silkroad.News.Cn: http://silkroad.news.cn/2016/0527/1438.shtml. Accessed 2 Aug 2016.

PART II

Critical Geographies on the Road

CHAPTER 4

The Belt and Road and the World: Why China's "One Belt, One Road" Initiative Is a Dilemma for Everyone

Quang Minh Pham and Le Hoang Giang

INTRODUCTION

What is China's Belt and Road Initiative (BRI), and what does it mean for the world? This question has been the topic of much debate since late 2013, when Chinese President Xi Jinping unveiled his vision of a land-based Silk Road Economic Belt and a twenty-first-century Maritime Silk Road that, if implemented, would together cover nearly the entire Eurasia and connect some of the world's largest economies into a massive economic zone. Almost immediately after the original announcement, steps have been taken to formalise the project, which has since greatly impacted the international level and within China itself, while generating different

Q. M. Pham (✉)
University of Social Sciences and Humanities,
Vietnam National University, Hanoi, Hanoi, Vietnam
e-mail: minhpq@ussh.edu.vn

L. H. Giang
International Cooperation Office, University of Social Sciences and Humanities,
Vietnam National University, Hanoi, Vietnam

© The Author(s) 2020
A. Chong, Q. M. Pham (eds.), *Critical Reflections on China's Belt & Road Initiative*, https://doi.org/10.1007/978-981-13-2098-9_4

responses from around the world. Due to the massive scale of this proposal as well as the rapidness with which it has been and is being implemented, it is imperative for all countries involved to get a clear sense of what the project and their participation therein will mean.

In this chapter, we focus on a key aspect of the BRI: how it can be a challenge for countries involved. On one hand, the BRI offers potentially lucrative economic benefits to its participants, but on the other hand entails serious political and security risks that they must take into account. As a result, countries included in China's "new Silk Road" ambition are caught within a dilemma of whether to reject BRI due to political concerns or to embrace the economic growth that it may bring about. Based on a multi-level analysis, we argue that the BRI is a dilemma for (1) China itself, (2) the existing global order, (3) a number of Eurasian states that are involved in China's vision, and (4) Vietnam. This approach allows for a holistic view on the BRI's impact and may reveal key strategic implications of each participant's role within the grand scheme.

The remainder of this chapter proceeds as follow. First, we provide an account of why BRI is a dilemma for China itself with a brief overview of its origin and its current status in China's policy. Next we argue that the BRI is a political challenge for the existing US-led global order, particularly in the era of President Donald Trump. What follows is an account of why the BRI is also a dilemma for Asian states (particularly those in Central Asia, South Asia, and Southeast Asia). Finally, we ponder how the BRI can be both an opportunity and a risk for Vietnam, who share an uneasy relationship with the Middle Kingdom. The chapter will conclude with some brief reflections.

DILEMMA 1: CHINA AND THE BRI

Known by many names, including "One Belt, One Road" until mid-2016, the Belt and Road Initiative (BRI) is an ambitious proposal championed by China that seeks to promote international and interregional trade and collaboration between European and Asian states. The project is composed of a land-based *Silk Road Economic Belt* that transcends continental Eurasia connecting China through Central Asia into Western Europe, and a *twenty-first-century Maritime Silk Road* that links Oceania and the South China Sea with the Indian Ocean, the Middle East, and the Mediterranean Sea. With this, 65 countries in total (including China) on the continents of Eurasia, Africa, and Oceania are involved, encompassing 62% of the world population and 30% of its economy (Chin and He 2016). In particular, the proposed "Belt and Road" consists of six continental corridors and one maritime route (China-Britain Business Council 2015, p. 9)[1]:

- New Eurasian Land Bridge
- China–Mongolia–Russia Corridor
- China–Central Asia–West Asia Corridor
- China–Indochina Peninsula Corridor
- China–Pakistan Corridor
- Bangladesh–China–India–Myanmar Corridor
- Maritime Silk Road

The origin and development of the Belt and Road Initiative is closely related to China's paramount leader since 2012—President Xi Jinping. On 7 September 2013, only ten months after becoming China's highest ranking decision-maker, Xi unveiled his plan for a "Silk Road Economic Belt" with Central Asia, and on 3 October 2013 continued to propose a "21st Century Maritime Silk Road" with Association of Southeast Asian Nations (ASEAN). Subsequently, the 3rd Plenary Session of the 18th Communist Party of China (CPC) on 9 November 2013 was an important milestone that marked the day the CPC officially called for the construction of "One Belt, One Road" (OBOR). On 13 December 2013, President Xi officially proposed the One Belt, One Road strategy. In reality, the implementation of the BRI is designated as follow: 2013 for proposing and finishing the initiative, 2014 for the promotion and promulgation of the BRI within all administrative levels of China, 2015 for completing the full action plan, and 2016 for the actual implementation (Pham 2017, pp. 84, 123–141). Although an unofficial initiative at first, the BRI was quickly formalised and in 2017 culminated in the Belt and Road Forum in Beijing in May 2017 where President Xi met with 29 world leaders from countries that are directly involved in the initiative.

---

[1] As mentioned earlier, the official English translation of the Initiative was changed from "One Belt, One Road" to "the Belt and Road" in mid-2016. This was due to the misleading implication that the Initiative only consists of one economic belt while in fact there were six proposed corridors. The original Chinese name, however, remained "yi dai, yi lu" or "one belt, one road."

What Is the BRI About?

The "Belt and Road" is a misleading name considering its essence and content. Essentially, the Initiative comprises a series of bilateral and multilateral deals between China and various countries in order to facilitate cross-border mobility. Its main content can be found in the *Vision and Actions on Jointly Building Silk Road Economic Belt and 21st-Century Maritime Silk Road*, issued jointly by China's Ministry of Foreign Affairs and Ministry of Commerce with authorisation of the State Council. Accordingly, five areas are identified as key cooperation priorities: (1) policy coordination between governments, (2) facilitating better connectivity through improving infrastructure, (3) unimpeded trade between states along the Belt and the Road, (4) financial integration, and (5) people-to-people bond (National Development and Reform Commission et al. 2015). Among these areas, the construction and enhancement of connectivity via infrastructure is considered the preeminent feature of the new Silk Road (Zhang 2016). Financing for the ambitious project is to be carried out through four primary mechanisms, being (1) specialised institutions (i.e. the Asian Infrastructure Investment Bank and the Silk Road Fund), (2) the Chinese banking system (including China Development Bank, China Exim Bank, and the Bank of China), (3) Chinese investment firms (namely CITIC Group, China Investment Corporation), and (4) a series of Chinese investment funds (Pham 2017, pp. 70–77).

What Does the BRI Mean for China?

First, it is necessary to point out that the BRI is as significant to China's domestic political and economic landscape as it is to the country's international integration. To begin with, one can see the proposed initiative's importance from the rapidity with which it was coined and developed. The transition of BRI from an initiative into a strategy took place in merely three months (September–November 2013), and its subsequent deployment was framed within a matter of years (2013–2016). The BRI was also included in China's 13th five-year plan for the first time (National Development and Reform Council 2016), signifying its importance as a blueprint for future economic development on one hand and the decisiveness of China's ruling circle on the other. Politically, the plan was also of great importance to President Xi, who intended it to be his personal legacy and an instrument to rally the CPC behind his cause (Bloomberg 2017).

The proposed plan also includes a goal to use connectivity enhancement to revitalise the underdeveloped Western provinces of China such as Xinjiang and, potentially, tighten the CPC's grip over the political unrest therein.

In terms of international relations, it is clear that China is using the BRI to assert itself as a major powerhouse of development and trade. Apart from the huge economic and financial benefit that the BRI—if executed successfully—can generate, the plan is also a key instrument to boost China's prestige and power worldwide. Over the first decade of the twenty-first century, China rose rapidly and became the world's second largest economy, and as a result has developed much potential for overseas investment and a need for larger markets. Within such a context the BRI may offer Chinese state-owned and private businesses a gateway to send their products, capital, technology, personnel, and other resources to Asia, the Middle East, Africa, and Europe. In strategic terms, such a grasp would extent Chinese influence far beyond the traditional Sinosphere and into the West, which in turn would most likely mean a pushback for the United States and its allies in the Eastern hemisphere. Parts of the Maritime Silk Road initiative include allowing China to utilise a series of naval ports in the Indian Ocean and its adjacent seas. This may result in a major shift in the global order, which will be dealt with in greater detail in the next section.

So Why Is BRI a Dilemma for China?

For all of its promises, the BRI is not without its challenges. These challenges make it difficult for China to come up with concrete action plans for implementing the BRI. First, there is the problem of its future prospect. As mentioned earlier, the BRI is the brainchild of Chinese President Xi Jinping and may well become his legacy, but there is no guarantee that the project may survive once Xi is no longer in power. The next generation of Chinese leaders can choose to continue Xi's vision, but they can equally choose to replace it with their own political ambition. Another problem involves the plan's enormousness, which leads to the fact that until now there have been few details of how the project can actually be implemented. In fact, it is so unclear that "Chenggang Xu, a professor of economics at the Cheung Kong Graduate School of Business, said it helps to think of OBOR as a 'philosophy' or 'party line', rather than anything concrete" (Griffiths 2017). Furthermore, China's goal of establishing international prestige may be undercut by past records of Chinese businesses' failures overseas, due to either poor technical capacity or unfavourable track records with local workers and environment. Finally, the BRI's financing mechanism is still heavily unilateral, with the Chinese accounting for much of the burden.

As a result, it is evident that the BRI is becoming a dilemma even for the Chinese themselves. To put in bluntly, China has done all it can to turn the BRI into their primary vision for development in the foreseeable future while it has not figured out what exactly should be done, hence a dilemma.

DILEMMA 2: THE WORLD AND THE BRI

Moving on from China to a greater scope, we argue that China's BRI is a dilemma for current major powers in the existing global order, represented by the United States. Scholars of the realist tradition of international relations have long been speaking of a rise of China challenging the United States' dominant role in the current global order, and when analysed with a realist lens one can see how China's BRI fits into such narrative.

In many ways, the BRI is a mysterious challenge for the United States—particularly under a Donald Trump presidency. This is not the least because Trump himself has been equivocal towards China and the BRI. On one hand, Trump has made no secret of his hostility towards China, labelling the latter a "currency manipulator" and staffing his cabinet with advocates of an aggressive stance towards China like Peter Navarro. On the other hand, Trump seems to have avoided direct criticism of the BRI, instead he has gone as far as sending a delegation of high-ranking officials to the Beijing Belt and Road Forum summit in May 2017 (Hsu 2017). As one of the highest priorities in Trump's administration so far has been the Korean nuclear crisis, one may be led to wonder whether Trump's support for China's BRI is a Nixonian tactic to get on China's good side and turn it against North Korea. Trump is, after all, not so much a man of strategy as a man of deal making.

With that being said, supporting the BRI may carry serious repercussions for the United States in the long run. If the Trump administration does turn away from free trade (like it did with the Trans-Pacific Partnership) and revert to protectionism, the BRI may present itself as an alternative to countries that depend heavily on free trade, and thereby gaining more support, giving way for China to assert itself as a new champion of free trade. A stronger BRI means a stronger Chinese influence and a weaker US dominance in Eurasia in particular and the world in general.

But this is not only in terms of the economic dimension. As mentioned earlier, parts of the BRI involve China's right to use a series of marine ports in Djibouti, Pakistan, and elsewhere around the world. And China has made no attempt to conceal its intention of using these ports as naval bases for its growing People's Liberation Army's Navy (Kynge et al. 2017). Should this intention be realised, China will have a firm basis to start challenging the United States' military presence around the world, thus risking a high likelihood of open conflict between the giants. Ironically, Trump's support for the BRI at the Belt and Road Forum in Beijing has been praised by Chinese media and would likely give legitimacy for the initiative, emboldening China as a result. And it seems that some people in Trump's administration also realise this irony, and speak up strongly against China's BRI, of which US Secretary of Defence James Mattis is an example (Economic Times 2017). Nevertheless, this internal disagreement among Trump's cabinet does little but highlight the strategic dilemma of the United States in the face of China's BRI.

DILEMMA 3: ASIA AND THE BRI

For Asian states, the BRI presents both challenges and opportunities but not in an equal manner. That is, while some countries are expected to gain much from the initiative, others may be prone to heavy losses economically and politically. Thus instead of a unifying force, the BRI may in fact be dividing Asia along sharp lines. This pattern also hints at (or, rather, gives credence to) the possibility of BRI actually becoming China's attempt to upset the status quo by rallying small and medium states towards its side as a counterbalance to other major powers in the region.

To get a sense of how this division is taking shape, it is important first to know who *is* and *is not* included in the BRI. Central Asia, the Middle East, some South and Southeast Asian nations (e.g. Pakistan and Thailand, respectively) belong to the former group, while Japan, South Korea, and other South and Southeast Asian nations (e.g. India, and briefly Singapore, respectively) fall into the latter. Here a pattern seems to emerge: rising economies and developing countries versus relatively powerful and developed countries. One dilemma, as a result, is how the group of developed economies can deal with China's initiative, and India provides an excellent example of this. For India, the dimensions of the Belt and Road are a direct geo-strategic threat as the land-based economic corridors and the Maritime Silk Road encircle India's continental and maritime borders, choking it from both directions. Moreover, China's plan for the land economic belt includes a route crossing the Pakistan-occupied Kashmir, and this alone was enough to enrage India to the point that it rejected participating in China's Belt and Road Forum summit in May 2017. As a result, India has already started on a countermeasure to China's BRI: its own version of infrastructure cooperative mechanism, known as the North-South Transport Corridor, that links India with Russia and Iran and facilitates better transportation of goods from India to Central Asia, Europe, Russia, and vice versa (Malmgren 2017).

The potentially divisive effect is even more evident as one looks to the Association of South East Asian Nations (ASEAN). As a regional organisation, ASEAN's most important principle is consensus, built upon every member's willingness to agree with one another for the greater good. Yet China's influence threatens to damage just that. For example, Singapore has long been profiting off the maritime traffic through the Straits of Malacca, but this revenue will be endangered if the Kra Isthmus Canal in Thailand is constructed as part of the Maritime Silk Road. As a result, Singapore is intensely concerned about the prospect of such a canal being built (Cheong 2016). In May 2017, Singapore was not invited to send its delegate to the Belt and Road Forum summit. While some ASEAN countries receive benefits from China's promise while some do not, China may very well exploit this gap as leverage to advance its strategic interests, such as in the South China Sea dispute. BRI thus does not promote connectivity for ASEAN in this case, but the opposite.

However, this is not to say that states which are included in China's BRI face no dilemma. On the surface, China's plan does seem appealing—particularly for developing countries—with its promises of better infrastructure, trade volume, and enhanced connection. In strategic terms, however, these promises entail an increase in China's economic and political presence. Specifically, Chinese investment could entail the risks of giving China access to these countries' natural resources and exclusive contracts for Chinese firms, which in the past have been proven to have damaging effects for the local environment and labour market (Pham 2017, p. 196). An increase in economic presence can also result in an increase in political influence, despite the claim by Beijing that no political strings are attached to BRI projects. The BRI is, therefore, a project that both attracts and repels politically, one that these countries can neither accept nor reject entirely without suffering some form of losses.

Dilemma 4: Vietnam and the BRI

Finally, the BRI proves to be a dilemma for Vietnam as well. As the Middle Kingdom's immediate neighbour to the South, Vietnam is among the most central actors within its proposed scheme, especially in the Maritime Silk Road proposal due to Vietnam's location relative to the South China Sea. The dilemma experienced by Vietnam is determined by (1) potential benefits of participating in the Maritime Silk Road, and (2) political risks of participating in the Maritime Silk Road.

Potential Benefits

Should Vietnam decide to become a part of the Maritime Silk Road, it will become part of one of the largest maritime trading networks in world history. This includes a surge in trade volume, better connectivity and traffic with other ports in the contiguous regions, easier circulation of goods and commodities, and enhanced regional integration.

Political Risks

Vietnam and China share a "special relationship" that has been both harmonious and tumultuous throughout history. Both countries have at various times been enemies at war or brothers in arms, but what never changes is Vietnam and China's shared fate as neighbours. As such, China plays a constantly significant—if not central—role in Vietnam's foreign policy.

When it comes to joining the Belt and Road Initiative, there are a number of factors Vietnam has to take into account. Firstly, before considering the economic benefits, Vietnam must prioritise how such an action would affect its territorial claim in the South China Sea. Particularly, it must consider how disputes between China are to be resolved in a way consistent with international law and regulations. If joining the Maritime Silk Road means sacrificing its rightful claims, Vietnam would never be a part of it. Secondly, Vietnam has to consider what joining the BRI in general would mean for the Vietnamese economy; that is, whether it will boost or impede Vietnamese products' competitiveness, and whether Vietnam would be more or less dependent on Chinese products, services, and capital. Finally, in calculating its next steps Vietnam has to consider what impacts it may have on China's reputation in the world. Due to China's proximity to Vietnam and influence in the world, it is best that despite whatever course it takes, it would still be able to avoid unnecessary hostility and resent-ment. And it is because such factors require careful consideration regard-ing the BRI that participation in the latter can be seen as a dilemma for Vietnam.

CONCLUSION

In summary, we argue that China's Belt and Road Initiative, despite its promises and potentials, is not without risks and challenges. When anal-ysed under a strategic lens, it is evident that all relevant actors have reasons to seriously consider participating or rejecting China's proposal. However, there are sufficient reasons for the BRI to be considered a dilemma for every party involved on the global, regional, and national levels. Thus it is up to policy planners and decision-makers to carefully weigh all relevant factors, so as to derive the optimal courses of action for their countries, regions, and the world.

REFERENCES

Bloomberg News. 2017. One Belt, One Road, One Man. *Bloomberg News*, May 16. https://www.bloomberg.com/news/articles/2017-05-15/one-belt-one-road-one-man-xi-lords-over-all-at-china-summit.

Cheong, Suk-Wai. 2016. The Thai Canal May Change Singapore Forever. *Strait Times*, April 30. http://www.straitstimes.com/lifestyle/arts/the-thai-canal-that-may-change-singapore-forever.

Chin, Helen, and Winnie He. 2016. *The Belt and Road Initiative: 65 Countries and Beyond.* https://www.fbicgroup.com/sites/default/files/B%26R_Initiative_65_Countries_and_Beyond.pdf. Accessed 6 Sep 2017.

China-Britain Business Council. 2015. *One Belt One Road: A Role for UK Companies in Developing China's New Initiative.* http://www.cbbc.org/cbbc/media/cbbc_media/One-Belt-One-Road-main-body.pdf. Accessed 6 Sep 2017.

Griffiths, James. 2017. Just What Is This One Belt, One Road Thing Anyway?. *CNN News*, May 12. http://edition.cnn.com/2017/05/11/asia/china-one-belt-one-road-explainer/index.html.

Hsu, Sara. 2017. Trump's Support For China's One Belt, One Road Initiative Is Bad For U.S., Good For World. *Forbes*, May 18. https://www.forbes.com/sites/sarahsu/2017/05/18/trumps-support-for-chinas-one-belt-one-road-initiative-is-bad-for-u-s-good-for-world/#4b63c9793402.

Kynge, James, Chris Campbell, Amy Kazmin, and Farhan Bokhari. 2017. How China Rules the Waves. *Financial Times*, January 12. https://ig.ft.com/sites/china-ports/?mhq5j=e5.

Malmgren, Pippa. 2017. Malmgren on China's OBOR and Its Impact on International Security. *Foreign Policy Concepts*, July 23. https://foreignpolicy-concepts.com/malmgren-obor-bri-international-security/.

National Development and Reform Commission. 2016. *The 13th Five-Year Plan for Economic and Social Development of the People's Republic of China, 2016–2020*. Beijing: Central Compilation and Translation Press. http://en.ndrc.gov.cn/newsrelease/201612/P020161207645765233498.pdf.

National Development and Reform Commission, Ministry of Foreign Affairs, and Ministry of Commerce of the People's Republic of China. 2015. *Vision and Actions on Jointly Building Silk Road Economic Belt and 21st-Century Maritime Silk Road*. http://en.ndrc.gov.cn/newsrelease/201503/t20150330_669367.html.

Pham Sy Thanh. 2017. *Mot vanh dai, mot con duong (OBOR): Chien luoc cua Trung Quoc va ham y chinh sach doi voi Viet Nam* [One Belt, One Road: China's Strategy and Policy Implications for Vietnam]. Hanoi: The gioi Publisher.

The Economic Times. 2017. On OBOR, US Backs India, Says It Crosses 'Disputed' Territory: Jim Mattis. *The Economic Times*, October 4. http://economictimes.indiatimes.com/articleshow/60932827.cms?utm_source=contentofinterest&utm_medium=text&utm_campaign=cppst.

Zhang, Junhua. 2016. What's Driving China's "One Belt, One Road" Initiative. *East Asia Forum*, September 2. http://www.eastasiaforum.org/2016/09/02/whats-driving-chinas-one-belt-one-road-initiative/.

CHAPTER 5

Infrastructure Construction as Empire Consolidation in Chinese History

Trinh Van Dinh

If we look back to Chinese history, it is interesting to note that every major dynasty in China, from the great Qin Dynasty onward, has built for itself a great legacy or a world-class strategy. For example, the Qin Dynasty was associated with the Great Wall; for the Han Dynasty, the opening of the world famous Silk Road; and the Sui Dynasty, in turn, is remembered for the opening and connecting of the world's largest river system at the time, the Grand Canal.[1] During the Tang Dynasty, the explorer Xuanzang traveled the Silk Road to India to read and acquire Buddhist sacred texts, and consequently, in doing so, ushered in a new era of Chinese culture. Likewise, Genghis Khan and his descendants traversed the Silk Road,

---

[1] The major Chinese river systems connected with each other include: Huanghe, Huaihe, Changjiang, and Qiantang and connected to the sea.

This research is funded by Vietnam National University, Hanoi (VNU) under project number QG.19.28.

T. Van Dinh
Office for Research Affairs, University of Social Sciences and Humanities, Vietnam National University, Hanoi, Vietnam

A. Chong, Q. M. Pham (eds.), *Critical Reflections on China's Belt & Road Initiative*, https://doi.org/10.1007/978-981-13-2098-9_5

leaving in their wake markers that created the basis for the trading networks that bound Asia intimately into European prosperity. During the Ming Dynasty, Admiral Zheng He connected China with Southeast Asia, South Asia, Europe, and Africa by the sea. Today, the geography of all these linkages is known under the label "The Belt and Road Initiative" (BRI).

Additionally, the idea of "connectivity" joins all the above-mentioned achievements. The nature of the "connectivity" can also be understood in its mechanical aspects: Interconnection, complementation to perfect the existing, build on the basis of the existing routes, or even initiate renewal. But the new story that has emerged with the Belt and Road Initiative is that it presents a way of survival and development for the State and its corresponding society, a theme repeated in many of China's strategic projects. The BRI transforms individual works into a massive, unified body that creates a new look, generates productivity, and imparts new vitality to China. *Secondly*, it restructures domestic interconnection in China. *Thirdly*, the BRI is geared toward connectivity between China and the world outside. *Fourthly*, each time the BRI makes such a connection, China undergoes a great renaissance. *Fifthly*, those connections, especially those that will serve as the precondition for China's historic expansion, are the lineage from the past to the present. The connectivity for change is therefore an operational thumb rule in China's development.

GRAND PROJECTS OF CONNECTIVITY IN CHINESE HISTORY

Connections Among the Mountain Peaks: The Great Wall

During the Zhou Dynasty, central and western Inner Mongolia (the Hetao region and surrounding areas) were inhabited by nomadic peoples such as the Loufan, Linhu, and Dí, while eastern Inner Mongolia was inhabited by the Donghu. During the Warring States period, King Wuling (340–295 BC) of the state of Zhao, based in what is now Hebei and Shaanxi provinces, pursued an expansionist policy toward the region. After destroying the Dí state of Zhongshan in what is now Hebei province, he defeated the Linhu and Loufan and created the commandery of Yunzhong near modern Hohhot. King Wuling of Zhao also built a long wall stretching through the Hetao region. After Qin Shihuang created the first unified Chinese empire in 221 BC, he sent the general, Meng

Tian, to drive the Xiongnu from the region, and incorporated the old Zhao wall into the Qin Dynasty's Great Wall of China. He also maintained two commanderies in the region, Jiuyuan and Yunzhong, and moved 30,000 households there to consolidate control over the region. After the Qin Dynasty collapsed in 206 BC, these efforts were abandoned (Many Authors 1999, p. 437).

Among the great works completed, the Great Wall is a special and highly differentiated type of monument. It is the largest type of border wall in China as well as outside it. The wall connects high mountain peaks and extends in record length across many countries. The wall is also ironic for manifesting a form of closed connectivity: It connects not to open up cross-border exchanges or trading, but to close off the exchanges between China and the West. It must be understood that this closure was enacted to ensure the survival of China in the face of the permanent threat of a Xiongnu invasion. The Great Wall served as an enduring legacy of imperial defense since every dynasty made it a standard policy to repair, embellish, and protect it. Therefore, we must understand the significance of the Great Wall as a symbol of imperial unity and extension sired by a highly centralized monarchy presided over by Qin Shihuang.

Linking among Rivers and Canals

Thus, if the Great Wall embodies the connection between mountainous peaks, the canal system erected by the various Chinese dynasties represents waterborne connectivity. We should understand the canal system as a riverine system artificially dug by human beings who link them together in tandem with the natural river tributaries. The foundation of the Grand Canal was laid in the sixth century BC. It was thus closely associated with the Sui Dynasty. It should be noted that the Grand Canal system, is on one hand, the connection and clearing of the new river system, and on the other hand, it is the connection of that canal system with China's large natural river system such as Yangtze and Yellow Rivers. The circulation of water across China has played an important role in the Chinese trade in the northern and southern parts of the country, creating a model for prosperity in the Tang Dynasty. This was especially evident during the An Lushan Rebellion, when both warlords and the state relied on the canals for improving their finances in their respective struggles. The network of canals during the Sui period reached from Daxing 大興 (i.e. Chang'an) in the west and linked the commandery of Zhuojun in the northeast (today's Bejing) and Yuhang in the southeast, and thereby connected the systems of Dagu River (today's River Haihe) with that of the Yellow River, the River Huai, the Yangtze River, and the Qiantang River (in modern Zhejiang). All important cities of the empire could be reached by this canal system: The metropolitan area (Jingshi 京師, i.e. Chang'an), the Eastern Capital (Luoyang), Zhuojun (Youzhou 幽州), Junyi (Bianzhou 汴州, i.e. Kaifeng), Liangjun 梁郡 (Songzhou 宋州, today Shangqiu, Henan), Shanyang 山陽 (Chuzhou 楚州, today Huai'an, Jiangsu), the "Yangtze Capital" Jiangdu (Yangzhou), Wudu 吳郡 (Suzhou), and Yuhang (Hangzhou). This system was an important component for the eventual revival of a nationwide economy under the Tang dynasty (Many Authors 1999, p. 491).

Connections with the Seaports and Deserts: The Silk Roads

If the Great Wall is the connection among the peaks, the Grand Canal system is a connection among the rivers, then the Silk Road at sea is symbolized by Zheng He's renowned trans-oceanic voyages. If the Great Wall is a fundamental connection within China, the Sea Road connects China's ports with the ports of other countries outside China. It consists mainly of links connecting the East and South East provinces of China to ports across the seas. The twin of the Silk Road on the sea is the connection among the deserts since this road passes mainly through the deserts of many countries. It can be said that the East-West road connects China and Europe through a series of countries in Central Asia on the basis of their common contiguity with many deserts cutting a unique path in a conjoined history.

Having set out a few historical precedents, we can now outline the connectivity aspects of the Belt and Road Initiative today as a premise for comment on China's longstanding connectivity rules.

CONNECTIVITY IN THE BRI

Based on the Act on *Vision and Action*, and based on the current practice up to this point, the Belt and Road Initiative (BRI) makes two main promises of improved communication: One connects China to the world, and the second, interconnects within China. The relevant policy statement from Beijing reads as follows:

The Belt and Road run through the continents of Asia, Europe and Africa, connecting the vibrant East Asia economic circle at one end and developed European economic circle at the other, and encompassing countries with huge potential for economic development. The Silk Road Economic Belt focuses on bringing together China, Central Asia, Russia and Europe (the Baltic); linking China with the Persian Gulf and the Mediterranean Sea through Central Asia and West Asia; and connecting China with Southeast Asia, South Asia and the Indian Ocean. The 21st-Century Maritime Silk Road is designed to go from China's coast to Europe through the South China Sea and the Indian Ocean in one route, and from China's coast through the South China Sea to the South Pacific in the other. (State Council of PRC 2015)

On the basis of that framework idea, the formation of specific cooperation corridors is as follows:

On land, the Initiative will focus on jointly building a new Eurasian Land Bridge and developing China-Mongolia-Russia, China-Central Asia-West Asia and China-Indochina Peninsula economic corridors by taking advantage of international transport routes, relying on core cities along the Belt and Road and using key economic industrial parks as cooperation platforms. At sea, the Initiative will focus on jointly building smooth, secure and efficient transport routes connecting major sea ports along the Belt and Road. The China-Pakistan Economic Corridor and the Bangladesh-China-India-Myanmar Economic Corridor are closely related to the Belt and Road Initiative, and therefore require closer cooperation and greater progress. (State Council of PRC 2015)

More specifically, the document proceeds to identify three key areas that need to be linked to outside China: The northwestern and northeastern parts of Asia, southwest Asia, and the coastal areas of Hong Kong, Macau, and Taiwan. For the Northwest and Northeast regions, the document identifies the following.

Concerning the structure of the connectivity, the frame literally consists of the Belt and the Road. The Belt includes roads, railways, connections to key cities, and logistics centers. The roads encompass not just sea routes but all the coastal cities, large industrial centers, key seaports, as well as the interconnected systems of the rivers flowing to the sea. The nature of the connectivity is such that both Belt and Roads meet at large junctions, joining landed roads, railways, and waterways with seaports.

Thus, in essence, it is a network, a circle connected or interconnected, so that truly it is the structure of a "crystal lattice", living organism or as iconographic as a strip of "a snake biting its tail" (Johnson 2016, pp. 1–25).

Thus, connectivity in the Belt and the Road continues to vindicate the rule of connectivity of Chinese tradition. In essence, the economic belt of the Silk Road is the renaissance of the ancient landed Silk Road. The Silk Road at sea of the twenty-first century is essentially a revival of the core of Zheng He's route. Thus, *The Belt and Road Initiative* is the continuation of the rule of interconnection in the Chinese tradition. In this sense, the Belt and the Road aim at restoring the past rather than an initiative. We can now review the precedents for the Belt and Road historically.

PRECEDENTS BEFORE *THE BELT AND THE ROAD INITIATIVE*

Qin Shihuang-Meng Tian: The "close connection" among the Pre-existing Forts and Linking them into the Great Wall

Meng Tian was a General during the Qin Dynasty, in 221 BC, after the reunification of China. Qin Shihuang ordered General Meng Tian to lead 30,000 troops to expel the Xiongnu, occupying Ha Nan (now the Ha Sa, on the Yellow River). Meng Tian directed the process of connecting the cities and forts of Qin, Zhao, and Yen. Besides his own troops, Meng Tian also directed many workers for ten years to complete the task.

Zhang Qian and Emperor Wu of Han Dynasty Who Connected West Asia and China

Zhang Qian (Chinese: 張騫; d. 113 BC) was a Chinese official and diplomat who served as an imperial envoy to the world outside of China in the second century BC, during the time of the Han dynasty. He was the first official diplomat to bring back reliable information about Central Asia to the Chinese imperial court, then under Emperor Wu of the Han Dynasty, and played an important pioneering role in the Chinese colonization of the region now known as Xinjiang. Today Zhang Qian's travels are associated with the major route of transcontinental trade, the Silk Road. In essence, his missions opened up to China the many kingdoms and products of a part of the world then unknown to the Chinese.

Father and Son of Sui Dynasty: Emperors Wen and Yang Build the Grand Canal Connecting the River System and Canals and with the Great Plains of China

The Sui Dynasty initiated the linking and digging of the previously existing river system in China, linking the northern waters and the South China Sea systems together with the river system. They established a solid foundation for a Chinese maritime route, a precondition for a shifting economy focusing on the south, and ultimately providing a sound basis for the Tang Dynasty's flourishing economy. While the pressing initial motives were for the shipment of grains to the capital, and for transporting troops and military logistics, the reliable inland shipment links would facilitate domestic trades, flow of people, and cultural exchange for centuries. Along with the extension of the Great Wall, and the construction of the eastern capital city of Luoyang, these mega projects, led by an efficient centralized bureaucracy, would mobilize millions of conscripted workers from the large population base, at a heavy cost in human lives.

Genghis Khan and Kublaï Khan as Builders of China-Europe Land Routes

Genghis Khan and his nephew, Emperor Kublai Khan, established a joint reputation for being builders of durable trade routes connecting China and Europe: "Under the Mongol Empire, the ruling scope has reached a new peak ... A 'pass' is well protected for the exchange of goods, people and ideas. Before Mongolian checkpoints, post offices, payment systems and credit cards (Paiza), trade and road transport had been well-governed, not seen [before] on this road" (Garten 2017, p. 41). Although known for the brutality of his campaigns and considered by many to have been a genocidal ruler, Genghis Khan and his descendants are also credited with bringing the Silk Road within one cohesive political environment. This brought communication and trade from northeast Asia into Muslim southwest Asia and Christian Europe, thus expanding the horizons of all three cultural areas.

Zheng He and Zhu Di, Who Connected China-Southeast Asia, South Asia, Europe, and Africa

From 1405 to 1433, the Yongle Emperor (2 May 1360–12 August 1424), Zhu Di, who reigned in the early Ming Dynasty, ordered Admiral Zheng

He to command seven expeditionary voyages to Southeast Asia, South Asia, Western Asia, and East Africa with a 27,000 strong crew on 162 boats.

The Dual Leadership Connecting the Belt and the Road in the 2000s

Continuing the tradition, the leadership duo of President Xi Jinping and Prime Minister Li Keqiang is associated with the new plans for connectivity. Yet, taking the historical perspective, one cannot fail to mention Deng Xiaoping, who opened up post-Mao China to the world, the trailblazer for the ideas circulated between Xi Jinping and Li Keqiang. In particular, Xi Jinping is the centerpiece of Deng-Xi-Li reform triad. In this "spindle of reform", Mr. Xi is in the middle, the center of the twin axis connecting the Belt and the Road.

Deng Xiaoping: Who "Opened" and "Connected" China with the Whole World

Deng Xiaoping is considered to be the second most open-minded character since the Chinese Han Dynasty. In view of Deng Xiaoping's position in Chinese history, Ezra Vogel offer his unique interpretation: "The structural changes that took place during Deng's leadership were ranked as the most radical changes since the Chinese empire formed in the Han dynasty two thousand years ago" (Garten 2017, p. 141).

Compared to Deng, Xi is a realist who has connected China with the rest of the world through the Belt and Road Initiative. Seen from this point of view, each plays a different role in the rise of China. But they both demonstrated a great desire to bring China back to the center and lead the world. The only difference is one thing, Mr. Deng instructed Xi to practice, "lower one's profile and wait for the right time", but Xi did not listen to Mr. Deng, he amended the historical precedent to facilitate China's rise to great power status earlier.

Xi Jinping: Li Keqiang: The Conceptual Design Person and the Implementer of Connecting Ideas

Based on the events that have taken place since the adoption of the *Vision and Action* document in China, since Mr. Xi addressed the idea of forming the 'unified generality', Mr. Li's office has consistently and strongly developed this idea of the Belt and Road Initiative.

Xi Jinping: The Connecting Character and the Soul of the Belt and Road Initiative

Strictly speaking, Beijing is neither the center nor the starting point of the BRI today. The heart of the Silk Road is Xi'an, capital of Shaanxi. Mr. Xi once said proudly: "My hometown, Shaanxi, is at the beginning of the ancient Silk Road. Standing here looking back at history, I listened to the sound of camels echoing in the middle of the hill, I saw the thin smoke scattered, scurrying, the way that birds fly in the desert wide. All that makes me feel very close" (Xi 2014, p. 287). As we know it, Xi'an (formerly known as Chang'an) is the oldest and richest traditional capital of China, the capital of the two most dynamic dynasties—the Han and Tang Dynasties. Not far away, Xianyang, also in Shaanxi, was the capital of the Qin Dynasty. The top three dynasties of China have been based in Shaanxi, which is understandable when Xi proudly praises his hometown of the three most lauded dynasties in Chinese history.

The Belt and Road augurs well for restoring Xi'an, Shaanxi's capital, to its former glory. Incidentally, the grave of Xi's father—Mr. Xi Zhongsun—is located there. In essence, it is a return to the homeland, a connection back to the past, taking and seeking inspiration from the glorious past of a wealthy man. With this revitalization, it is also easy to understand the Xi'an action plan as a key to the Silk Road, in particular, the Xi'an Transportation University serves as the focal point for international academic exchanges about the Silk Road (Thanh 2017, p. 127). Hundreds of universities are involved in shaping that academic dimension of the BRI. Xi's special publicized affection for his hometown is a deliberate move. At one stroke, he resurrected dynastic tradition and added vitality to his traditional homeland. In many ways, Xi Jinping is the new Chinese Emperor, connecting and revitalizing his homeland.

Not only that, we must acknowledge the legacy of the Han Dynasty, since Xi'an was also its capital. The Han Dynasty Emperor Zhang Qian was dubbed the "Tracer" opening the Han empire to the world, and this policy was strongly continued under Emperor Wu. Zhang Qian, interestingly, is a Shaanxi "citizen" again. Today, the Shaanxi Museum features both the Zhang Qian statue and Zhang Qian tomb. Therefore, the many symbolisms of the road, and of cultural exchanges in the past, will guide Xi Jinping to the crossroads of cultural exchanges at Xi'an University of Transportation.

Besides Xi'an in Shaanxi, Fujian and Zhejiang are also mentioned as the focal points of China's twenty-first century Silk Road. It is known that Fujian and Zhejiang were the famous ports of China in the past where Zheng He started and built the boats in history, but the connection of these places together with Xi'an creates a new layer of meanings in restoring and connecting them, because Xi Jinping, the designer of the BRI was once the Secretary of Fujian and Zhejiang.

CONCLUSION: AN OVERVIEW OF THE BRI's HISTORIC SIGNIFICANCE

The Role of Connectivity: Reviving China and Maintaining China's Global Leadership

In retrospect, every time China appears to fulfill its projects for pioneering connectivity, it marks the zenith of the reigning Chinese empire. The Great Wall was successfully completed during the reign of Qin Shihuang, unifying the whole of China while also concentrating the authority and power at the top. Zhang Qian opened the Silk Road, linking China with the world, and implementing all these during the peak of the Han Dynasty. The river system that was connected by canals was also completed during the most glorious part of the Sui Dynasty. Admiral Zheng He ventured out to sea seven times in the Zhu Di period, which was also widely regarded as the peak of the Ming Dynasty. The BRI today arises at the end of 30 years of China's most uninterrupted phase of modern development. Hence, it is difficult to avoid linking the BRI to China as the world's number two economy and its aspirations toward global dominance.

On the other hand, the completion of connectivity projects exerts multi-dimensional effects on China. The Great Wall helped to shape the "Look South" development of China. As a defensive wall, it virtually eliminated the Xiongnu "barbarians" as a threat to the stability of the empire. The Silk Road opened up the celestial kingdom even further by throwing open the doors of the Chinese market to the world. The gold and silver of the outside world poured into China since Chinese products were sold outside the kingdom with great financial gain. Arriving on the Silk Road, Buddhism changed the face of Chinese culture and inculcated the idea of harmony (*hexie*). Merchants trading within China lent a social and cultural unity to its people.

In the same way, trade with foreign merchants enriched Chinese culture both materially and ideologically. Unfortunately, all this took place during the peak of the respective dynasties. But the demonstration effects of grand connectivity projects persisted into the country's modern era. Hence, the BRI can be considered as a marker of the peak of the modernization of the People's Republic of China, but at the same time, it will provide China with the foundation to build the Chinese dream for its population. More realpolitik-minded observers will however observe that if gold and silver from other parts of the world pour into China, it also means that other places will run short of money and resources. This is especially the strategic fear today regarding natural resources, gems, and oil from all over the world flowing to China (Cardenal and Araújio 2015, p. 162).

The Origin of Connectivity Redux: From Obsession and Fear of Separation and Schizophrenia

It is a fact that China is the second largest economy in the world, and the third largest nation in the world by territorial size. But it remains a divided and unstable country which faces latent separatist tendencies. This is the source of the deep rooted desire to unite the Chinese people in the mind of the new paramount leader Xi Jinping. The elite leading scholars of Tsinghua University, led by Hu Angang, reflect this strategic obsession insightfully. In the section *"Assessing China's Changes in Strategic Resources"*, the authors write: "China is the third largest country in the world and borders dozens of countries, and furthermore, [it] is still divided, requiring the state to pay the necessary defense costs, but the central budget is too small to address these issues. This is the 'Death Penalty' of China's strategic resource" (Hu 2003, p. 90). The story of centrifugalism has proven to be a historical obsession resonating through China's imperial tradition of juxtaposing unity and division. It will be an insult[2] to any Emperor or any state institution if China remains in disunity for a considerable period of time. For instance, the story of Taiwan's unification has become a core interest of China, because the plot is not just about territorial imperfection. More importantly, it involves the question of the incapacity of national unification efforts by one of the world's leading powers.

---

[2] This obsession is so great that the Chinese have compiled a dictionary called "National Shame".

As a symbol connected to the question of national unification the Great Wall of China should conclude our final reflection. The Wall was built up as a product of the schizophrenic era of the Spring and Autumn Wars of ancient China. But the era of the construction of the Wall also coincided with the flourishing of the essence of Chinese ideology and elitism: Confucianism, Taoism, Confucius, Lao Tzu, Trang Tu, and Zonghengjia (縱橫家/纵横家). The Great Wall served as a link to unity, symbolizing political awareness, political aspirations, and political persistence formed on the basis of the historical experiences of this period. Before that, the small cities and kingdoms thrived in atomistic fashion. On the other hand, the Wall was a direct military response to the Xiongnu threat. While the Wall did not eliminate the invasion of these "barbarians", its defensive presence crucially confined the latter's space for maneuver, enabling successive dynasties to marshal time and resources to wipe out the Xiongnu completely over time. On another level, the symbolic defensiveness of the Great Wall has completely eradicated the so-called the political spring associated with the "Hundred Flowers' Bloom", the only period of democracy and freedom in Chinese history to date. The special culture of the countries in Spring and Autumn War also eliminated with the Wall's construction. In sum, the Great Wall is a symbolic representation of China's fragmented obsession with modernization, unity, stability, and innovation among its people.

Today, the BRI, as a successor to the Wall, strengthens the central government, unites the inland regions, expands the area of influence, joins up the underdeveloped regions, and empowers a new empire. After 30 years of development at all costs, China seems to be losing the driving force of development, a worrying prospect for a Chinese Communist Party that has survived on the basis of continuous economic development for over 30 years. The BRI is the trump card that can supply a new glue for bonding the Chinese people against the temptations of separatism and disillusionment with progress. China's participation in the Belt and Road will produce a renewed motivation to obtain loans from banks and the Silk Road Funds of foreign governments and international financial organizations. It will relieve the national economy of excess capacity. China thereby creates a new impetus for connectivity and unification while Chinese businesses are encouraged to invest abroad and obtain capital support. The risk of disintegration is minimized if important economic and political segments of the population are engaged in deeper exploitation of their resources, in addition to putting the excess labor, even criminals, prisoners, the homeless and the unemployed, the potential hazards of domestic risks to productive use. If the BRI succeeds, it will help in maintaining the existing identity of the Chinese Communist Party, including the absolute survival of President Xi Jinping. The BRI is the new impetus for China's development, eliminating the centrifugal threat of multi-party demands across the Chinese population.

REFERENCES

Cardenal, Juan Pablo, and Heriberto Araújio. 2015. *China's Silent Army.* Trans. Nguyen Dinh Huynh. Hanoi: Publishing House of Vietnam Association of Writers Vinh.

Garten, Jeffrey E. 2017. *From the Silk to Silicon, The Story of Globalization Through Ten Exotic Lives.* Trans. Nguyen Tuan Viet. Hanoi: Young Publisher.

Hu, Angang. 2003. *Chinese Great Strategies.* Trans. Tran Khang and Bui Xuan Tuan. Hanoi: Publishing House of News Agency.

Johnson, Christopher. 2016. *President Xi Jinping's Belt and Road Initiative: A Practical Assessment of the Chinese Communist Party's Roadmap for China's Global Resurgence.* A report of Center for Strategic and International Studies. https://www.csis.org/analysis/president-xi-jinping%E2%80%99s-belt-and-road-initiative. Accessed 8 Jan 2019.

Many Authors. 1999. *Cultural History of China.* Trans. Tran Ngoc Thuan, Dao Duy Dat, and Dao Phuong Chi. Hanoi: Publishing House of Culture.

State Council of PRC. 2015. Action Plan on the Belt and Road Initiative. http://english.gov.cn/archive/publications/2015/03/30/content_281475080249035.htm; http://dantri.com.vn/the-gioi/chuyen-ve-mo-bo-ong-tap-can-binh-1413886096.htm; http://www.au.af.mil/au/awc/awcgarte/congress/mos021406.pdf. Accessed 8 Jan 2019.

Thanh, Pham Sy. 2017. *A Strategic OBOR One Belt One Road of China and Policy Implications for Vietnam.* Hanoi: World Publisher.

Xi Jinping. 2014. *Xi Jinping tan zhi guo li zheng.* Beijing: 外文出版社有限责任公司 [Wai wen chu ban she].

CHAPTER 6

Rail Developments Under the BRI

Shang-su Wu

INTRODUCTION

Since at least half of the Belt and Road Initiative (BRI) is based on land transportation, the railway is an unavoidable subject of interest. Although motor highway systems occupy a larger share of land transport than their rail counterparts in most countries, the latter enjoys some advantages such as cost savings and capacity in long-distance situations (Pyrgidis 2016, 29–34). Furthermore, China's domestic rail reform, modernization, and expansion have created the largest rail industry in the world (Nikkei Asian Review 2019). As such, BRI rail projects will not much rely much on non-Chinese technology and they will promote Beijing's domestic economy. Finally, with its increasingly huge economy, Beijing's rail links to its neighbours will undoubtedly strengthen various bilateral and multilateral relations which also serve its diplomatic purposes.

China's location naturally suggests four main directions of developing rail connections to North, Central, South, and Southeast Asia. Through better connectivity, these rail lines between China, the world's second largest economy, and its neighbours would considerably strengthen the

S. Wu (✉)
Regional Security Architecture Programme, S. Rajaratnam School of International Studies, Nanyang Technological University, Singapore, Singapore
e-mail: issswu@ntu.edu.sg

© The Author(s) 2020
A. Chong, Q. M. Pham (eds.), *Critical Reflections on China's Belt & Road Initiative*, https://doi.org/10.1007/978-981-13-2098-9_6

former's economic and political influence on the latter. Thus, the BRI rail projects are more than pure infrastructure, but involve "railpolitics" (Wu and Chong 2018, 505–508). Within just a few years following the announcement of the BRI in 2013, substantial rail projects involving Mongolia, Central, South, and Southeast Asia are taking shape. This chapter will survey the progress and challenges of building railways in these four directions, as rail systems are also constrained by various physical factors, such as gauges and topography. This chapter concentrates on China's contiguously neighbouring countries where they are indispensable for further rail connections. Therefore, some countries with salient footprints of the BRI and/or the Chinese rail industry, such as Iran, will not be treated here. By the same token, those BRI rail projects which require sea transport to link to China, such as the high speed rail (HSR) in Indonesia, will be excluded from this chapter as well.

THE RAIL OUTLOOK IN CHINA'S NEIGHBOURHOOD

The divided rail networks in the Asian Continent both throw up challenges and yet leave some room for China to promote BRI to connect them. Geographic obstacles and distinct political landscapes have contributed four separate operational groups distinguished by different rail gauges: the Russian gauge (1520 mm), the South Asian gauge (1676 mm), the standard gauge (1435 mm), and the metre and cape gauges (1000 and 1067 mm) (United Nations Economic and Social Commission for Asia and the Pacific 2016; Pyrgidis 2016, 27). The Russian Empire, and subsequently the Soviet Union, built its unique 1520 mm network to deliberately increase the logistical difficulty for external invasion (Carter 2018). All former Soviet bloc countries therefore have the Russian gauge, and hence they complicate the connectivity of the standard gauge network in the eastern and western sides of the Eurasian Continent. The South Asian countries have also separately inherited the rail network of the British colonial legacy: the broad rail gauge. Despite the similar gauge, the connection between the three countries, India, Pakistan, and Bangladesh, are limited due to political reasons (Khan 2017; Deb 2018). In addition, other narrow gauges, such as 1000 and 610 mm, were adopted for local uses in all these countries, but India has striven for a policy of unifying most of its rail network to the wide gauge (Jha 2018). The standard gauge networks are distributed in East Asian countries, such as both Koreas and China, and West Asian ones, such as Iran and Turkey, with links to most of the European network through Turkey (Fender 2013). The cape gauge was selected to fit mountainous terrain while maintaining relatively low building costs, in Indonesia, the Philippines, Japan, and Taiwan (Saito 1979). The countries using the metre gauge (i.e. 1000 mm) are Vietnam, Cambodia, Laos, Myanmar, Thailand, and Malaysia, for similar reasons (Pyrgidis 2016, 324). The main trade-offs for adopting such narrow gauge systems lie in speed and capacity (Conles and Novales 2011).

From Beijing's perspective, continental rail transport would mainly represent four advantages: rail is an alternative to sea transport, serves regional economic development, exports domestic industrial capacity, and furthers China's political influence. Until the People's Liberation Army Navy (PLAN) achieves substantive superiority vis-à-vis its maritime rivals, China's sea lines of communication (SLOCs) could be under threat, and rail lines are the most effective alternatives on land. Despite their much higher costs, well equipped and managed rail systems have potential to reach similar capacity as sea transport (Smyth 2018).[1] In the face of the strategic dilemma of using the Malacca Strait, rail lines to Central Asian and Middle East countries, as well as to Russia, for energy and other resources would be critical for strategic consideration, as access to the major market in Europe would moderate the disruption of SLOCs (Storey 2006).

To realize Beijing's alternative strategy, the cooperation of all countries through which the rail lines pass is indispensable, and the latter have to be persuaded that China's national interest aligns with theirs. The BRI rail projects can therefore be rendered politically feasible. China has to make the argument that infrastructure improvement can offer a positive multiplier solution for neighbouring countries facing difficulties in enticing or accommodating investment due to their insufficient infrastructure. Improvement of their land transportation, especially to markets and ports for connection with sea lanes of communication (SLOCs), will serve as a net economic contribution. Additionally, China's investment in rail and other BRI projects linking into its huge market and various coastal ports would be a huge attraction in itself (Chen 2018, Hillman 2018a, 3–4).

If a sufficient number of countries join the BRI rail projects, there may be enough demand to sustain China's own national railway and other related industries. The massive modernization and expansion of Chinese

---

[1] For example, a freight train of the Rio Tinto is usually comprised of 238 wagons, with each wagon having a capacity of 100 tons. Thus, the train provides a capacity larger than many cargo ships. Jamie Smyth, "How robot trains are boosting Australia's mining industry," *Financial Times*, November 23, 2018, https://www.ft.com/content/b71db1fa-ed3d-11e8-89c8-d36339d835c0.

rail networks have resulted in boosting the large rail sector and other related industries (Pyrgidis 2016, 299–300). Since domestically driven demand will not last indefinitely, the overseas market is becoming important for such industries to retain their economies of scale as well as to continue their research and development. Aside from the substantial construction business, infrastructure projects are usually involved with loan or investment arrangements that would benefit Chinese financial industries. As a main investor, Beijing's influence on infrastructure recipient states would naturally increase. China's expansion of its geo-economic sphere could contribute to its rising status as a global power through diplomacy, economy, and security.

As for the problem posed by different railway gauges, although China is developing trains with adjustable wheels for different gauges, such sophisticated devices would only make economic sense for passenger services, as freight ones require large numbers of various types of carriages (National Company Kazakhstan Temir Zholy joint stock company 2018; Wang 2016).[2] Chinese policy makers are also thinking of standardizing those countries' rail systems with the standard gauge, but the policies for Central Asia have not been clearly enunciated to date (United Nations Economic and Social Commission for Asia and the Pacific 2018). Therefore, some grand projects, such as the high speed rail (HSR) between Xinjiang and Europe across Central Asia, mentioned in the initial stage of the BRI, have not been mentioned further (Cai and Zhao 2014). Transferring cargo and passengers at break-of-gauge border crossings is the only feasible solution so far.

Northern Approach: Mongolia

Mongolia serves as a potential multirole junction to the BRI's northern rail connection. Since 1955, the Trans-Mongolia Railway has been a major bridge between Russia and China, and this route is still theoretically important for the BRI (Soucek 2009, 301). Despite longer than normal routes through Central Asia connecting Europe, Russia's established rail system and single custom and tariff system simplifies the trips in comparison to routes passing through several countries. In order to shorten the

---

[2] Usually, rail operators possess many more freight carriages than passenger ones. For example, the Kazakhstan Temir Zholy joint stock company possesses only 2089 passenger carriages, but boasts 53,000 freight carriages in its holdings.

current route, the most salient BRI rail project in Mongolia is the Northern Rail Corridor, between Erdenet and Arts Suuri on the Russian border, from where lines could be linked with Kyzyl on the Trans-Siberia Railway. This project, a major part of the China-Mongolia-Russia Economic Corridor (CMREC), has been agreed to by Beijing, Ulaanbaatar, and Moscow, and invested in by Chinese and Australian companies (Edwards 2016; Aspire Mining Limited 2018). In the long term, the CMREC plans to build two additional rail routes between China and Russia across Mongolia (Ganbold 2017). As a major exporter of coals to China, Mongolia also builds two rail lines, Tavan Tolgoi-Gashuun Sukhait and Khuut-Bichigt, to replace the current highway transport. In order to create seamless connectivity with the Chinese network, the new lines are built at the standard gauge (Ewers 2014; National Development Agency n.d.-a, b, Stanway, Mongolia plans coal rail link to China by 2021: official 2018b) This Tavan Tolgoi-Gashuun Sukhait line may connect to the main network through another proposed line between Tavan Tolgoi and Sainshand, a project under the China-Mongolia-Russia Economic Corridor (Center for Strategic and International Studies 2019). Apart from coal, Ulaanbaatar also attempts to overcome its landlocked geographical circumstances with a joint project with China of a transport and logistics centre in Tianjin, the port closest to Mongolia (Styles 2013; M.Unurzul 2018; Stanway, China's Caofeidian port launches new rail freight link to Mongolia 2018a) As for rolling stock, the Chinese products, such as diesel locomotives, carriages, and bogies, contributes to the modernization of the Mongolian rail fleet (Railway Gazette 2008, 2010; Mongolian Railway 2019; Zhang 2018).

Despite such achievements, Beijing's rail influence on Ulaanbaatar remains constrained by gauge, external competition from Russia and other countries. Aside from the new lines of the standard gauge for exporting coals to China, the rest of the Mongolian rail network is still operating the broad gauge, including the Northern Rail Corridor (Styles, Mongolia Railway Assessment 2018; Stanway 2018b). In other words, Beijing's influence is not overwhelming enough to persuade or push Ulaanbaatar to massively change gauge. Mongolia's policy of retaining the broad gauge could be attributed to China's non-monopolistic role as an entrepôt for the Mongolian economy, along with other external influences, especially from Russia. Although the route to Tianjin is shorter, Russia provides tariff discounts for Mongolian exports through its rail networks (Russian Business Today 2018). Regarding rail construction, facilities, and rolling stock, the Russian Railways (Российские железные дороги, known as RZD) and other related industries are main suppliers to Ulaanbaatar (Transmash Holding 2011; Railway Gazette 2014a; RZD 2015). Besides the Russian source, the American General Electric (GE) has also emerged as a major supplier to the Mongolian railway (GE 2009; GE Mongolia 2014). In addition, South Korea also participates in the construction of the Tavan Tolgoi-Gashuun Sukhait and Tavan Tolgoi-Sainshand lines in southern Mongolia (Yi 2019).

China's limited influence on Mongolia's rail sector may be chiefly explained by geopolitical considerations. Clearly, the route through Mongolia and then Russia would be simpler than those through several Central Asian and other countries, and the Northern Rail Corridor will further shorten the travel time. However, this route would endow Moscow, a rival to Chinese great power, with a critical role, if not a veto, on Beijing's BRI. It would be in China's interest to develop a route that bypasses Russian territory (Hillman 2018b). Similarly, given that the whole Mongolian rail network was converted to the standard gauge, it is still impossible to transfer to the Russian one according to the current conditions. Therefore, given this mixed landscape, Mongolia would likely not be a target of high priority for the BRI, despite some attractions.

CENTRAL ASIA

In contrast to the lines to South and Southeast Asia, the westward rail connection serves the highest national interests of China, in terms of access to Europe, the Middle East and other areas for markets, energy, and resources. Furthermore, China's rising economy could naturally overshadow its Russian counterpart, and subsequently become the largest market and source of investment to the region. Moreover, since none of the Central Asian countries qualify as great or medium powers, Beijing would enjoy a relatively superior position in negotiation, in contrast to dealing with Russia. Nonetheless, Central Asia also presents some challenges to rail transport under the BRI. The rail networks in this area were built for serving Moscow and some are reported to be in poor maintenance. Moreover, despite the collapse of the Soviet Union, Russia still enjoys considerable political influence in addition to connectivity to the broad gauge still in use throughout Central Asia (Putz 2016). There are also a number of break-of-gauge border crossings that are placed on the borders between former Soviet states, namely Azerbaijan, Turkmenistan, Georgia, Armenia, Belarus, Ukraine, and their neighbours, China, Iran, Turkey, and Poland (United Nations Economic and Social Commission for Asia and the Pacific 2017, 95).

Beijing adopts a practical approach to Central Asian countries by transferring cargo at the border crossings between different gauges, through two main routes. Firstly, the continental one starts from China, and threads through Kazakhstan, Russia, Belarus, and to Poland where it enters into the European network. Secondly, the multimodal one starts from China, through Kazakhstan, crossing the Caspian Sea to Azerbaijan, Georgia, Turkey, and then connects with the European network (Hillman 2018b). The continental route passes directly under Moscow's sovereignty, hence Beijing has relatively limited influence. The large number of countries in the multimodal routes pose considerable challenges on coordination for China since one of them is enough to thwart or delay the entire service. It must be noted that there is more than one port on the shore of the Caspian Sea for the multimodal route, as Turkmenistan also builds its own port for a shipping route to Baku (Gerden 2017). Such an alternative would provide flexibility for the BRI project. Beijing has also opened alternative highway routes for shorter travel time, despite higher costs and greater fuel emissions from vehicular traffic (Lennane 2018). As such, China has invested in the countries along the routes to improve their rail infrastructure.

China has in fact emerged as the top source of investment in Kazakhstan's transportation infrastructure. This is directly attributable to its strategic position of accommodating the two routes. Some of the Chinese investment projects, such as the Khorgos Dry Port and related special economic zones (SEZs), the Kazakhstan-Turkmenistan-Iran rail link, and the Aktau port on the Caspian shore, are related to international rail connectivity (人民交通网 (People's Transportation Net) 2018). The Khorgos dry port is linked up to China's Lianyungang through rail lines, and Kazakhstan itself also invests in the facilities dedicated towards providing greater capacity for reloading cargo between trains of broad and standard gauges (Altynsarina 2018). The 914 km of the Kazakhstan-Turkmenistan-Iran railway, a part of the North-South International Transportation Corridor, provides the linkage to the Iranian rail network and then onto seaports in the Persian Gulf (Uysal 2014; Vakilov 2019). The Aktau port provides the transferring between trains and ships for crossing the Caspian Sea, a key section of the multimode route (NDTV 2018).

Apart from Kazakhstan, China also plans to open another rail route from Southern Xinjiang through Kyrgyzstan to Uzbekistan. The 900 km rail line across various ridges has been a top construction priority among these countries since the feasibility report completed in 2003, as it represents a shorter trip between China and Europe, as well as Middle East (Rail Freight 2018b). In addition to these three countries, Turkmenistan and Russia may be involved as well (KABAR 2018). However, the rising estimated costs, potential instability, geopolitical competition, national debts, and the dilemmas of adopting broad or standard gauges have been the main disputes between Bishkek and Beijing (News Central Asia 2018; Goble 2019). In the meantime, China has invested in the alternative highway link through Kyrgyzstan (Levina 2018). In addition, Uzbekistan's rail network also facilitates the freight service between China and Afghanistan (Azer News 2019).

More than investment, the Chinese rail industry also expands its weight in the region. The China Railway Rolling Stock Corporation (CRRC) has supplied diesel and electric locomotives as well as passenger and freight carriages to all the Central Asian countries (Railway Gazette 2012; China Railway Rolling Stock Corporation 2018). Those deals involve training and other commercial activities, including the opening of branch offices in regional countries. This would amplify Beijing's influence on Central Asian rail transport. China's investments will also endow Chinese contractors with priority access for participation in construction (China Railway Group Limited 2018).

Today, after years of sustained contributions by China, other related countries and the Eurasian Economic Union (EEU), the travel time has significantly shortened across Central Asia. For example, the train service between Shanghai and Hamburg was 36 days back in 2006, and 16 days in 2018 (Hillman 2018b). Correspondingly, the volume of transport has increased: there was no Chinese container passing through Kazakhstan in 2010, but 200,000 were counted in 2017. In 2018, more than 223,348 containers were transported from China to Europe and 152,846 in the opposite direction (Gotev 2018; Kozhanova 2019). With the Chinese subsidy, the overall number of Twenty Foot Equivalent Unit (TEU) containers passing through the broad gauge networks in Russia, Belarus, and Kazakhstan grew 58% in 2018 compared to the previous year (Rail Freight 2018a). Further demands for shorter trips are likely to spur demand for better infrastructure and greater inter-state cooperation, particularly in the continental route for the Eurasian Rail Alliance of Russia, Belarus, and Kazakhstan (Eurasian Rail Alliance Index 2018). Moreover, China has become one of the top trade partners to some regional countries, such as Kazakhstan and Kyrgyzstan (World Trade Organisation 2018).

Judging from the BRI as well as its earlier efforts at cultivation of the region, China's achievements in Central Asia are therefore considerable. But these achievements have not translated into dominance due to a range of counter factors. None of the Central Asian countries have adopted any policy of changing their rail network from the Russian gauge to the standard one. Therefore, the costs and delays in transferring and reloading at border crossings will not be fully mitigated. In addition, the costs for the continental rail freight services is still double or more than that for sea transport (Mooney 2018). This requires the rail operators to attract mostly customers who prioritize time savings over cost savings, and who do not wish to spend on vastly more expensive airfreight services (Todd 2019). Although the currently slowing growth of rail transport could be attributed to various factors, such as the Sino-US trade war and break-of-gauge, the limited market potential also matters (Suzuki 2019).

Distance factors also favour the existing landscape of rail gauges, as China does not provide the shortest access to SLOCs. The routes through China are rather longer than the others heading towards Iran, Russia, and other East European countries (United Nations Economic and Social Commission for Asia and the Pacific 2017, 33). The Trans-Caspian route between several Russian and Iranian ports means that a substantial project will be available for Central Asian countries' collaboration outside of the BRI framework (Mammadov 2018). The Indian and Iranian joint venture of Chabahar Port with an additional rail line linking to the existing network would further shorten the distance between Central Asia and the seas (Joy 2018). As long as China is unable to dominate the entrepôt trade with Central Asian countries, the former's influence on the latter would be restricted.

Additionally, Beijing lacks pre-eminence in supplying capital and equipment in the region. In addition to accepting Chinese capital, Central Asian countries, especially Kazakhstan, also invest in themselves for improving their rail network. Relatively poor regional countries, such as Kyrgyzstan, are keenly aware of the dangers of falling into debt trap and extending their national debts to China. Hence they are cautious towards embracing BRI projects (News Central Asia 2018). The CRRC also does not dominate the supply of rolling stock and other rail technology to Central Asian economies. Following the Soviet legacies, the Russian and Ukrainian rail industry continue to deliver related products to Central Asian countries, as the EEU serves an advantageous framework for the Russian one (Azer News 2018; Buyers 2003, 76–77; Dolukhanov 2018; Transmash Holding 2018). Kazakhstan also has something of its own incipient rail industry, equipped with a capacity for manufacturing locomotives and carriages through joint venture with foreign companies, such as General Electric

(GE) and European Alstom. This goes some way to providing regional countries a local and competitive option in contrast to Chinese products (ALSTOM 2018; Railway Gazette 2011a, 2014b).

Beyond the rail sector, the complicated geopolitics would not favour China's expansion of its sphere of influence in Central Asia. Despite the large amount of capital and attraction of the second largest economy in the world, it would take time for Beijing to overtake Moscow's influence, as the later retains considerable security ties with the regional countries. Thanks to the Soviet legacy, many regional political elites maintain tangible ties with Moscow. Militarily, the armed forces of several regional countries still operate a great deal of Russian-made arms, holding joint exercises with their Russian counterparts, and some are still accommodating Russian deployments (The International Institute for Strategic Studies 2019, 191, 193, 209–210, 217; Stefanovich 2018). This simply means that Central Asian states can still play the Moscow "card" to balance Beijing. Although Russia's economic capacity cannot match with China's in all dimensions of national power status, it would still be difficult for the latter to capitalize upon the spill-over effects from economic investments to effect overall change in the geopolitical picture. Following the *status quo*, the BRI will not be likely to deliver enough momentum or interest for regional countries to change their Russian rail gauge, a fundamental strategic fixture, to interoperate seamlessly with the Chinese network.

SOUTH ASIA

The geopolitical circumstances in South Asia are more challenging for BRI rail projects than in Central Asia in both geographical and political dimensions. Various mountain ridges, such as the Himalayas, between China and South Asia form a natural obstacle for trains. Railways that climb mountainous terrain will constrain the efficiency of operation, limiting locomotives' speed and capacity, or require building long tunnels to penetrate these barriers for more flat routes. Correspondingly, the scale of construction will be technologically challenging and accompanied by high costs. For instance, despite some plans for rail linkages between China and Pakistan, the majority of the ongoing projects under their China-Pakistan Economic Corridor are aimed at domestic services (Zhen 2015; Pakistan Government 2018). Without linkage to the Chinese networks, the geopolitical impacts of those BRI rail projects in Pakistan would be mostly self-contained without extra-regional benefit.

As the largest power and economy in South Asia, India's responses matter to those BRI rail projects. Despite some recent rapprochements in the bilateral relations, it would not be surprising for New Delhi to continue harbouring significant reservations about Beijing's expansion in its neighbourhood, particularly in Pakistan. At the minimal level, India can just assert its sovereignty in rejecting all BRI rail connections at its borders. Its negative attitude on BRI could render all rail links to South Asia less tenable due to the inability to connect with the largest economy in the region (Prasad 2018). Moreover, the existing colonial-inspired gauge of South Asian rail networks are not compatible with their Chinese counterparts. New Delhi's policy of promoting the unification of its own broad gauge would reinforce the obstacles for Beijing to connect with the former's rail network. Currently, rail projects with linkage to the Chinese network exist only in Nepal, and perhaps in Myanmar, as all rail projects in Pakistan are domestic in nature. Although Myanmar is a Southeast Asian country, it is grouped under a BRI corridor stretching towards South Asia, and thus it is discussed in this section.

After completing the long construction of the rail line to Lhasa in Tibet in 2006, and then to Xigaze in 2014, China has reached a feasible position of connecting Nepal with railways (Railway Gazette 2014c). Furthermore, the other rail line under construction from Chengdu to Lhasa will provide a shorter trip to Tibet (Reuter 2016). Kathmandu hopes to ameliorate its landlocked disadvantage with the rail link to Lhasa, especially after the lessons arising from the fuel dispute with New Delhi in 2015–2016. In 2018, the China and Nepal inked an agreement on the Trans-Himalaya railway between Xigaze and Kathmandu. This was to be about 660 km in length. Due to the topographic constraints, the costs of this line would be expensive for tunnels and bridges covering more than 98% of the route, and Chinese capital will be the mainstay of the expenditure (Miyamoto 2018; Global Construction Review 2019). Although it is technologically possible to conduct trade through rail lines across the Himalayas, for most companies currently doing business with India and Nepal, the existing SLOCs from China are much more economical, in contrast to a long rail trip through climbing ridges and break-of-gauge transition points. In other words, the geopolitical impacts on connecting New Delhi's northern neighbours may matter more than economic considerations for Beijing (Mahato 2018). That said, India has not completely abandoned Nepal to Chinese railpolitics. Since Nepal is the most successful case for the BRI rail linkage in South Asia so far, India is also extending five rail lines into Nepal under a rapprochement initiative. Thus far the government in Kathmandu welcomes such improvements in transportation on the basis of geopolitical balancing (The Indian Express 2018). Judging from the sheer numbers of existing rail lines coupled to the distance to ports and major markets, most Nepalese trade would currently go through India rather than China. If Beijing is unable to create enough positive economic externalities through rail construction, it would not develop long term spill-over political influence on Kathmandu. However, Nepal's current selection of the standard gauge compatible with the Chinese network instead of the Indian one suggests China's strong influence (Sharma 2019). Since the Kerung-Kathmandu rail is still under the feasibility study, it must be noted that the selection of the gauge may not be permanent since the substantial construction has not yet begun at the time of writing (Giri 2019).

On another front, the rail linkage between Myanmar and China is also strategically meaningful but its progress has been intermittent. From Beijing's perspective, the rail line to the shores of the Indian Ocean serves not only as a solution to the Malacca Straits Dilemma, it also raises a threshold to other South and Southeast Asian countries. Myanmar's metre gauge rail system lacks modernization and efficiency due to its poor management and maintenance (Asian Development Bank 2014; Thant 2019). As the top trade partner and source of foreign investment to Nay Pyi Taw, Beijing can leverage upon certain niches for building a separated rail system of standard gauge which would revolutionize Myanmar's railways through providing greater speed and capacity. Needless to say, this will also facilitate a smoother linkage with the Chinese rail network which would in turn expedite bilateral economic ties (China Central Television 2016). Nay Pyi Taw's dependence on Beijing further favoured the latter's promotion of the rail project to the former, as evidenced in the bilateral memorandum of understanding (MOU) signed in 2011. With democratization in play after 2011, a newly elected administration in Nay Pyi Taw placed Chinese rail projects on hiatus after heeding public opposition and concerns about financial affordability that were raised in 2014. In 2019, the China Railway Eryuan Engineering company completed a feasibility study of rail lines between Muse, a place on the bilateral border, and Mandalay, a major inland city in Myanmar. This report indicates that the progress of the rail project was tied in with a plan to eventually connect Kyaukpyu, a coastal town with a Chinese invested deep-water port and special economic zone (Chan 2019). Some Myanmar officials further highlighted the value of rail transport in the China Myanmar Economic Corridor (CMEC), paving the foundation for resuming the HSR or standard gauge rail project

(Wan 2018; Xinhua 2018). The current situation reveals some hope for further progress, but the sluggish development of the Chinese HSR project in neighbouring Thailand demonstrates the unpredictable nature of such inter-state joint ventures, with Myanmar's much weaker financial capacity compounding the difficulties with a joint venture.

Myanmar's government still has other concerns even if China is willing to jumpstart the country's rail renaissance. Myanmar's existing metric gauge network has yet to reach a bottleneck despite its dilapidated quality. And Myanmar's decision makers therefore may not want to build redundancy into their railways in anticipation of explosive growth in usage bearing in mind their limited financial resources and in the shadow of some well known BRI-related debt traps in South Asia (Chaudhury 2018). The endless insurgencies in Myanmar, especially those close to the Chinese borders, also pose potential threats to the construction and operation of proposed new rail links (Martina 2018). Given this mixed picture, the potential for BRI rail projects to structurally reshape the regional situation in China's favour remains quite uncertain despite some promising projections for China's great power ambitions.

SOUTHEAST ASIA

The Southeast Asian rail networks are characterized by a self-contained geopolitical context. Without a uniform legacy like Central or South Asia, the divided histories left the regional countries with fragmented rail networks. The political and economic separation imposed by the Cold War denied the chance to achieve regional connectivity among some regional countries. In Indochina for instance, despite sharing the metric gauge most of the new states born after decolonization do not join their networks comprehensively. Thailand, the geographical centre of Indochina, has developed connections with Laos and Cambodia after the Cold War, in addition to the link to Malaysia harking back to the colonial era (Robinson 1991, 191; Janssen 2018). However, Vietnam and Myanmar are isolated from any connection to Thailand (United Nations Economic and Social Commission for Asia and the Pacific 2016). As the metric gauge is relatively slow and incompatible with the Chinese network, Beijing can technically offer separated rail systems of standard gauge for seamless connection and bypass existing networks altogether. But this blank slate solution can only work if Southeast Asia can muster the political will to accept a Chinese rail masterplan. Politically, Southeast Asia offers a far more benign geopolitical environment than South and Central Asia as there are no local great powers that can pose "peer competition" to Beijing. That said, the USA and Japan do retain some interest in the region, but unlike China, they cannot provide direct rail links with Southeast Asian networks to compete with China.

By and large, the primary BRI rail project in the region is the Singapore-Kunming Rail Link (SKRL), as others in Indonesia and the Philippines would not generate high geopolitical impacts for the archipelagic locations. The SKRL is planned with three main routes in Indochina, respectively through Vietnam, Thailand, and Myanmar (Ganjanakhundee 2018). As it was with the situation of Myanmar mentioned earlier, that of Vietnam is also complicated. Before the BRI, Hanoi already rejected the HSR project in 2010, and the renewed plan may yet be contracted out to Japan (Le 2018). At the same time, there has also been piecemeal progress in linking up with China. Two standard gauge lines have been extended from two Chinese provinces, Yunnan and Guangxi, into the Red River Delta (Asian Development Bank 2006). Separately, Hanoi and Beijing have reached a few deals on further upgrades for the economic corridors along the two lines (Barrow 2017). Using these two lines connected to the Chinese networks, Vietnam has started international freight services to Europe through Kazakhstan (KAZ Inform 2019). Despite the absence of a substantial policy, China also promotes the rail links between Vietnam and Cambodia (Railway Gazette 2011b). Furthermore, the Chinese rail industry has emerged as a major supplier to the Vietnamese rail system, including the metro project in Hanoi (Railway Gazette 2017a, b; Lam 2018). China also retains the metre gauge rail line in the Yunnan Province for direct freight services into Vietnam (Xinhua 2019). In other words, the BRI rail projects in Vietnam may not directly work towards the SKRL route to the east, but they contribute to greater connection with the Chinese network in bits and pieces.

The middle portion of the SKRL is built upon several projects based on their locations and hosting countries, namely Laos, Thailand, Malaysia, and Singapore. Due to Laos' landlocked environment and shortage of capital, Vientiane generally accepts Beijing's conditions on building the 409 kilometre HSR line, and the project is progressing smoothly (Phouthonesy 2018). On the other end, the Singapore-Kuala Lumpur HSR project is suspended for two years out of consideration for the new Malaysian administration's financial situation (Land Transport Authority 2018). Given its wary attitude towards the HSR project to Singapore, it is improbable that the Pakatan Harapan government in Kuala Lumpur will proceed with any substantial development of the HSR project to Bangkok, despite some earlier discussions aired by its predecessor, the Barisan Nasional government (The Star 2016).

As a result, the SKRL spotlight remains on Thailand. Since the bilateral MOU of 2014, the joint HSR project did not directly proceed but ran into several disputes and changes of the plan, until reaching the current two stages of construction. One stretch of a 253 km line from Bangkok to Nakhon Ratchasima and another 606 km stretch from Nakhon Ratchasima to Nong Khai on the Lao border. The former is under construction and the latter is expected to be completed in 2024, despite current delays (Ministry of Transportation 2015; Jotikasthira 2018). Beijing, through the cooperation with the Charoen Pokphand Group, has also participated in the upcoming HSR project connecting the three airports between Bangkok and Rayong, while the Bangkok-Chiang Mai project has been assigned to a Japanese consortium. The latter project remains in stagnation due to the poor financial expectations on both sides, and Japan's rejection of Thailand's proposed investment plans, despite Tokyo's offer of low interest loans to Bangkok (Kotani 2018; Takahashi 2018; Bangkok Post 2018; Kishimoto 2019). Thailand also has a plan to establish a southbound HSR line between Bangkok and Hua Hin. But this has not been opened for tender yet. It is also widely known that this projected Bangkok-Hua Hin line is more domestic oriented rather than connecting to Malaysia (The Nation 2018). In short, it is a remote prospect for the SKRL to achieve completion. Currently, there are also no substantive ongoing projects connecting China and the Indian Ocean to avoid the Malacca Straits.

The stagnation of the SKRL vision indicates that despite China's overwhelming economic weight vis-à-vis Southeast Asia, the lack of political willpower can pose serious obstacles to functional integration. Except for Laos, other regional countries rely relatively less on railways for internal or external transport. This stands in marked contrast to the other regions studied in this chapter. Hence adapting Southeast Asian railways to the standard gauge from China would be less urgent. Moreover, HSR projects built from scratch would bring in considerable financial burdens for host countries. This was already exemplified through Bangkok's bargaining for better deals in obtaining loans from Beijing (Wu and Chong 2018, 512–514). Such expensive projects are often hot button issues in democracies and likely to be affected by changes of administration after major elections, as evident in the cases of Malaysia and Myanmar. For many Southeast Asian governments, any rail project will also be politically less attractive or legitimate without a HSR label. The Chinese end of the SKRL is not economically feasible either. Since Yunnan Province is less developed than the coastal ones, the potential interests in transiting goods through the route would be limited for the former province, and more costs will be stacked up for transporting goods to the coastal zones which already enjoy significant seaborne commercial access (National Bureau of Statistics of China 2018).

Conclusion: China's Rail Impacts Abroad as a Mixed Picture

Rail developments under the BRI cannot be conclusively treated as auguring an era of Chinese dominance in the political economy of China's Asian neighbours. Extending economic and political integration through rail connectivity is nonetheless a crucial step in forging stronger ties between China and the BRI associated states. Just as importantly, the BRI brings a group of landlocked countries, which were previously marginalized by globalization, to the attention of the international community. There is also a demonstration effect arising from China's rail investments. Powers such as Russia and India, along with many regional players, are inspired to work on their own rail projects to improve domestic and bilateral connectivity, in addition to cooperation with the BRI (Garibov 2016). If Beijing stops being a leading promoter of international rail transport on the Asian Continent, the momentum can be sustained by other countries involved.

In any case, even if all of these rail projects were successfully completed by China, they would not effectively secure China's dominance in specific areas or create reliable alternative routes to the Malacca Straits. Undeniably, modern rail technologies have narrowed the gap in capacity between ships and trains, but the linear nature of rail transport renders it vulnerable to political disruptions. Sovereign governments can interdict Chinese commerce on the rail routes and place all manner of bans on transit at will. In a hypothetical crisis involving rival great powers in Eurasia or South Asia, it would not be surprising if China's adversaries attempt to persuade one or more of their neighbours to disrupt rail transport as a sanction against Beijing. Others may equally blackmail Beijing by merely threatening to restrict train travel across "the iron Silk Road" where circumstances permit. To hedge against these extreme scenarios, China would likely have to prepare "the alternative to the alternative." From the route involving with fewest countries through Mongolia and Russia to the multimodal one involving six or more countries, Beijing has indeed explored many possibilities of a fall-back plan for railway snafus. Given the unstable nature of most of the governments along the new Silk Road, Beijing may have to continually worry if all of its insurance policies might just fail at the same time.

In all the four directions surveyed in this chapter, China is never the only power providing capital, connection, or rail technology. In Mongolia and Central Asia, Russia's influence is still significant, and so is India in relation to South Asia. These geopolitical powers operate rail gauges different from China's standards. As long as Moscow and New Delhi exercise sufficient soft power towards their proximate regions, whether through connectivity, trade, investment, or material supply, the *status quo* of non-standard gauges would remain. Beijing consequently cannot push for full transformative impacts through railway construction due to the persistence of break-of-gauge border crossings. Additionally, the field remains wide open for European, American, and Japanese companies to present credible, if not better, alternatives to the Chinese suppliers. For countries, such as Mongolia, that judiciously wish to avoid overdependence on China, the involvement of non-Chinese entities evokes some semblance of "balancing" in the rush to embrace the BRI. Some countries interested in building up indigenous capabilities, such as Kazakhstan, can even utilize the improving regional connectivity to build up its own rail industry.

In the foreseeable future, several indicators would be useful to gauge the deliverable promises of the development of the BRI rail projects. Firstly, the change of gauge does not translate only into technological or operational considerations, but also the shaping of the geopolitical picture. Among China's neighbouring countries connected through rail, Vietnam and Kyrgyzstan would be most critical for their currently planned projects. If Hanoi and Bishkek accept the standard gauge for connection with the Chinese network, Beijing's sphere of influence would be accordingly expanded. Secondly, despite the technological challenges involved, China's invention of cheap and convenient devices, such as adjustable bogies for different gauges, should not be excluded. Provided that such devices are economical enough for most freight carriages to adopt, Beijing's influence on the countries operating the broad gauges would be reinforced. Finally, other alternatives to rail transport on land, such as driverless trucks powered by electricity, may narrow the gap of efficiency between highway and railway (ZumMallen 2018). As a result, China may shift the focus of BRI connectivity more towards highways or other forms of passage instead of rail. Incidentally, this scenario of a shift away from rail connectivity will correspond to Beijing's other ambitious plan of promoting electric vehicles on a global scale (Rapoza 2017).

REFERENCES

ALSTOM. 2018. *Alstom in Kazakhstan.* https://www.alstom.com/alstom-kazakhstan. Accessed 21 Dec 2018.

Altynsarina, Elya. 2018. Key Belt and Road Node Bears Potential. *The Astana Times*, October 9. https://astanatimes.com/2018/10/key-belt-and-road-node-bears-potential-for-much-gain-for-kazakhstan-china-and-beyond/. Accessed 20 Dec 2018.

Asian Development Bank. 2006. *Proposed Loan and Administration of Loan from Agence Française de Développement Socialist Republic of Viet Nam: Greater Mekong Subregion Kunming–Hai Phong Transport Corridor: Yen Vien–Lao Cai Railway Upgrading Project.* Manila: Asian Development Bank.

———. 2014. *Myanmar Transport Sector Policy Note.* Manila: Asian Development Bank. https://www.adb.org/sites/default/files/publication/184794/mya-transport-policy-note-es.pdf. Accessed 30 Dec 2018.

Aspire Mining Limited. 2018. *Northern Railways LLC.* https://aspiremininglimited.com/northern-railways-llc/. Accessed 24 Dec 2018.

Azer News. 2018. Turkmenistan, Ukraine Aim at Mutually. *Azer News*, December 15. https://www.azernews.az/news_print.php?news_id=142680. Accessed 22 Dec 2018.

Azer News. 2019. First Container Train from Afghanistan to China Launches Through Uzbekistan. *Azer News*, September 6. https://www.azernews.az/region/155591.html. Accessed 1 Oct 2019.

Bangkok Post. 2018. Japan Reaffirms Rejection of Rail Investment Proposal. *Bangkok Post*, October 24. https://www.bangkokpost.com/thailand/general/1563270/japan-reaffirms-rejection-of-rail-investment-proposal. Accessed 3 June 2019.

Barrow, Keith. 2017. China and Vietnam to Study Standard-Gauge Link. *International Rail Journal*, November 13. https://www.railjournal.com/regions/asia/china-and-vietnam-to-study-standard-gauge-rail-link/. Accessed 5 Jan 2019.

Buyers, Lydia M. 2003. *Central Asia in Focus: Political and Economic Issues.* New York: Nova Science.

Cai, Xiao, and Yinan Zhao. 2014. More Talks 'Needed on High-Speed Rail Link' Between Xinjiang, Europe. *China Daily*, July 5. http://www.chinadaily.com.cn/china/2014-07/05/content_17649707.htm. Accessed 23 Dec 2018.

Carter, Ian. 2018. *Operation 'Barbarossa' and Germany's Failure In The Soviet Union*, June 27. https://www.iwm.org.uk/history/operation-barbarossa-and-germanys-failure-in-the-soviet-union. Accessed 16 Dec 2018.

Center for Strategic & International Studies. 2019. Tavan Tolgoi – Sainshand Rail Route. *Reconnecting Asia.* https://reconnectingasia.csis.org/database/projects/tavan-tolgoi-sainshand-rail-route/9e9ea448-d818-4bf7-934c-367ec355d2e5/. Accessed 1 June 2019.

Chan, Mya Htwe. 2019. Initial Technical Report on Muse-Mandalay Railway Project Submitted. *Myanmar Times*, May 29. https://www.mmtimes.com/ news/initial-technical-report-muse-mandalay-railway-project-submitted.html. Accessed 3 June 2019.

Chaudhury, Dipanjan Roy. 2018. India Keeps a Close Watch on Kenya as It Falls Under China's Debt Trap. *The Economic Times*, December 24. https://economictimes.indiatimes.com/news/politics-and-nation/india-keeps-a-close-watch-on-kenya-as-it-falls-under-chinas-debt-trap/articleshow/67224761.cms.

Chen, Maggie Xiaoyang. 2018. Foreign Investment Growth in the Belt and Road Economies. *The Trade Post*, November 10. http://blogs.worldbank.org/trade/ foreign-investment-growth-belt-and-road-economies. Accessed 20 Dec 2018.

China Central Television. 2016. China: Myanmar's Largest Trading Partner. *China Central Television*, August 18. http://english.cctv.com/2016/08/18/ VIDElca99EPoHiGIeFF9QliJ160818.shtml. Accessed 1 Jan 2019.

China Railway Group Limited. 2018. *Electrified Railway Tunnel Project in Uzbekistan*, December 18. http://www.crecg.com/english/2745/2808/10049686/index.html. Accessed 20 Dec 2018.

China Railway Rolling Stock Corporation. 2018. *Worldwide*. http://www.crrcgc. cc/g6782.aspx. Accessed 20 Dec 2018.

Conles, Emilio, and Margarita Novales. 2011. Study on Narrow Gauge Track Mechanics for Speeding-Up to 160 KM/H. *Rail Knowledge Bank*. http:// railknowledgebank.com/Presto/content/Detail.aspx?ctID=MTk4MTRjND UtNWQ0My00OTBmLTllYWUtZWFjM2U2OTE0ZDY3&rID=MTM3Mg ==&qrs=RmFsc2U=&q=Z2F1Z2UsIHNwZWVk&ph=VHJ1ZQ==&bckToL =VHJ1ZQ==&rrtc=VHJ1ZQ==. Accessed 20 Dec 2018.

Deb, Debraj. 2018. *Tripura: Test Run Kindles Hopes of Reviving an Old Rail Route to Bangladesh*, December 6. https://indianexpress.com/article/north-east-india/tripura/belonia-santirbazaar-agartala-bangladesh-rail-route-5482053/. Accessed 15 Dec 2018.

Dolukhanov, Fikret. 2018. Russia's Altaivagon to Supply Railways Cars for Uzbekistan's First Private Car Park. *Trend*, December 5. https://en.trend.az/ business/economy/2989338.html. Accessed 23 Dec 2018.

Edwards, Terrence. 2016. *Mongolia to Pitch Railway Projects to China-Backed AIIB – Govt Adviser*, September 20. https://www.reuters.com/article/mon-golia-railways/mongolia-to-pitch-railway-projects-to-china-backed-aiib-govt-adviser-idUSL3N1BW2KQ. Accessed 24 Dec 2018.

Eurasian Rail Alliance Index. 2018. *Eurasian Rail Alliance Index*. http://www. index1520.com/. Accessed 5 Jan 2019.

Ewers, Larry. 2014. *Mongolia Approves Standard Rail Gauge to Match China*, October 29. https://www.speroforum.com/a/DRYATPBEZC50/75296-Mongolia-approves-standard-rail-gauge-to-match-China#.XCyA7017k5t. Accessed 2 Jan 2019.

Fender, Keith. 2013. Standard Gauge Rail Connection from Asia to Europe Opens in Turkey. *Trains*, October 29. http://trn.trains.com/news/news-wire/2013/10/standard-gauge-rail-connection-from-asia-to-europe-opens-in-turkey. Accessed 7 Jan 2019.

Ganbold, Ulziisaikhan. 2017. Mongolia Russia China. *United Nations Economic and Social Commission for Asia and the Pacific*, November 28. https://www.unescap.org/sites/default/files/4.3%20Mongolia.pdf. Accessed 2 June 2019.

Ganjanakhundee, Supalak. 2018. Completion of High-Speed Southeast Asian Rail Link Is Still Far Down the Track. *The Nation*, January 22. http://www.nationmultimedia.com/detail/asean-plus/30336801.

Garibov, Azad. 2016. The Trans-Caspian Corridor: Geopolitics of Transportation in Central Eurasia. *Caucasus International* 6 (1): 67–83.

GE. 2009. *GE Transportation Delivers First Evolution® Series Locomotive to Mongolian Railways*, September 24. https://www.genewsroom.com/Press-Releases/GE-Transportation-Delivers-First-Evolution%C2%AE-Series-Locomotive-to-Mongolian-Railways-245548. Accessed 4 Jan 2019.

GE Mongolia. 2014. *2 Zagal Locomotive*, November 24. https://www.facebook.com/pg/General-Electric-Mongolia-757018301039337/photos/?tab=album&album_id=757023061038861. Accessed 4 Jan 2019.

Gerden, Eugene. 2017. Turkmenistan Port Opens New China-Europe Rail. *The Journal of Commerce*, November 30. https://www.joc.com/rail-intermodal/international-rail/asia/turkmenistan-port-opens-new-china-europe-rail-corridor_20171130.html. Accessed 23 Dec 2018.

Giri, Anil. 2019. Nepal Presents Visiting Chinese Foreign Minister A Long Wish-List of Projects. September 10. https://newsin.asia/nepal-presents-visiting-chinese-foreign-minister-a-long-wish-list-of-projects/. Accessed 1 Oct. 2019

Global Construction Review. 2019. Nepal to Begin Work on Rail Links to China and India "Within Two Years." *Global Construction Review*, May 8. http://www.globalconstructionreview.com/news/nepal-begin-work-rail-links-china-and-india-within/. Accessed 3 June 2019.

Goble, Paul. 2019. China's Plan for Railway to Uzbekistan Is Transforming Central Asian Geopolitics. *The Jamestown Foundation*, March 21. https://jamestown.org/program/chinas-plan-for-railway-to-uzbekistan-is-transforming-central-asian-geopolitics/. Accessed 3 June 2019.

Gotev, Georgi. 2018. China's Belt and Road Initiative, Explained by Kazakhstan. *Euractiv*, July 4. https://www.euractiv.com/section/central-asia/news/chinas-belt-and-road-initiative-explained-by-kazakhstan/. Accessed 22 Dec 2018.

Hillman, Jonathan E. 2018a. China's Belt and Road Is Full of Holes. *CSIS Brief*, September.

———. 2018b. The Rise of China-Europe Railways. *Center for Strategic and International Studies*, March 6. https://www.csis.org/analysis/rise-china-europe-railways. Accessed 21 Dec 2018.

Janssen, Peter. 2018. *Misaligned Rails Keep SEAsia Delinked from China*, 4 May. http://www.atimes.com/article/misaligned-rails-keep-seasia-delinked-from-china/. Accessed 4 Jan 2019.

Jha, Srinand. 2018. *India to Scrap Its Narrow Gauge Train Lines*, June 12. http://www.atimes.com/article/india-to-scrap-its-heritage-listed-narrow-gauge-train-lines/.

Jotikasthira, Om. 2018. Somkid Rips Thai-Sino Rail Holdup. *Bangkok Post*, October 9. https://www.bangkokpost.com/news/general/1554282/somkid-rips-thai-sino-rail-holdup. Accessed 4 Jan 2019.

Joy, Santosh Koshy. 2018. *India, Kazakhstan Mull Starting Work on*, November 26. https://sputniknews.com/analysis/201811261070143422-india-kazakhstan-extension-of-instc/.

KABAR. 2018. Turkmenistan Offered to Take Part in Construction of China-Kyrgyzstan-Uzbekistan Railway. *KABAR*, August 24. http://kabar.kg/eng/news/turkmenistan-offered-to-take-part-in-construction-of-china-kyrgyzstan-uzbekistan-railway/. Accessed 21 Dec 2018.

KAZ Inform. 2019. Vietnam-China-Kazakhstan-Europe Rail Route Launched. *KAZ Inform*, March 6. https://www.inform.kz/en/vietnam-china-kazakhstan-europe-rail-route-launched_a3505064. Accessed 3 June 2019.

Khan, Atir. 2017. *Bus and Rail Links Between India and Pakistan Are Placed on High Alert After 'Intelligence Warns Terrorists Could Target Republic Day Celebrations'*, January 17. https://www.dailymail.co.uk/indiahome/indianews/article-4133728/India-Pakistan-bus-rail-links-high-alert.html. Accessed 15 Dec 2018.

Kishimoto, Marimi. 2019. Thai CP Group Wins Government Approval on High-Speed Airport Rail. *Nikkei Asian Review*, May 29. https://asia.nikkei.com/Business/Companies/Thai-CP-Group-wins-government-approval-on-high-speed-airport-rail. Accessed 3 June 2019.

Kotani, Hiroshi. 2018. Thailand on Track to Develop into Regional Rail Hub. *Nikkei Asian Review*, December 7. https://asia.nikkei.com/Economy/Thailand-on-track-to-develop-into-regional-rail-hub. Accessed 4 Jan 2019.

Kozhanova, Nazira. 2019. China-Europe Railroad Shipment Route Through Kazakhstan, Russia, Belarus Exceeds Expectations in 2019, Says UTLC ERA President. *The Astana Times*, May 20. https://astanatimes.com/2019/05/china-europe-railroad-shipment-route-through-kazakhstan-russia-belarus-exceeds-expectations-in-2019-says-utlc-president/. Accessed 3 June 2019.

Lam, Tue. 2018. Road, Rail Investment to Push Vietnam Infrastructure Growth. *VN Express*, August 6. https://e.vnexpress.net/news/business/industries/road-rail-investment-to-push-vietnam-infrastructure-growth-3788331.html. Accessed 5 Jan 2019.

Land Transport Authority. 2018. Kuala Lumpur-Singapore High Speed Rail. *Land Transport Authority*, December 3. https://www.lta.gov.sg/content/ltaweb/en/featured-projects/hsr.html. Accessed 4 Jan 2019.

Le, Hong Hiep. 2018. Vietnam's North-South High-Speed Rail Project: A Renewed Opportunity for Japan? *ISEAS – Yusof Ishak Institute*, August 21. https://www.iseas.edu.sg/medias/commentaries/item/8146-vietnams-northsouth-highspeed-rail-project-a-renewed-opportunity-for-japan-by-le-hong-hiep.

Lennane, Alex. 2018. China-Europe Truck Service Gear Up for January Launch After Successful Pilot. *The Load Star*, November 28. https://theloadstar.co.uk/china-europe-truck-service-gears-january-launch-successful-pilot/.

Levina, Maria. 2018. China-Kyrgyzstan-Uzbekistan Railway to Improve Attractiveness of Central Asia. *The Times of Central Asia*, January 13. https://www.timesca.com/index.php/news/26-opinion-head/19193-china-kyrgyzstan-uzbekistan-railway-to-improve-attractiveness-of-central-asia. Accessed 22 Dec 2018.

M.Unurzul. 2018. Agreement on Establishment of Mongolia-Tianjin Transportation and Logistics Center Signed. *MONTSAME News Agency*, October 24. https://montsame.mn/en/read/168877. Accessed 2 Jan 2019.

Mahato, Rubeena. 2018. Proposed China-Nepal Railway Expected to Be Game-Changer, May Reduce India's Influence on Himalayan Nation. *First Post*, December 29. https://www.firstpost.com/world/train-to-kathmandu-proposed-china-nepal-railway-expected-to-be-game-changer-may-reduce-indias-influence-on-himalayan-nation-5805791.html. Accessed 30 Dec 2018.

Mammadov, Seymur. 2018. The Trade Corridor that Connects Russia, Iran, India & Azerbaijan. *Madras Courier*, December 18. https://madrascourier.com/opinion/the-trade-corridor-that-connects-russia-iran-india-azerbaijan/. Accessed 24 Dec 2018.

Martina, Michael. 2018. China Condemns Myanmar Border Violence. *Reuters*, May 13. https://www.reuters.com/article/us-myanmar-insurgency-china-idUSKCN1IE05B. Accessed 2 Jan 2019.

Ministry of Transportation. 2015. Background. *Railway Cooperation Between Thailand and China*. http://maps.mot.go.th/pao/about_EN.html. Accessed 4 Jan 2019.

Miyamoto, Hidetake. 2018. Nepal to Join Hands with China on Tibet-Kathmandu Railway. *Nikkei Asian Review*, November 22. https://asia.nikkei.com/Editor-s-Picks/Interview/Nepal-to-join-hands-with-China-on-Tibet-Kathmandu-railway. Accessed 29 Dec 2018.

Mongolian Railway. 2019. *Company Introduction*. http://www.mtz.mn/content/8. Accessed 3 Jan 2019.

Mooney, Turloch. 2018. China-Europe Rail on Track for Long Term Despite Headwinds. *The Journal of Commerce*, September 20. https://www.joc.com/rail-intermodal/china-europe-rail-track-long-term-despite-headwinds_20180920.html. Accessed 23 Dec 2018.

National Bureau of Statistics of China. 2018. http://data.stats.gov.cn/english/easyquery.htm?cn=E0103. Accessed 7 Jan 2019.

National Company Kazakhstan Temir Zholy Joint Stock Company. 2018. Annual Report 2017. *NC KTZ JSC.* https://www.railways.kz/reports/2017/?page_id=2124&lang=en. Accessed 24 Dec 2018.

National Development Agency. n.d.-a. Khuut-Bichigt Railway Base Infrastructure. *Invest in Mongolia.* http://en.investmongolia.gov.mn/109.html. Accessed 2 June 2019.

———. n.d.-b Tavantolgoi-Gashuunsukhait Railway Base Infrastructure. *Invest in Mongolia.* http://en.investmongolia.gov.mn/106.html. Accessed 2 June 2019.

NDTV. 2018. Idle Cranes at Kazakh Port Reveal Something About China's New Silk Route. *NDTV,* August 26. https://www.ndtv.com/world-news/idle-cranes-at-kazakh-port-reveal-something-about-chinas-new-silk-route-1906318. Accessed 18 Dec 2018.

News Central Asia. 2018. China-Kyrgyzstan-Uzbekistan Railway Line—Risks and Rewards. *News Central Asia,* June 22. http://www.newscentralasia.net/2018/06/22/china-kyrgyzstan-uzbekistan-railway-line-risks-and-rewards/. Accessed 21 Dec 2018.

Nikkei Asian Review. 2019. CRRC Corp. Ltd. *Nikkei Asian Review,* January 4. https://asia.nikkei.com/Companies/CRRC-Corp.-Ltd.

Pakistan Government. 2018. *CPEC Projects.* http://cpec.gov.pk/#. Accessed 26 Dec 2018.

Phouthonesy, Ekaphone. 2018. The Train of Opportunities as Laos Builds Rail Link with China: Vientiane Times Contributor. *The Strait Times,* October 8. https://www.straitstimes.com/asia/se-asia/the-train-of-opportunities-as-laos-builds-rail-link-with-china-vientiane-times. Accessed 4 Jan 2019.

Prasad, K.V. 2018. India-China Ties on Upswing, but Concerns on BRI Remain. *The Tribune,* December 31. https://www.tribuneindia.com/news/nation/india-china-ties-on-upswing-but-concerns-on-bri-remain/706428.html. Accessed 28 Dec 2018.

Putz, Catherine. 2016. Can China Fix Central Asia's Soviet Rail Legacy? *The Diplomat,* January 14. https://thediplomat.com/2016/01/can-china-fix-central-asias-soviet-rail-legacy/. Accessed 25 Dec 2018.

Pyrgidis, Christos N. 2016. *Rail Transport System.* New York: CRC Press.

Rail Freight. 2018a. *Eurasian Rail Traffic in 2018,* December 24. https://www.railfreight.com/specials/2018/12/24/eurasian-rail-traffic-in-2018-heading-to-a-million-teus/. Accessed 23 Dec 2018.

———. 2018b. Uzbekistan, China One Step Closer to Building Railway Corridor via Kyrgyzstan. *Rail Freight,* October 8. https://www.railfreight.com/beltandroad/2018/10/08/uzbekistan-china-one-step-closer-to-building-railway-corridor-via-kyrgyzstan/. Accessed 17 Dec 2018.

Railway Gazette. 2008. *Rolling Stock Market*, March 7. https://www.railwaygazette.com/news/single-view/view/rolling-stock-market.html?sword_list[]=16&sword_list[]=coaches&sword_list[]=supplied&sword_list[]=by&sword_list[]=CNR&sword_list[]=Tangshan&sword_list[]=Railway&sword_list[]=Vehicle&no_cache=1. Accessed 3 Jan 2019.

———. 2010. *World Rolling Stock Market February 2010*, February 12. https://www.railwaygazette.com/news/single-view/view/world-rolling-stock-market-february-2010.html?cHash=f66031939aa1657de7cdcb1afb3ff20c&sword_list[]=World&sword_list[]=rolling&sword_list[]=stock&sword_list[]=market&sword_list[]=February&sword_list[]=201. Accessed 3 Jan 2019.

———. 2011a. Investment Spurs Kazakh Rolling Stock Industry. *Railway Gazette*, November 8. https://www.railwaygazette.com/news/business/single-view/view/investment-spurs-kazakh-rolling-stock-industry.html.

———. 2011b. News in Brief. *Railway Gazette*, September 13. https://www.railwaygazette.com/news/single-view/view/news-in-brief-62.html?cHash=640e865579ca5032c31d0892f6aef3cd&sword_list[]=Vietnam&no_cache=1. Accessed 5 Jan 2019.

———. 2012. *World Rolling Stock Market August 2012*, August 14. https://www.railwaygazette.com/news/single-view/view/world-rolling-stock-market-august-2012.html?cHash=89326f0f72c26eeed4e341da4702dce8&sword_list[]=CSR&sword_list[]=Ziyang&sword_list[]=is&sword_list[]=to&sword_list[]=supply&sword_list[]=64&sword_list[]=m. Accessed 22 Dec 2018.

———. 2014a. *Ulaanbaatar Railway Orders Coaches*, March 13. https://www.railwaygazette.com/news/passenger/single-view/view/ulaanbaatar-railway-orders-coaches.html?cHash=b6ef7522916a2c3c138823c6ef09fb4f&sword_list[]=Ulaanbaatar&sword_list[]=Railway&sword_list[]=orders&sword_list[]=coaches&no_cache=1. Accessed 4 Jan 2019.

———. 2014b. *World Rolling Stock Market May 2014*, May 11. https://www.railwaygazette.com/news/traction-rolling-stock/single-view/view/world-rolling-stock-market-may-2014.html?cHash=73a015ec7359ef148c134ccdcd92e79c&sword_list[]=KTJ&no_cache=1. Accessed 21 Dec 2018.

———. 2014c. World Rolling Stock Market May 2014. *Railway Gazette*, May 11. https://www.railwaygazette.com/news/traction-rolling-stock/single-view/view/world-rolling-stock-market-may-2014.html?cHash=73a015ec7359ef148c134ccdcd92e79c&sword_list[]=KTJ&no_cache=1. Accessed 29 Dec 2018.

———. 2017a. Bo-Bo-Bo Locomotives Shipped to Myanmar. *Railway Gazette*, February 21. https://www.railwaygazette.com/news/traction-rolling-stock/single-view/view/bo-bo-bo-locomotives-shipped-to-myanmar.html?sword_list[]=Myanmar&no_cache=1. Accessed 2 Jan 2019.

———. 2017b. World Rolling Stock Market January 2017. *Railway Gazette*, January 29. https://www.railwaygazette.com/news/traction-rolling-stock/

single-view/view/world-rolling-stock-market-january-2017.html?sword_
list[]=Vietnam&no_cache=1. Accessed 5 Jan 2019.

Rapoza, Kenneth. 2017. To Promote Electric Cars, China Considers Move to Ban
Gas Guzzlers. *Forbes*, September 11. https://www.forbes.com/sites/ken-
rapoza/2017/09/11/to-promote-electric-cars-china-considers-move-to-ban-
gas-guzzlers/#578ffa2851b7. Accessed 6 Jan 2019.

Reuters. 2016. *China to Build Second Railway Line into Tibet*, March 5. https://
www.theguardian.com/world/2016/mar/05/china-to-build-second-
railway-line-into-tibet.

Robinson, Ronald E. 1991. "Conclusion: Railways and Informal Empire." In
Railway Imperialism, by Clarence B. Davis and Kenneth E. Wilburn, Jr., 175-
196. New York: Greenwood.

Russian Business Today. 2018. Mongolia, Russia Sign Rail Freight Deal Negotiated
for Ten Years. *Russian Business Today*, June 22. https://russiabusinesstoday.
com/infrastructure/mongolia-russia-sign-rail-freight-deal-negotiated-
for-ten-years/.

RZD. 2015. *"Our Investment in Infrastructure Shows We Are Maintaining Our
Development Course" Says Yakunin*, June 5. http://eng.rzd.ru/newse/public/
en?STRUCTURE_ID=15&layer_id=4839&id=106629. Accessed 4 Jan 2019.

Saito, Akira. 1979. *Why Did Japan Choose the 3'6" Narrow Gauge?* http://www.
ejrcf.or.jp/jrtr/jrtr31/f33_sai.html. Accessed 17 Dec 2018.

Sharma, Gopal. 2019. Nepal to Use Chinese Gauge for Its Railway, Not the One
India. *Reuters*, March 5. https://www.reuters.com/article/us-india-nepal/
nepal-to-use-chinese-gauge-for-its-railway-not-the-one-india-uses-idUSKC-
N1QM16Y. Accessed 3 June 2019.

Smyth, Jamie. 2018. How Robot Trains Are Boosting Australia's Mining Industry.
The Financial Times, November 23. https://www.ft.com/content/b71db1fa-
ed3d-11e8-89c8-d36339d835c0. Accessed 7 Jan 2019.

Soucek, Svat. 2009. *A History of Inner Asia*. Cambridge: Cambridge
University Press.

Stanway, David. 2018a. China's Caofeidian Port Launches New Rail Freight Link
to Mongolia. *Reuters*, March 27. https://af.reuters.com/article/commodi-
tiesNews/idAFL3N1R92ZO. Accessed 4 Jan 2019.

———. 2018b. *Mongolia Plans Coal Rail Link to China by 2021: Official*,
November 8. https://www.reuters.com/article/us-china-coal-mongolia-
tavan-tolgoi/mongolia-plans-coal-rail-link-to-china-by-2021-official-
idUSKCN1ND0HP. Accessed 2 Jan 2019.

Stefanovich, Dmitry. 2018. Russia's Military Cooperation Goals in Central Asia.
The Diplomat, January 31. https://thediplomat.com/2018/02/russias-mili-
tary-cooperation-goals-in-central-asia/. Accessed 25 Dec 2018.

Storey, Ian. 2006. China's "Malacca Dilemma." *Association for Asian Research*, May
17. http://www.asianresearch.org/articles/2873.html. Accessed 20 Dec 2018.

Styles, Lucy. 2013. Mongolia Port Assessment. *Logistics Capacity Assessment*, September 26. https://dlca.logcluster.org/display/public/DLCA/2.1+Mon golia+Port+Assessment. Accessed 2 Jan 2019.

———. 2018. Mongolia Railway Assessment. *Logistics Capacity Assessment*, May 31. https://dlca.logcluster.org/display/public/DLCA/2.4+Mongolia+Railw ay+Assessment;jsessionid=4D9A75997A6033E1D109026D7559FFE2. Accessed 4 Jan 2019.

Suzuki, Wataru. 2019. China's Belt and Road Hits a Speed Bump In. *Asia Nikkei*, April 24. https://asia.nikkei.com/Spotlight/Belt-and-Road/China-s-Belt-and-Road-hits-a-speed-bump-in-Kazakhstan. Accessed 3 June 2019.

Takahashi, Toru. 2018. Sino-Japanese Cooperation Thrown Off Track Over. *Nikkei Asian Review*, December 16. https://asia.nikkei.com/Politics/International-Relations/Sino-Japanese-cooperation-thrown-off-track-over-Thai-rail-project. Accessed 4 Jan 2019.

Thant, Htoo. 2019. Railway Works to Recover Lost Transport Market Share. *Myanmar Times*, January 2. https://www.mmtimes.com/news/railway-works-recover-lost-transport-market-share.html. Accessed 7 Feb 2019.

The Indian Express. 2018. Nepal, India to Expedite Raxaul-Kathmandu Rail Project. *The Indian Express*, July 11. https://indianexpress.com/article/world/delhi/nepal-india-raxaul-kathmandu-bihar-rail-project-kp-oli-modi-5255184/. Accessed 2 Jan 2019.

The International Institute for Strategic Studies. 2019. *Military Balance 2018*. London: The International Institute for Strategic Studies.

The Nation. 2018. Somkid Calls for High-Speed Rail Action. *The Nation*, July 12. http://www.nationmultimedia.com/detail/Economy/30349861. Accessed 4 Jan 2019.

The Star. 2016. M'sia, Thailand to Begin Talks on Bangkok-KL HSR Project – Thai Minister. *The Star*, November 23. https://www.thestar.com.my/business/business-news/2016/11/23/msia-and-thailand-to-begin-talks-on-bangkok-kl-hsr-project%2D%2D-thai-minister/. Accessed 4 Jan 2019.

Todd, Stuart. 2019. Gefco Sets Up Forwarding Subsidiary in Central China. *Lloyd's Loading List*, May 31. https://www.lloydsloadinglist.com/freight-directory/news/Gefco-sets-up-forwarding-subsidiary-in-central-China/74381.htm#.XPTJuf4RWM8. Accessed 3 June 2019.

Transmash Holding. 2011. *BMZ Has Delivered a Batch of Shunting Diesel Locomotives to Ulan-Bator Railway*, April 11. http://www.tmholding.ru/en/press_office/events/2711.html?sphrase_id=14262. Accessed 4 Jan 2019.

———. 2018. *Geography of Deliveries*. http://www.tmholding.ru/en/commer-cial_activities/geography/index.php?sphrase_id=14262. Accessed 2 Jan 2019.

United Nations Economic and Social Commission for Asia and the Pacific. 2016. *Trans-Asian Railway Network*, November 1. https://www.unescap.org/resources/trans-asian-railway-network-map. Accessed 4 Jan 2019.

————. 2017. *Review of Developments in Transportation in Asia and the Pacific.* Bangkok: United Nations Economic and Social Commission for Asia and the Pacific.

————. 2018. Capacity Building Seminar on Railway Network Connectivity and Interoperability Challenges. *United Nations Economic and Social Commission for Asia and the Pacific,* September 5. https://www.unescap.org/sites/default/files/China%27s%20presentation%20Dushanbe.pdf. Accessed 22 Dec 2018.

Uysal, Onur. 2014. Kazakhstan-Turkmenistan-Iran Railway to Open Today. *Rail Turkey En,* December 3. https://railturkey.org/2014/12/03/kazakhstan-turkmenistan-iran-railway/. Accessed 18 Dec 2018.

Vakilov, Fakhri. 2019. Uzbekistan Joins China-Kazakhstan-Turkmenistan-Iran Railway Corridor. *Trend,* April 2. https://en.trend.az/business/economy/3041770.html. Accessed 3 June 2019.

Wan, Debby Chan Sze. 2018. China-Myanmar High-Speed Railway Quietly Back on Track. *Myanmar Times,* July 6. https://www.mmtimes.com/news/china-myanmar-high-speed-railway-quietly-back-track.html. Accessed 1 Jan 2019.

Wang, Brian. 2016. China Developing Faster High Speed Trains with Adjustable Wheels for Different Gauges from China to Europe. *Nextbigfuture,* June 6. https://www.nextbigfuture.com/2016/06/china-developing-faster-high-speed.html. Accessed 23 Dec 2018.

World Trade Organisation. 2018. *Members and Observers.* https://www.wto.org/english/thewto_e/whatis_e/tif_e/org6_e.htm. Accessed 23 Dec 2018.

Wu, Shang-su, and Alan Chong. 2018. Developmental Railpolitics: The Political Economy of China's High-Speed Rail Projects in Thailand and Indonesia. *Contemporary Southeast Asia* 40 (3): 503–526.

Xinhua. 2018. China, Myanmar Sign MoU on Feasibility Study of Muse-Mandalay Railway. *Xinhua Net,* October 23. http://www.xinhuanet.com/english/2018-10/23/c_137550972.htm. Accessed 1 Jan 2019.

Xinhua. 2019. China facilitates meter-gage railway freight transportation to Vietnam. Xinhua Net. September 24. http://www.xinhuanet.com/english/2019-09/24/c_138418806.htm. Accessed 1 Oct. 2019.

Yi, Whan-woo. 2019. Mongolia, Korea Discuss Railway Cooperation. *The Korean Times,* May 17. https://www.koreatimes.co.kr/www/nation/2019/05/176_268345.html. Accessed 1 June 2019.

Zhang, Lipeng. 2018. *Having Obtained Rights for Operating CRRC ZK1-K Bogies on North American Railways,* March 19. http://www.crrcgc.cc/en/tabid/7389/sourceId/10408/infoid/291220/Default.aspx. Accessed 3 Jan 2019.

Zhen, Summer. 2015. Chinese Firm Takes Control of Gwadar Port Free-Trade Zone in Pakistan. *South China Morning Post,* November 11. https://www.scmp.com/business/companies/article/1877882/chinese-firm-takes-control-gwadar-port-free-trade-zone-pakistan. Accessed 26 Dec 2018.

ZumMallen, Ryan. 2018. German Auto Supplier ZF Prepares Electric, Autonomous Truck Takeover. *Trucks*, July 16. https://www.trucks. com/2018/07/16/german-auto-supplier-zf-electric-autonomous-truck/?utm_referrer=https%3A%2F%2Fwww.bing. com%2Fsearch%3Fq%3Ddriverless%2Btruck%252C%2Belectric%2Bpower%26 qs%3Dn%26form%3DQBRE%26sp%3D-1%26pq%3Ddriverless%2Btruck%252 C%2Belectr. Accessed 6 Jan 2019.

人民交通网 (People's Transportation Net). 2018. 中国是哈萨克斯坦交通基础设施的最大投资国 (China Is the Largest Investor to Kazakhstan's Transportation Infrastructure). 人民交通网 *(People's Transportation Net)*, November 16. http://www.rmjtxw.com/news/cj/62341.html. Accessed 17 Dec 2018.

PART III

Critical Political Economy
on the Road

The Belt and Road Initiative and China's Relations with Iran and Saudi Arabia: A Delicate Balancing Act

Manochehr Dorraj

CHINA'S RISE AND ITS EXPANDING INFLUENCE

China's expanding power and presence in the Middle East has been aided by several factors. First, its impressive rate of growth of six–ten percent since 1976 and its mercurial economic rise on the global stage, which changed its status as energy self-sufficient to a net importer by 1993, inaugurated its "going out" strategy in pursuit of new energy supplies. Second, the declining US and European influence in the region, which accelerated after the US invasion of Iraq in 2003, provided a vacuum for China to step in. China's lack of a colonial history and its policies of "respect for sovereignty", "non-intervention", "offend no one", and "win-win economic ties" have served it well in a region with a bitter memory of colonialism and a strong anti-colonial sentiment. Third, China's massive financial

M. Dorraj (✉)
Department of Political Science, Texas Christian University,
Fort Worth, TX, USA
e-mail: m.dorraj@tcu.edu

© The Author(s) 2020
A. Chong, Q. M. Pham (eds.), *Critical Reflections on China's Belt & Road Initiative*, https://doi.org/10.1007/978-981-13-2098-9_7

assets (more than US$2 trillion surplus) as compared to the current US national debt of US$22 trillion in 2018 allow it to provide the region with investments and loans. The energy-rich Middle East, in turn, not only provides China with energy security but also a lucrative market for trade, investment, and exports for its excess capacity.

The Belt and Road Initiative (BRI) is going to be much larger and more expansive in its reach, breadth, and ambitions than the US Marshall Plan, initiated in the aftermath of the Second World War to rebuild the devastated European economies. Once fully implemented, it would indeed be a transformative phenomenon for the regions of West Asia and North Africa and the world at large. This initiative also signifies China's mercurial rise on the global stage in the last four decades, changing its strategy from "going out" to "going global". Hence, there would be winners and losers in the path of the BRI. Geography, assets, compatibility in trade and commerce, and political stability would go a long way to determine who would be a more viable partner for China in its BRI initiative. Both Iran and Saudi Arabia possess many of the assets, including vast energy resources, a history of trade and financial transactions with China and a healthy consumer-based market, ready to absorb the export of Chinese investments, goods, services, and commodities and become major players in the regional success of the BRI.

China-Iran Relations

The history of China's relations with Iran is elaborate and goes back to the pre-Islamic Persia, prior to the seventh-century Arab conquest of the country, and the cordial relations between the Tang dynasty and the Persian Empire. This period witnessed the flourishing of trade, diplomatic ties, and numerous mutual cultural influences and exchanges, between the two grand empires of East and West Asia. With this illustrious history of commercial, political, and cultural relations that date back to 2100 years, the Chinese and Persian Empires enjoyed good ties and partnership through the ancient Silk Road that endured for centuries. After the Mongol invasion of both empires in the thirteenth century, these ties expanded (Garver 2006, 3–14). The fact that this long history of mutually beneficial relations is complemented by the lack of any war or major conflict between the two countries, and both nations suffering the humiliation of Western neo-colonial rule, together with aspirations for the creation of a multipolar world, helped to rekindle their ties in the twenty-first century (Garver 2006, 3–14).

While this history remains a significant topic of scholarly investigation, due to the limited scope of this chapter, we would leave that worthy endeavor to historians. Our focus here is on the relationship between the People's Republic of China and the Islamic Republic of Iran after the Iranian revolution of 1979. Although the former Shah of Iran formally established relations with China in 1971, it was under the Islamic Republic that the relations between the two countries flourished and expanded substantially.

In the immediate aftermath of the Iranian revolution of 1979, China recognized the Islamic Republic and expressed its aspirations for expansion of relations between the two countries. After the hostage crisis of 1980, whereby a group of militant Iranian students took the American embassy personnel as hostages, Iran experienced a major fall-out with its erstwhile ally, the US. With the imposition of sanctions and the threat of military force against the Islamic Republic, and the escalation of tensions, Iran-US bilateral ties deteriorated rapidly, forcing the Islamic Republic to opt for an "Eastern Strategy", seeking closer ties with China and the Soviet Union. In the ensuing Iraq-Iran war (1980–1988), Iran suffered major destruction of its cities. Thus, in the aftermath of the war, the Iranian government needed to rebuild its war-torn cities and their infrastructures. This provided China with the opportunity to step in and provide the major investments and services, and in the process, expand its trade and commercial ties with the Islamic Republic (Bin Huwaidin 2002, 57–72).

Possessing the fourth largest oil reserves and the second largest gas reserves in the world, Iran is a major energy powerhouse. The fact that Iran's production capacity is only about 3 million barrels a day, as opposed to Saudi production of 11.2 million barrels a day, may mean that, because of its smaller volume of current production, its reserves are likely to last longer, thus making it a more reliable source of energy supply for the long run once it acquires the necessary technological capability to expand its production. In the aftermath of the Iraq-Iran war that saw the devastation of significant Iranian production capacity and facilities, China helped Iran to rebuild its energy infrastructure, and its production capacity gradually began to recover. In 1994, Iran was responsible for one percent of China's oil imports, while, by 2011, China was the destination for 22 percent of Iranian oil exports and nine percent of China's global imports. In 2004, Iran signed a US$20 billion contract with China to sell it 2.5 metric tons of natural gas, over the next 25 years, starting in 2008. This was followed by another deal a few years later that would allow China to import 250 million tons of Iranian gas, a deal estimated to be worth between US$70 and US$100 billion (Jin 2005, 1–2; Garver 2006, 270–275).

While Iran's oil exports to China under the US-UN-EU sanctions that encompassed its energy sector was diminished, since the nuclear agreement of 2015 and the removal of energy-related sanctions, Iran's oil exports to China began to expand. In 2016, the Iranian oil minister announced that Chinese companies were scheduled to develop the two giant Iranian oil fields, North Azadegan and Yadavaran. Prior to the 2018 Trump administration's abrogation of Iran's nuclear deal and its intent to impose new set of sanctions on the Iranian government that encompasses its energy sector, the Iranian government was in cooperation with China, hoping to increase its oil production of about 3 million barrels a day to 5.7 million barrels a day and its gas production to 1.4 billion cubic meters a day by 2021 ("China to Develop two Iranian Giant Oil Fields" 2016). However, with the new US sanctions in place, in addition to the threat of imposing extraterritorial sanctions on nations that do business with Iran, it remains to be seen if China would be able to deliver on its aspirations of expanding economic ties with Tehran.

In 2017, China emerged once more as the number one importer of Iranian oil in the world when Chinese energy companies announced that they would expect to lift between three million and four million barrels more Iranian oil each quarter than the year before (Chen 2017). China has also emerged as the largest market for the growing Iranian petrochemical exports, especially methanol. Iran is currently the biggest methanol exporter to China in the Middle East and plans are underway for Chinese companies to build a US$5 billion methanol plant in Mahshahr (Harold and Nader 2012, 10–11).

China's interest in the Iranian market is not confined to energy. The two nations enjoy an extensive trade relationship in other sectors of the economy as well. Whereas prior to the Iranian revolution of 1979, the value of China's trade with Iran was less than one percent of its total trade, but by 1991, bilateral trade doubled. By 2003, China was responsible for eight percent of Iran's global trade. By 2006, China overtook Japan as Iran's number one trade partner. By 2007, the three major East Asian economic powerhouses, namely, China, Japan, and South Korea were, respectively, Iran's number one, two, and three trade partners in the world, a position that was held previously by European powers (Garver 2013, 76–77). In May 2011, China signed a US$20 billion agreement to expand the bilateral cooperation in Iran's mining and industrial sectors

(Garver 2013, 77). The bilateral trade has expanded ever since. In 2015, the value of this bilateral trade was estimated to be about US$52 billion dollars. During President Xi Jinping visit to Tehran in January of 2016, the two sides pledged to expand the value of bilateral trade to US$600 billion by 2025 (Clover et al. 2016).

China has also played a significant role in the development of Iran's nuclear program in the early stages of its development, training Iranian scientists, providing nuclear technology, and building research facilities such as the research reactor in Isfahan. China played a key role in the development of Iran's missile system as well (Currier and Dorraj 2010). Because Iran's air force is weak compared to its neighbors, its long-range missiles are its strategic weapons of deterrence and self-defense. Currently, China ranks as the number two provider of armaments to Iran after Russia. The value of China's arms' transfers to Iran between 1980 and 2010 is estimated to be between US$ 4–10 billion (Dorraj 2013, 16–20). However, when compared to the US$95 billion US-Saudi arms' transfers between 2009 and 2016, this amount is very small. Iran and China's security ties involve joint anti-terrorism cooperation as well as joint naval exercises.

CHINA-SAUDI RELATIONS

Unlike the pervasive common perception, China-Saudi relations are not merely commercial. As a part of the larger Arab World, the Saudis have a relationship with China that goes back to the seventh century and the ancient Silk Road, buttressed by a long history of commercial and cultural ties and exchanges that existed between ancient China and Arabia (Bin Huwaidin 2002). In more recent times, since the ascendance of Communism in China in 1949, and as a close ally of the US, the politically conservative Saudi monarchy was averse to the establishment of relations with Beijing. Communist China's support of the radical regime in South Yemen and the guerrilla movement in Oman in the 1960s and early 1970s made the Saudi monarchy very suspicious of Communist China and its intentions. However, the ensuing political developments, such as the US normalization of relations with China in 1972, the collapse of Communism in Central and Eastern Europe in 1989 and the steady economic rise of China and its expanding demand for energy, convinced Riyadh to establish relations with Beijing in 1990 (Currier and Dorraj 2011, 69).

Once the diplomatic ties were established, the relations grew rapidly. Several factors worked as the catalyst for the rapid expansion of bilateral ties. First, China's economic rise and its transformation from an energy self-sufficient state to a net importer of oil in 1993 elevated the search for long-term suppliers of energy on top of its economic and national security agenda. Second, the financial strength of Riyadh as a trade partner added to its allure. Third, Beijing's abandonment of the "export of socialism" and support for radical regimes and its integration into the global system laid Saudi suspicions about China's malignant political intentions to rest. Fourth, in the aftermath of the 2001 terrorist attacks against the US and the rise of anti-Saudi sentiments there, Riyadh decided to diversify its international partnership. The unpopular US invasion of Iraq in 2003 affirmed and solidified this policy. Fifth, with the rise of the "shale revolution" in the US and its diminishing demand for oil imports from Saudi Arabia, China began to look even more attractive as a partner who would lead the world in energy demand for the decades to come. With the overall decline of the Western influence in the region, Beijing, now flush with cash—in clear contrast to the massive US deficit—stepped in to fill the vacuum.

Thus, the energy and trade ties between the two countries expanded rapidly. Saudi Arabia, with the estimated oil reserves of 262 billion barrels a day (the second largest in the world), as opposed to Iran's estimated reserves of 132.6 billion barrels a day (the fourth largest), and, respectively, a production capacity of 11–11.5 million barrels a day for Saudi Arabia, as opposed to Iran's 2.3–3.6 million barrels per day, was even a bigger prize and the most significant player in providing China with the largest share of its energy imports globally. Whereas in 2014, the Saudis were on top of the list of global oil exporters to China, providing it with 16 percent of its global oil imports as opposed to Iran's 9 percent, in 2017 they trailed Russia and Angola and became the third largest source of China's energy imports. Nonetheless, the Saudis' large reserves and production capacity renders them a "swing producer" that can have a great impact on oil prices. This is an important consideration for a major energy consumer like China. The Chinese were also interested in the Saudi national oil company ARAMCO's refining and petrochemical production capabilities, as demonstrated by numerous joint venture partnerships developed between the two countries in this area. Hence, early on in the relationship, the fact that Saudi Arabia as a close ally of the US and its European allies did not carry the anti-American political baggage often associated with Iran, rendered it a less "complicated or problematic partner" (Currier and Dorraj 2011, 69).

With the establishment of the bilateral relations, in the 1990s, trade ties between the two countries expanded rapidly. Whereas the value of Saudi-Chinese bilateral trade was a mere US$71 million in 1989, in 1991, it reached US$525 million, and climbed to US$1.027 billion in 1994. By 1996, Saudi Arabia became China's leading trade partner in the Middle East, accounting for more than 30 percent of Beijing's total export to the region (Bin Huwaidin 2002, 228–236). By 2010, the bilateral trade reached US$40 billion. This amount climbed to US$60 billion in 2015, and climbed to US$64 billion in 2017. Currently, China is Saudi Arabia's number one trade partner in the world (Chaziza 2016, 176).

The energy ties have also expanded exponentially. Whereas in 1995, China ranked 25th on the list of the countries importing oil from Saudi Arabia, by 2002, China assumed the mantle of number one on this list. In 2014, the Saudis were the top exporter of oil to China, accounting for 16 percent of its global imports (Energy Information Administration 2014). Although by 2017, Saudi Arabia was relegated to number three exporter to China, trailing Russia and Angola, the Saudis are still a significant source of energy supply to China for the reasons discussed above.

China also enlisted Saudi ARAMCO's expertise and capital to expand and modernize its refining capacity. Saudi Arabia has built a refinery in Fujian region of China and is operating more than 600 gas stations there. Another refinery, that was scheduled to be built in Qingdao province, is designated to process the Saudis' heavier crude for the Chinese market. The two countries have also created numerous joint ventures in petrochemicals that are primarily used in Chinese textile industries (China Daily 2006). Since the Saudis have built numerous refineries in China to process their heavier exports of crude oil, China is likely to import the Saudi crude for decades to come.

Belt and Road Initiative and China's Expanding Ties with Iran and Saudi Arabia

China's ambitious initiative, announced for the first time by President Xi Jinping in 2013, is an "all-inclusive" project that is going to connect three continents, Asia, Africa, and Europe, that encompasses more than four billion people, and produce one-third of the global GDP (Ferdinand 2016, 950). China would implement this plan through trade, investments in infrastructure, energy, and communication technology in order to create a new global supply chain, while expanding the political, security, cultural, and people-to-people connections between China and the BRI partners. The BRI is projected to cost US$1.7 trillion annually. It is intended to increase connectivity and linkages among the nations that are stakeholders in this project by building high-speed railways, ports, roads, highways, as well as broadband and the expansion of communication networks. These are all a part of Chinese leadership's global strategy for the twenty-first century. BRI is not just a trade initiative. It heralds the dawn of a new Sino-centered global order that is going to transform the international system (Ehteshami 2017, 193–194). No matter where one stands politically, BRI is going to have a transformative impact globally as well as regionally. Here, however, our focus is on its impact on Iran and Saudi Arabia. As moving parts in this larger scheme, Iran and Saudi Arabia have much to offer as trade partners for China as well each posing distinct challenges for China's diplomacy to ensure the success of Belt and Road.

As the BRI unfolds in connecting the Urumqi-Central Asia-Iran-Turkey-Russia-Europe trade corridor, Iran expects to receive much larger amounts of Chinese investment and business flows. As one Iranian official stated in 2015, "Iran and China have so far had trade ties but from now on our expectation is to see Chinese investments in our infrastructure projects. We need between US$30 and US$50 billion foreign investments annually, a big chunk of which can be secured by China for such sectors like road, rail and air transportation, agriculture and industries such as household, textile and ceramics" (The Iran Project 2015).

Boasting the longest coastline on the Persian Gulf and the control of the strategically significant Straits of Hormuz that much of the oil shipment to China goes through and serving as gateway to Central Asia and the Caspian Sea with a consumer base of 83 million people, Iran is a key player in the success of the BRI in West Asia. As a *New York Times* columnist on July 25 2017 observed, "For China's Global Ambitions, 'Iran is at the Center of Everything'" (Erdbrink 2017). One evidence for this assertion is that China's investments in Iran since the second half of 2016 have increased by 43.5 percent (Financial Tribune 2017).

China's attempt to revive the ancient Silk Road has also manifested itself through a railway system that connects Yiwu region in Eastern China to Tehran, and through Turkey, to Europe and Russia. Combined with the 2000-mile Urumqi-Mashad railway, these developments are likely to transform Iran as a major hub of regional trade and a transit point to Europe. In February 2016, the first cargo train service to enhance the trade ties between the two countries was inaugurated (Chaziza 2016).

China is building major railways in East and Western Iran to connect it respectively to Central Asia and Turkey and Europe, and in the process, connecting the major Iranian cities of Tehran and Mashhad to the Southern ports of the country and rebuilding and expanding the Iranian ports in the Persian Gulf and the Caspian Sea to expand their capacity to handle larger cargoes and expedite the flow of goods and commodities from China to Central Asia and from there to Iran, and through Turkey to Europe. This expanding flow has also increased the number of students and cultural exchanges between the two countries.

The BRI initiative is also transforming Saudi Arabia. China successfully completed the Kingdom's first high-speed railway that was inaugurated by King Salman in September 2018. Dubbed the Haramain High Speed Rail, the Spanish-built trains operate through stations and civil works constructed by a Saudi-Chinese consortium. The Haramain Line has the capacity to transport 60 million people annually between the two holy cities of Mecca and Medina. Although the new trains are currently running at 200 kilometers per hour, they are expected to operate at much higher speeds of up to 300 kilometers per hour once the systems are fully run in (Railway Gazette 2018). It was therefore no surprise that on the eve of his visit to Saudi Arabia in January 19–20, 2016, the Chinese president, Xi Jinping, declared that the two countries should expand their bilateral trade ties, and push for further progress in the China–GCC Free Trade Agreement Talks. They should also establish the China-Saudi Energy Cooperation Community. He expressed his appreciation for Saudi Arabia's joining the Asian Infrastructure Investment Bank as a founding member in 2015 and contributing US$20 billion to funding the bank (People's Daily 2016).

This was followed by King Salman's trip to China in March 2017 that culminated in the signing of US$64 billion worth of economic and trade deals between the two countries. King Salman also expressed his interest in building synergy between the Saudi Vision 2030 and China's Belt and Road initiative. The Saudi leadership is particularly interested in the expansion of Chinese investment in diversifying the Saudi economy, and they have discussed the possibility of converting some of their sovereign wealth assets into Renminbi, as they anticipated that the value of the Chinese currency would appreciate in the future. China has in turn offered Renminbi bonds to any nation that would partner with it in the BRI.

China's rapidly expanding economic influence in the region in part reveals the financial and political windfalls of abstaining from military intervention and respecting sovereignty. Unlike the West and Russia, China lacks a history of war and conflict with West Asia and North Africa. The policies of respect for sovereignty and non-intervention in the internal affairs of other nations, keeping a low political profile and accentuating trade, have served Beijing's diplomacy very well so far. China has accumulated a good deal of political capital in the region. How it spends this capital would go a long way to determining the future viability of the BRI and China's political fortunes in the region, including its relations with Iran and Saudi Arabia. If successfully implemented, this initiative is going to change China and the world.

CHINA'S BALANCING ACT

While Iran's tensions with the US and its politics of "resistance" pose one set of challenges for Chinese foreign policy, Saudi Arabia's close political and military alliance with the US poses another set of challenges for Chinese foreign policy. But so far Beijing has attempted to stay above the fray and remain neutral. China refuses to take sides between such antagonists as Iran and Saudi Arabia, and the Palestinians and the Israelis. Hence, China's mediation of regional conflict renders it as an impartial broker in a polarized region. Beijing's constructive role in bringing Iran's nuclear deal to fruition and its invitation to the leaders of Syria and the opposition to come to China for negotiation, and its attempt to hold negotiations between the leaders of Israel and the Palestinian Authority after President Trump's divisive policy of declaring Jerusalem as the capital of Israel, all serve as recent examples of its balanced diplomacy and judicious exercise of its soft power.

Another example of China's balancing act is its provision of missile and nuclear technology to both Iran and Saudi Arabia. As mentioned previously, China played an important role in the development of Iran's nuclear program in the early stages of its development, and was equally instrumental in the progress of the country's missile defense system. China has also sold Saudi Arabia long-range missiles in 1998, in 2007, and in 2014. In 2017, China even agreed to build its first drone factory in the Middle East in Saudi Arabia. Beijing has consistently argued that access to such technologies should not be a monopoly of powerful Western nations alone (Currier and Dorraj 2011). Iran, which until July 2018 was an observer in the Shanghai Cooperation Organization—a collective security pact that includes China, Russia, India, Pakistan and several Central Asian countries—is poised to join the organization as a permanent member sometime in the future. All this was ostensibly facilitated by Beijing. China has also held joint naval exercises with Iran in 2014 and 2017 and has expressed its intentions to do the same with the GCC countries, including Saudi Arabia.

Chinese leaders would probably agree with the former US President Barack Obama's suggestion that Iran and Saudi Arabia should "share the neighborhood" and coexist through a "cold peace" (The Atlantic 2016). However, it is not likely to get involved directly in this conflict or spend any of its political capital trying to resolve it. Chinese leadership is too cautious to be bogged down in the quicksand of Middle East conflict and turmoil.

Clearly, China's political positions on Syria, Yemen, Iraq, and ISIS are more aligned with Iran than Saudi Arabia. But so far, China has refused to take a strong position on these civil wars and conflicts, perhaps fearing that such a stand may lead to alienating potential trade partners and needlessly making enemies. It is also the case that economic prerogatives, and the Saudi position as the number one energy supplier and trade partner for China in the region has trumped any political unease Beijing may harbor against Saudi policies.

Some energy observers believe that with the current rate of consumption, China is likely to run out of its domestic sources of oil in the next 15 years. This in turn would make China more dependent on oil imports from the Middle East. The latter currently provides it with 55 percent of its oil imports. As the country with the largest oil reserve in the region, and massive financial assets, the Saudis are likely to continue to loom large in Beijing's political calculus for the near future.

As the BRI takes off and transforms the region, it would have a more profound and distinct impact on the economic and political realignment of great powers underway in the Middle East. This is a realignment that involves a more prominent Chinese role in the region in the future. This is already evident through Beijing's more pro-active political diplomacy and increasing naval presence and joint naval exercises in the regions of the Persian Gulf and the Indian Ocean.

The January 2016 Xi Jinping trip to Saudi Arabia, Iran and Egypt was in large part designated to promote China's BRI and enlist the partnership of these three key nations for this project. The success of this initiative, however, cannot be achieved merely by economic means alone. China's successful balancing act must be sustained and refined, so that at the end of the day it is not led by events, as might be entailed by a reactive policy. Instead, Beijing leads by charting a role that is more proactively in consort and consultation with its partners.

CONCLUSION

The mutually beneficial energy and trade ties that China maintains with Iran and Saudi Arabia are sustained by the two energy giants of the region. Both Tehran and Riyadh provide China with the security of supply, and China in turn provides them with the security of demand by signing long-term energy contracts with them and becoming the largest importer of their oil in the world. The future threat to the disruption of these energy ties may stem as much from the political turmoil in the Middle East as from China's ability to tap into its own massive supplies of shale oil and gas, if and when the higher prices for oil and gas would make exploring its massive shale deposits viable economically.

The lingering dark horse for the future of the Iranian and Saudi economies would lie with the current energy exports of the US and Canada to the Asian markets, including China, thanks to the "shale revolution". If this scenario plays out, North American oil supplies would expand substantially and emerge as the major competitor for Iranian and Saudi exports of energy to East Asian markets. However, President Trump's inauguration of a trade war with China and the imposition of tariffs on Chinese goods have already culminated in Chinese retaliation against US goods and decreases in the import of American oil. Another unknown factor is the Trump administration's pledge to prevent the selling of the Iranian oil on the global market in light of abrogation of the nuclear deal. It remains to be seen as to how successful Trump's administration would be in implementing its economic strangulation of the Islamic Republic and ushering in regime change in Iran.

In addition, in the post-Paris climate change conference of November 2015, pressure is building on nations to reduce their carbon footprint and diminish the share of fossil fuel in their energy mix in favor of renewables and other alternative sources of "green energy". All of these developments could leave an indelible mark on the future course of bilateral ties between China, Iran and Saudi Arabia. A countervailing factor might yet ameliorate this trend. As the BRI gains momentum, and the projected soaring Chinese demand for energy in the next two decades and the new markets for its excess economic capacity materializes, ties between China and its two most important Middle Eastern partners will remain steady. Moreover, China has prudently refused to take sides on the conflicts between Saudi Arabia and Iran. This delicate balancing act has enabled Beijing to maintain cordial relationships with both countries' leadership. This has also served China's overall regional strategy, dictated by the aphorism "accentuate the trade and maintain a low political profile".

For Iran, in the post-nuclear deal era, so long as the mistrust and tensions with the US linger under the Trump administration, China would remain an indispensable insurance policy, and a vital potential partner countering the US policy of economic strangulation and political containment. For Saudi Arabia, in contrast, its close economic and security ties with the US, culminating in the purchase of US$95 billion worth of arms under the Obama administration alone, imposes some limitations on the degree of its security partnership with China. For Riyadh, Beijing is just one more partner among many of its energy consumers and trade partners, albeit a significant one.

Within the geographical scope of the BRI, Iran would also play a directly beneficial role in China's Urumqi-Central Asia-Iran-Turkey-Russia-Europe Corridor. Saudi Arabia, in contrast, only tangentially straddles the path of the Maritime Silk Road, and does not occupy any important direct link in any of the designated BRI corridors. Instead, it has decided to tendentiously join the China-Pakistan corridor. Theoretically, the BRI offers sufficient economic and political room to accommodate both Iran and Saudi Arabia. Should the current rift between Saudi Arabia and Iran deepen, it might test China's policy of "non-intervention" and "offend no one". If such a scenario materializes in the future, it is likely that China would assume a higher profile political role in the region as a mediator. Going forward, it is less likely that Beijing could afford to remain politically aloof and neutral as its economic investment in the region deepens. We would all have a privileged seat of observation, as the drama of China's global rise unfolds in the Middle East and redefines its foreign policy posture. We are currently witnessing the early stages of this change.

REFERENCES

Bin Huwaidin, Mohammad. 2002. *China's Relations with Arabia and the Gulf.* London: Routledge Curzon.

CCTV.com. 2016, May 17. China to Develop two Iranian Giant Oil Fields. http://www.cihan.com.tr/en/worldNews. Accessed 5 Dec 2017.

Chaziza, Mordechai. 2016. Sino-Turkish 'Solid Strategic Partnership': Chinas Dream or a Reality? *China Report* 52 (4): 265–283. https://doi.org/10.1177/0009445516661812. Accessed 5 Jan 2017.

Chen, Alzhu. 2017. China's Iran Oil Imports to Hit Record on New Production: Sources. *Reuters*, January 5.

Clover, Charles, Heba Saleh, Najmeh Bozorgmehr, and Simeon Kerr. 2016. Xi Faces Diplomatic Test on First Middle East Visit. *The Financial Times*, January 18.

Currier, Carrie, and Manochehr Dorraj. 2010. In Arms We Trust: The Economic and Strategic Factors Motivating China-Iran Relations. *Journal of Chinese Political Science* 15 (1): 49–69.

———. 2011. China's Quest for Energy Security in the Middle East; Strategic Implications. In *China's Energy Relations with the Developing World*. London and New York: Continuum.

Dorraj, Manochehr. 2013. Iran's Expanding Relations with China and Their Strategic Dimensions. *The Emirates Center for Strategic Studies and Research* 112: 16–20.

Ehteshami, Anoushrivan. 2017. The One Belt, One Road in China's Grand Strategy. In Anoushrivan Ehteshami and Niv Horesh, *China's Presence in the Middle East: The Implications of One Belt, One Road Initiative*. New York: Routledge.

Erdbrink, Thomas. 2017. For China's Global Ambitions, 'Iran is at the Center of Everything'. *New York Times*, July 25. https://www.nytimes.com/2017/07/25/world/middleeast/iran-china-business-ties.html. Accessed 28 Nov 2019.

Ferdinand, Peter. 2016. Westward HO—The China Dream and 'One Belt, One Road': Chinese Foreign Policy Under Xi Jinping. *International Affairs* 92 (4): 950.

Garver, John W. 2006. *China and Iran: Ancient Partners in a Post-Imperial World*. Seattle: University of Washington Press.

———. 2013. China-Iran Relations: Cautious Friendship with America's Nemesis. *China Report* 1 (49): 76–77.

Goldberg, Jeffrey. 2016. The Obama Doctrine. *The Atlantic*, March 10.

Harold, Scott, and Alireza Nader. 2012. China and Iran: Economic, Political, and Military Relations. *Rand Corporation, Occasional Paper Series* 11–12.

Jin, liangxiang. 2005. Energy First: China and the Middle East. *Middle East Quarterly* X11 (2): 1–2.

People's Daily. 2016. Xi's Visit to Improve Ties with Saudi Arabia: Envoy. *The People's Daily* (China), January 18. http://en.people.cn/n3/2016/0118/c90780-9005339.html. Accessed 14 Jan 2019.

Railway Gazette. 2018. King Inaugurates Haramain High Speed Rail. *Railway Gazette*, September 25. https://www.railwaygazette.com/news/high-speed/single-view/view/king-inaugurates-haramain-high-speed-rail.html. Accessed 14 Jan 2019.

CHAPTER 8

Australia and China's Belt and Road Initiative: Economic Opportunities and Geo-Strategic Concerns

Carlyle A. Thayer

INTRODUCTION

This chapter discusses the contending factors at play that have influenced Australia's coalition Liberal-National Party government to decline to join China's Belt and Road Initiative (BRI) despite the obvious economic opportunities and support from the business community.

Geo-strategic concerns of the Australian government over the BRI have led to deterioration in bilateral relations with China. In 2018, Beijing declined to issue visas for Australian ministerial visits to China (Shanahan and Riordan 2018; Riordan and Baxendale 2018; Hewett et al. 2018). Chinese officials and state-owned media were critical about what they viewed as anti-Chinese rhetoric and implied that Australia could suffer sanctions as a result (Riordan et al. 2017; Tillett 2017; Grigg 2017; Saunokonoko 2018; Wood 2018; Korporaal 2018). The former Labor

C. A. Thayer (✉)
School of Humanities and Social Sciences, The University of New South Wales, Australian Defence Force Academy, Canberra, NSW, Australia
e-mail: c.thayer@adfa.edu.au

© The Author(s) 2020
A. Chong, Q. M. Pham (eds.), *Critical Reflections on China's Belt & Road Initiative*, https://doi.org/10.1007/978-981-13-2098-9_8

139

Party premier of Victoria observed that relations had reached a 'tipping point' (Kelly 2017a; Kehoe 2018c).

Australia-China economic ties are substantial. China is Australia's largest trading partner and, as noted below, their economies are complimentary. China provides the largest number of foreign students attending Australian universities and the income they generate is important for their hosts (Dodd 2018a, b; Stewart 2018). In addition, Chinese tourism is on the increase.

After the election of Donald Trump as president of the U.S., his pursuit of America First and Make America Great Again resulted in the U.S. withdrawing from the Trans-Pacific Partnership and the Paris Accord on Climate Change. Trump's actions reinforced the shared commitment of Australia and China to oppose protectionism and to support policies designed to mitigate climate change.

How then do we explain Australia's reluctance to join the BRI and the current downturn in bilateral relations?

This chapter is divided into five parts: Part 1 provides a broad overview of Australia-China relations. Part 2 explores the opportunities for cooperation. Part 3 examines the domestic debate over the pros and cons of joining the BRI. Part 4 discusses the major geo-strategic obstacles to Australia's formal participation in the BRI. Part 5 offers some concluding observations.

PART 1: OVERVIEW OF AUSTRALIA-CHINA RELATIONS

According to the Australian Department of Foreign Affairs and Trade:

> The Australia-China bilateral relationship is based on strong economic and trade complementarities, a comprehensive program of high-level visits and wide-ranging cooperation. In 2014, the Australian Prime Minister and Chinese President agreed to describe the relationship as a "comprehensive strategic partnership". (Australian Government Department of Foreign Affairs and Trade 2017)

In 2014, Australia initially declined to join China's Asian Infrastructure Investment Bank (AIIB) under pressure from the U.S. and Japan. However, when France, Germany, Italy and the United Kingdom joined in March 2015, Australia reversed course and became a member in June 2015. Australia contributed US$930 million.

On 20 December 2015, Australia and China signed a Free Trade Agreement (ChAFTA). This agreement provided three major benefits to

Australia: the removal of regulatory barriers on financial and legal services; fewer limits on cash transactions; and lower tariffs on agricultural goods. China gained greater access to Australia's markets for direct and indirect investments, a higher threshold for investment in Australian assets before triggering a government review, and greater use of the renminbi as a transaction currency of choice.

One year after ChAFTA came into force, over eighty-five per cent of Australian goods by value exported to China entered duty free or at preferential rates. Australian exports of wine, pharmaceuticals and skin-care products shot up dramatically. Bilateral two-way trade reached US$151 billion in 2015–2016 with Australia enjoying a surplus of US$51 billion. In 2016, Chinese investment in Australia reached US$11.49 billion the highest level since 2008, a peak year with record investment going to agriculture and infrastructure. Two-way trade in goods and services was valued at more than US$155 billion in 2016–2017 (Thayer 2018, 3).

Approximately thirty per cent of Australia's merchandise and sixteen per cent of services exports go to China. Merchandise exports are concentrated in a few key sectors. For example, iron ore comprises half of merchandise exports, with gold, coal and wool comprising fifteen per cent. China imports two-thirds of its iron ore of which Australia supplies sixty per cent (Thayer 2018, 3).

By 2019, ChAFTA will cover ninety-four per cent of Australian goods by value exported to China and rise to ninety-six per cent by 2029 when ChAFTA will be fully implemented. One major challenge for Australia is to get China to remove non-trade barriers over quarantine and safety standards.

PART 2: CHINA'S BRI: OPPORTUNITIES FOR COOPERATION

In September-October 2013, President Xi Jinping proposed the Silk Road Economic Belt while visiting Kazakhstan and the twenty-first-century Maritime Silk Road while visiting Indonesia (Thayer 2016, 3). In November 2013, the Chinese Communist Party (CCP) Central Committee approved these initiatives under the banner of One Belt, One Road (later referred to as the Belt and Road Initiative).

Australia did not feature on maps illustrating the One Belt, One Road issued at this time. This was puzzling because of the proximity of northern Australia to Indonesia and the significance to China of Australian exports of resources from Western Australia and Queensland. These factors were certainly known to Xi Jinping who, as Vice President, paid several visits to Australia.

The neglect of Australia was rectified in November 2014 when President Xi addressed the Australian Parliament. Xi stated:

> Oceania is a natural extension of the ancient maritime Silk Road, and China welcomes Australia's participation in the twenty-first century maritime Silk Road. Our two countries should enhance cooperation in humanitarian disaster relief, counter-terrorism and maritime safety to jointly meet various security challenges to our region. (Xi 2018)

Xi is reported to have suggested privately that Darwin might serve as a hub to service the Maritime Silk Road (Thayer 2018, 4).

In May 2015, the Treasurer, Joe Hockey, announced the Northern Australia Infrastructure Facility (NAIF) in his budget speech for 2015–2016 (Australian Government 2015). Hockey outlined funding for the NAIF in five areas: AUD$101.3 million over four years for cattle supply chains (roads); AUD$15.3 million for tropical health research into threats from exotic diseases; AUD$5 billion in concessional loans for private sector investment; AUD$3.7 million to draw up an Infrastructure projects pipeline priority list; and AUD$2.1 million to fund a taskforce into insurance premium reduction measures.

Later the Australian Government (Department of Industry, Innovation and Science, 2015) issued *Our North, Our Future White Paper on Developing Northern Australia Overview* that outlined funding of AUD$916.3 million over four years including AUD$600m on a roads programme. Hockey's initiative was enacted into legislation with the passage of the Northern Australia Infrastructure Facility Act on 3 May 2016 (Australian Government 2016a). This act established an independent board that established its headquarters in Cairns in July 2016. Infrastructure priorities included: airports, communications, energy, ports, rail and water.

NAIF is an initiative of the federal government. But many of the key project developments are the prerogatives of the Western Australia, Northern Territory and Queensland state governments. For example, in 2017 Queensland Deputy Premier and Minister for Trade and Investment, Jackie Trad visited China to explore investment opportunities arising from China's BRI and the Annastacia Palaszczuk's government's North Queensland development priorities.

In October 2015, the Northern Territory government made the decision to lease the Port of Darwin to the Chinese Landbridge Group for ninety-nine years, in part to position itself to secure a place on China's Maritime Silk Road trade route. That same month, China and Australia began discussions on aligning the BRI with the NAIF.

A year after the passage of the Northern Australia Infrastructure Facility Act, the initiative achieved scant progress due to lack of interest, complex investment barriers and the dearth of infrastructure projects that would generate ongoing financial returns. In fact, more money was spent on salaries for board members than on actual projects (Wen and Blanchard 2017). At the end of the 2017–2018 financial year, only AUD$800 million had been allocated despite a commitment to spend AUD$2 billion (Ludlow 2018).

In February 2016, China's Foreign Minister Wang Yi hosted Australia's Foreign Minister Julie Bishop at the third round of the China-Australia Foreign and Strategic Dialogue held in Beijing. At a joint press conference held after the dialogue, Minister Wang Yi announced that "the two sides have established a working group to pair up China's Belt and Road Initiative and the northern Australia initiative" (Australian Government 2016b).

In April 2016 Prime Minister Malcolm Turnbull, flew to Beijing to meet President Xi. Prior to their meeting, the Australia-China Senior Business Leaders' Forum, that included participants from Xi's Central Leading Group on Economics and Finance, endorsed linking the BRI with the NAIF and encouraged Chinese participation in major water conservation projects in northern Australia.

At the meeting between Xi and Turnbull the two leaders talked at cross-purposes. For the first time, President Xi included Australia within the single most important policy priority of his presidency, the BRI. Not only did Xi give his imprimatur to Chinese investment in northern Australia's infrastructure, but he also committed his prestige to aligning the BRI with Northern Territory development. Turnbull, however, failed to pick up on this and focused his comments on innovation, science and education.

Chinese media coverage highlighted Xi's call for the "alignment of China's Belt and Road initiative with Australia's northern development plan" and virtually passed over Turnbull's stress on innovation (Xinhua 2016). In hindsight, the Turnbull-Xi meeting may be viewed as both a major turning point and perhaps a missed opportunity of major consequence. If the BRI and the northern Australia infrastructure development were linked, this would likely spark greater interest from potential Chinese investors because it would improve the likelihood of receiving official funding.

Xi's Belt and Road Initiative also offered Australia much more, a major opportunity to cooperate with Beijing to assist with infrastructure development in China, Eurasia and the South Pacific. On 27 May 2016, the Australian government launched the Australia-China Belt & Road Initiative (ACBRI) to explore these opportunities. ACBRI came under the auspices of the Australia-China Council funded by the Department of Foreign Affairs and Trade. The former Minister for Trade, Andrew Robb, was appointed chairman.

At its launch ACBRI issued its inaugural report, *China's One Belt One Road*. ACBRI's remit was to promote infrastructure development, engagement with China, and public education on the BRI. For example, ACBRI assembled a Senior Executive Delegation to engage with Chinese counterparts on an annual basis. ACBRI also formulated a strategy to promote Australia's involvement with the BRI such as identifying Chinese priority projects and determining Australian capability.

In addition, ACBRI sought to build awareness through boardroom briefings held in Sydney, Melbourne, Canberra, Brisbane and Perth from May to August 2016. ACBRI negotiated a formal advisory role with the Victorian government. ACBRI led a cluster of agriculture-focused companies and a delegation of Australian banks and services companies to Beijing in September and October 2016, respectively, to explore BRI opportunities. It was also in October 2016 that Australia and China commenced discussions on a Memorandum of Understanding on the Belt and Road Initiative. Finally, Australia became an unofficial One Belt, One Road partner in 2016 with the launching of the public-private non-governmental organisation the Australia-China OBOR Initiative or ACOBORI (Australia-China One Belt One Road Initiative 2016).

In 2017, Australia and China exchanged several high-level visits. China once again sought Australia's involvement in the BRI and linkage with development in northern Australia. The Commonwealth government repeatedly sidestepped the issue. For example, in February 2017, Australia hosted the fourth round of the China-Australia Diplomatic and Strategic Dialogue in Canberra. At a joint press conference Foreign Minister Wang Yi stated, "We are willing to align the 'Belt and Road' initiative with the

'Northern Development' plan of Australia" (Ministry of Foreign Affairs of the People's Republic of China 2017).

Foreign Minister Julie Bishop responded by noting:

> We talked about the need for greater infrastructure, both regionally and in our respective countries—China's One Belt One Road initiative, Australia's Developing Northern Australia initiative—and *we commit to the principles of transparency, private sector engagement and ensuring that infrastructure investment leads to strong development outcomes.* (Australian Government Department of Foreign Affairs and Trade 2018, emphasis added)

In March 2017, on the eve of Premier Li Keqiang's official visit to Australia, China's Vice Minister Zheng Zeguang observed that there are "many opportunities and space for cooperation" (Dziedzic 2017) between China and Australia on the BRI and that Premier Li would raise this during his visit. Australia's trade Minister Steve Ciobo opined, "Obviously Australia has a high degree of expertise both in relation to execution but also financing of infrastructure. So there will be scope for Australian businesses in the future to be involved in belt-road initiative projects" (Dziedzic 2017). The media quoted an anonymous Australian official, "No formal memorandum on this issue will be signed during the visit" (Smyth 2017). Premier Li Keqiang visited Canberra from 24–28 March 2017 to attend the high-level dialogue under the Comprehensive Strategic Partnership. As foreshadowed, Australia once again declined to link the BRI with the NAIF.

On 14 May 2017, China hosted the BRI Forum in Beijing. Australia was represented by Trade Minister Steve Ciobo, Andrew Robb (former Minister for Trade and Investment), Kevin Rudd (former Prime Minister and Foreign Minister) and Daniel Andrews (Premier of Victoria). No Australian companies were invited. Australia supported the "Initiative on Promoting Unimpeded Trade Cooperation along the Belt and Road" statement issued at the end of the trade session despite European protests over lack of clauses on transparency and tendering standards.

Andrew Robb suggested that there were joint venture opportunities for Australian businesses to build hospitals, schools and aged care services along the BRI trade route while Trade Minister Ciobo clearly spelled out Australia's reservations about linking the BRI with northern Australia development. He noted that:

Australian participation is to put further meat on the bone for BRI. Given the strong relationship between Australia and China, it is important [that] Australia is there to learn more... [Australia has experience in] financing, designing and the construction of major infrastructure... There are complementarities between northern Australia and Belt and Road, but they are separate initiatives... We've seen much merit in the BRI Initiative. We see opportunities for collaboration. But we take decisions about initiatives in Australia on the basis of what's in Australia's national interest and I think we don't need to view everything through one lens. (Quoted in Needham 2017a)

Following the BRI Forum, China hosted the BRI Summit in Beijing, on 15 May 2018. This meeting was attended by twenty-nine heads of government and representatives from seventy other countries, the United Nations, World Bank and International Monetary Fund. Australia was not represented. At the summit, President Xi announced a further US $124 billion for BRI initiatives.

PART 3: AUSTRALIA'S DOMESTIC DEBATE OVER JOINING THE BRI

Generally, the debate over the BRI within Australia has seen the business community, especially those involved in trade with China, and state leaders in the Northern Territory and Victoria, argue that the Coalition Government should temper its critical comments about China and get on with the job of promoting trade.

The defence and security community, on the other hand, is very concerned about the threats to Australia's sovereignty by Chinese interference in Australia's internal affairs (Clark 2018). Peter Jennings and Malcolm Davis of the Defence Department-funded Australian Strategic Policy Institute are most vocal in this respect. They are countered by Bob Carr, former Minister for Foreign Affairs and now head of the Australia-China Relations Institute at the University of Technology, Sydney. But there are also dissenting voices amongst defence analysts. Hugh White and Paul Dibb, two former deputy secretaries in the Department of Defence, have squared off in a public debate about the pros and cons of economic engagement with China versus national security.

Those in favour of associating Australia with China's BRI advance the following seven points:

First, by signing up early Australia can help shape the BRI. This now appears a lost opportunity.

Second, by formally joining the BRI Australian businesses can attract Chinese partners in Australian-based projects particularly in northern Australia.

Third, Australian businesses can form joint partnerships with their Chinese counterparts to develop infrastructure such as roads, bridges, schools and hospitals in China and countries participating in the BRI.

Fourth, the BRI provides opportunities for Australian businesses to contribute their skills in service industries such as banking, finance, resources, tourism, education, healthcare, management of public-private partnerships, legal services, professional management and consulting on technical trade-related businesses, agriculture, engineering, and energy (de Jonge 2018).

Fifth, participation in the BRI will contribute to improved connectivity and market access across the BRI network as well as enhance policy coordination, financial integration, infrastructure connectivity, unimpeded trade and people-to-people networks.

Sixth, the development of regional infrastructure under the BRI umbrella will result in more demand for Australian iron ore and coal.

Seventh, by participating in the BRI Australia can boost its standing and influence in the region.

Those who oppose or have reservations about associating Australia with China's BRI make the following arguments:

First, the BRI is so unprecedented in scope that there is a real question about the feasibility of many projects as most target countries have a poor sovereign risk rating, thus creating major investment risks.

Second, the BRI will give preference to Chinese companies.

Third, there is a lack of Chinese reciprocity in investment access.

Fourth, the BRI lacks a reciprocal flow of two-way trade.

Fifth, the BRI will enhance China's strategic and economic domination over Eurasia and beyond. The BRI will weaken the Bretton Woods financial institutions; and the BRI will undermine the U.S. leadership role in the region by extending Chinese influence at expense of the U.S.

Sixth, foreign ownership of critical infrastructure (ports, power grids, roads etc.) is a potential threat to national security, and China will use joint BRI projects as economic leverage to influence Australia's decision-making.

Seventh, the BRI will have an adverse impact on human rights and the environment in host countries.

PART 4: GEO-STRATEGIC CHALLENGES TO COOPERATION

In the midst of a domestic debate in Australia over the merits of joining the BRI, a number of security and geo-strategic challenges arose that contributed to government criticism of China and this in turn led to a deterioration of bilateral relations. Part 4 focuses on three major geo-strategic challenges that arose during this period: Chinese ownership of critical infrastructure, Chinese interference in Australia's domestic affairs and strategic challenges to the rules-based international order.

The 2015 decision by the Northern Territory government to lease the Port of Darwin to China's Landbridge Group provoked protests to the Australian government by President Barack Obama and other U.S. officials because U.S. naval vessels regularly called in at these port facilities. It was later revealed that the Chinese lease was only reviewed at the lowest levels of the Department of Defence and focused mainly on operational aspects of the transaction rather than any larger strategic implications.

A public debate erupted in Australia about the security implications of a Chinese presence in such a sensitive area. It is commonly assumed in Australia that private and state-owned Chinese businesses are used by China's security apparatus for intelligence purposes.

Security concerns raised by the lease of the Port of Darwin immediately led to a review of foreign investment in critical infrastructure. The Foreign Investment Review Board (FIRB) directed that Australian states and territories must now receive Government approval before selling critical infrastructure to offshore buyers. David Irvine, the former head of Australian Security Intelligence Organisation (ASIO) and former Ambassador to China, was appointed to the FIRB to ensure that security implications were factored into foreign investment and ownership of critical infrastructure such as electric power grids and telecommunications. The Defence Department placed bans on the WeChat App and phones produced by Huawei (Grigg 2018).

The Australian Security Intelligence Organisation stated in its 2016–2017 annual report, "We identified foreign powers clandestinely seeking to shape the opinions of members of the Australian public, media organisations and government officials in order to advance their country's own political objectives. Ethnic and religious communities in Australia were also the subject of covert influence operations designed to diminish their criticism of foreign governments" (Australian Government 2017c). In addition, China's Ministry of State Security is alleged to have conducted covert operations in Australia against Chinese citizens without conducting liaison with the Australian Federal Police.

In May 2017, Dennis Richardson, a senior Australian Defence official and the Secretary of the Department of Defence, said on his retirement that China is conducting extensive espionage against Australia and exerting unreasonable influence over Chinese communities and media (Reuters 2017). In 2016, former Chinese diplomat Chen Yonglin, now resident in Australia, warned that the number of Chinese spies and agents working in Australia was growing.

Although China was not explicitly named by ASIO it is widely held that China, Russia and North Korea are the main but not only foreign powers interfering in Australia's internal affairs. In late January 2018, it was reported that ASIO listed China as an extreme threat on a secret country-by-country counter-intelligence index, the highest level. Chinese entities have been implicated in hacking defence contractors, defence industries and the Commonwealth Scientific Industrial Research Organisation or CSIRO (Grigg et al. 2018a, b).

ASIO's assessment was backed by widespread Australian media reports of Chinese influence operations in Australia primarily directed by the CCP's United Front Work Department (Murray 2017; Needham 2017b; Dotson 2018; Hamilton 2018, 29–34). Chinese businessmen were identified as agents of influence in activities designed to influence Australian politicians, the Chinese community including Chinese students studying in Australia and the Chinese-language media (Maley and Berkovic 2017; Australian Associated Press 2017; Garnaut 2018). In addition, there have been several cases where Chinese diplomats have instigated and/or supported Chinese students involved in the disruption of university lectures when they disagree with the lecturer's point of view on an issue related to China (Hamilton 2018, 219–220).

In 2017, in a high-profile case, a Labor Party frontbencher, Senator Sam Dastyari, resigned from Parliament after it was revealed he accepted cash donations from a Chinese businessman reportedly in return for supporting China's territorial claims in the South China Sea and that Dastyari warned a Chinese business associate that Australian security officials were tapping his phone (McKenzie et al. 2017, 2018; Riordan and Brown 2017).

In June 2018, the Australian Parliament enacted legislation requiring the registration of foreign political agents and imposing harsh penalties on foreign espionage and domestic interference, the Foreign Influence Transparency Scheme and National Security Legislation Amendment (Espionage and Foreign Interference), respectively.

In March 2017, Foreign Minister Julie Bishop stated in her Fullerton Lecture:

The importance of liberal values and institutions should not be underestimated or ignored.

While non-democracies such as China can thrive when participating in the present system, an essential pillar of our preferred order is democratic community.

Domestic democratic habits of negotiating and compromise are essential to powerful countries resolving their disagreements according to international law and rules.

History also shows democracy and democratic institutions are essential for nations if they are to reach their economic potential. (Australian Government 2017a)

In November 2017, the Australian government released its Foreign Policy White Paper. The overview of this document stated unequivocally "[t]oday China is challenging America's position". In Chap. 2, A Contested World, the White Paper asserted "[t]he United States remains the most powerful country but its long dominance of the international order is being challenged by other powers" that openly contest the principles and values on which international order is based (Australian Government 2017b).

Australia's 2017 Foreign Policy White Paper assessed that China's power and influence will grow to match "and in some cases exceed" that of the U. S. in the Indo-Pacific Region. Australia is particularly concerned that China, a signatory to the United Nations Convention on the Law of the Sea (UNCLOS), chose to adopt a policy of three no's—non-recognition, non-participation and non-compliance—towards the Arbitral Tribunal's Award (Jin 2016). UNCLOS is widely referred to by legal specialists as the Constitution of the World Oceans. China's militarisation of the South China Sea is viewed by the Australian government as an egregious violation of the international rules-based order (see below).

The 2017 White Paper depicted territorial disputes in the South China Sea as a "major fault line" in the region and noted that Australia was "particularly concerned by the unprecedented pace and scale of China's activities… (and) opposes the use of disputed features and artificial structures in the South China Sea for military purposes" (Australian Government 2017b). Various reports in 2018 indicate that Chinese installed anti-ship cruise missiles, and surface to air missiles have been widely viewed as a major provocation (Macias 2018; Baxendale and Callinan 2018).

The White Paper stressed the importance of U.S. leadership of and participation in a rules-based international order. At a time of growing strategic uncertainty by the Trump Administration, Australia has picked up the strategic slack and engaged more with like-minded democracies such as Japan (Murray and Grigg 2017; Coorey 2017b; Riordan 2017b, 2018a, b, d; Tillett 2018a, b; Stutchbury and Grigg 2018), India (Medcalf 2018; Sheridan 2018a), France (Packham 2018c; Tillett 2018d; Higgins 2018) and the United Kingdom (Packham 2018a; Tillett 2018c; Shanahan 2018a, b; Coorey 2018; Sheridan 2018b) to push back against Chinese political and military influence.

The Quadrilateral Security Dialogue (Australia, India, Japan and the U.S.) is considering a Japanese proposal to mobilise funds from the World Bank to provide alternate funding to China's BRI for infrastructure development (Riordan 2017a; Coorey 2017a; Medcalf 2017; Fontaine 2017; Callick 2017; Kehoe 2018a; Kehoe 2018b; Earl 2018; Thayer 2018; Murray 2018).

In 2018, Chinese investment and influence peddling in Papua New Guinea, the Solomon Islands and elsewhere in the South Pacific (Packham 2018b; Riordan and Callick 2018b) became a subject of contention between Australia and China when Australia's Minister for International Development Conceta Fierravanti-Wells accused China of lending funds to Pacific nations on unfavourable terms and constructing "useless buildings…and roads to nowhere" (Riordan 2018c; Riordan and Callick 2018a). Greater concern was aroused in Australia when the media published reports that China was seeking to establish a naval base in Vanuatu and Fiji and a multi-use port in Papua New Guinea (Maley and Riordan 2018, Riordan 2018e; Wroe 2018). This led Australia and France to confer on cooperation in the South Pacific to protect their national interests.

PART 5: CONCLUSION

On 7 August 2018, Prime Minister Turnbull gave a speech at the University of New South Wales in Sydney that was complimentary towards the Chinese student community in Australia and upbeat in its tone on future relations. Turnbull stated,

> We're committed to working with China's leaders to advance our Comprehensive Strategic Partnership, a great framework within which to advance our mutual and complementary interests. And along with ChAFTA, the China-Australia Free Trade Agreement, another legacy of President Xi's historic 2014 visit to Australia. (Australian Embassy, Chian 2018)

China's positive media reaction was taken as a sign that relations with China were on the mend. Yet, later that month, in a development that provoked a strong reaction from China, the Australian Cabinet announced that it was banning Chinese companies from Australia's 5G Network (Grigg and Murray 2018; Riordan and Korporall 2018). On 24 August, in an internal Liberal Party leadership contest, Scott Morrison replaced Turnbull as Prime Minister. Julie Bishop, Deputy Prime Minister and Minister for Foreign Affairs declined to stay on as minister. Steve Ciobo lost his portfolio as Minister for Trade in the new Cabinet.

In May 2019, Morrison's coalition government won a landslide victory in federal elections. Not only has the Morrison government continued to keep China's BRI at arm's length, but also Australia has joined Japan and the United States in a Trilateral Infrastructure Partnership to provide alternate funding for infrastructure investment needs in the Indo-Pacific. In July 2019, the newly rebranded Export Finance Australia set up the Australian Infrastructure Financing Facility for the Pacific under an expanded mandate and financing capacity.

As of this writing, there have been no meetings between government leaders in Australia and China for three years. Australia continues to be embroiled in a domestic debate about the merits of pursuing economic opportunities with China under the umbrella of the BRI against the costs to Australia's national interests arising from security and strategic challenges posed by China's rise. One of the most cogent analyses of the state of play on Australia's participation in the BRI, written three years ago by veteran political commentator Paul Kelly, remains valid today:

> It is absurd to say Australia cannot be involved [in the BRI] for strategic reasons and equally absurd to say we should blindly sign any memorandum China wants, regardless of its abuse of economic principles. Both the anti-

China nay-sayers and pro-China glad-handers are wrong. Australia is biding its time on Belt and Road, and that is sensible... it is far better that China's investment proposals for Australia be assessed on merit alone, and not be branded as part of a grand scheme to enhance China's regional interests. Such branding would only be counter-productive. (Kelly 2017b)

REFERENCES

Australia-China One Belt One Road Initiative. 2016. *China's One Belt One Road: Opportunities for Australian Industries.* http://www.acbri.org.au/report/ACBRI_Report-Final1-1054-56.pdf. Accessed 2 Aug 2018.

Australian Associated Press. 2017. ASIO Alert to Foreign Heat on Campuses. *The Australian*, October 25.

Australian Embassy China. 2018. Prime Minister of Australia The Hon Malcolm Turnbull MP, Speech at the University of New South Wales, August 7. https://china.embassy.gov.au/bjng/180807pmspeech.html. Accessed 10 Sept 2018.

Australian Government. 2015. The Honourable J. B. Hockey MP, Treasurer of the Commonwealth of Australia, Budget Speech 2015, delivered on 12 May 2015. http://www.budget.gov.au/2015-16/content/speech/html/speech.htm. Accessed 2 Aug 2018.

———. 2016a. Federal Register of Legislation 2016. Northern Australia Infrastructure Facility Act 2016, No. 41. https://www.legislation.gov.au/Details/C2016A00041. Accessed 2 Aug 2018.

———. 2016b. Joint Media Conference with Foreign Minister Wang Yi – Beijing, China. Minister of Foreign Affairs, The Hon Julie Bishop MP, 2016. February 17. https://foreignminister.gov.au/transcripts/Pages/2016/jb_tr_160217a.aspx. Accessed 2 Aug 2018.

———. 2017a. Change and Uncertainty in the Indo-Pacific: Strategic Challenges and Opportunities. Minister of Foreign Affairs The Hon Julie Bishop MP, 28th IISS Fullerton Lecture, Singapore, March 13, 2017, https://foreignminister.gov.au/speeches/Pages/2017/jb_sp_170313a.aspx. Accessed 2 Aug 2018.

———. 2017b. *2017 Foreign Policy White Paper.* https://www.fpwhitepaper.gov.au/foreign-policy-white-paper. Accessed 2 Aug 2018.

———. 2017c. Australian Security Intelligence Organisation. *ASIO Annual Report 2016–2017.* https://www.asio.gov.au/sites/default/files/Annual%20Report%202016-17.pdf. Accessed 2 Aug 2018.

Australian Government, Department of Foreign Affairs and Trade. 2017. *China Country Brief*, July 10. http://dfat.gov.au/geo/china/pages/china-country-brief.aspx. Accessed 2 Aug 2018.

———. 2018. Australia-China Foreign and Strategic Dialogue – Joint Press Conference with Chinese Foreign Minister Wang Yi. Minister of Foreign Affairs The Hon Julie Bishop MP, Parliament House, Canberra, 7 February 2017. https://foreignminister.gov.au/transcripts/Pages/2017/jb_tr_170207.aspx. Accessed 2 Aug 2018.

Australian Government Department of Industry, Innovation and Science. 2015. *Our North, Our Future White Paper on Developing Northern Australia Overview*, June 2015. https://www.industry.gov.au/data-and-publications/our-north-our-future-white-paper-on-developing-northern-australia. Accessed 7 Sept 2018.

Baxendale, Rachel, and Rory Callinan. 2018. Warning for China on Missiles. *The Weekend Australian*, May 5–6.

Callick, Rowan. 2017. Renewed Talks Rock Beijing's Boat. *The Australian*, November 15.

Clark, Andrew. 2018. China Doves and Hawks Go to War. *The Australian Financial Review*, May 5–6.

Coorey, Phillip. 2017a. Australia Backs Revival of 'Anti-China' Security Group. *The Australian Financial Review*, November 8.

———. 2017b. Australia, Allies Face Up to China, N Korea. *The Australian Financial Review*, November 14.

———. 2018. UK Bid to Join TPP May Help Counter China. *The Australian Financial Review*, April 21–22.

Dodd, Tim. 2018a. Top Brass on a Mission to Ease China Tensions. *The Australian*, April 11.

———. 2018b. Chinese Defy Warnings and Flock to Aussie Unis. *The Australian*, April 18.

Dotson, John. 2018. The United Front Work Department in Action Abroad: A Profile of the Council for the Promotion of Peaceful Reunification of China. *China Brief* 18 (2).

Dziedzic, Stephen. 2017. Li Keqiang Visit: Chinese Premier Arrives in Australia for Five-Day Tour. *ABC News*, March 23. http://www.abc.net.au/news/2017-03-23/chinese-premier-li-keqiang-in-canberra-for-five-day-visit/8378146. Accessed 2 Aug 2018.

Earl, Greg. 2018. Abe's Misfiring Quad Finally Discovers a Strong Base. *The Australian Financial Review,* January 22.

Fontaine, Richard. 2017. Why Washington and Australia Urgently Need the Quad. *The Australian Financial Review*, November 11–12.

Garnaut, John. 2018. How China Interferes in Australia. *Foreign Affairs*, March 9. https://www.foreignaffairs.com/articles/china/2018-03-09/how-china-interferes-australia.

Grigg, Angus. 2017. Angry China Blasts Australian Media. *The Australian Financial Review*, December 12.

———. 2018. Defence Bans WeChat App. *The Australian Financial Review,* March 12.

Grigg, Angus, and Lisa Murray. 2018. Huawei, ZTE Barred. *The Australian Financial Review*, August 24.

Grigg, Angus, Ben Potter, and Nick McKenzie. 2018a. Chinese Data Breach Riled CSIRO. *The Australian Financial Review*, April 4.

———. 2018b. It Was a 'Wake-Up Call': CSIRO Spent Millions After Chinese Data Breach. *The Australian Financial Review*, April 4.

Hamilton, Clive. 2018. *Silent Invasion: China's Influence in Australia*. Richmond: Hardie Grant Books.

Hewett, Jennifer, Michael Smith, and Phillip Coorey, 2018. China's Big Snub to Australia. *The Australian Financial Review*, April 12.

Higgins, Ean. 2018. Macron Tackles Flashpoints as Paris Burns. *The Australian*, May 3.

Jin, Yongming. 2016. Ruling Won't Calm Disputes in South China Sea. *China Daily*, June 7. http://europe.chinadaily.com.cn/opinion/2016-06/07/content_25632134.htm. Accessed 2 Aug 2018.

de Jonge, Alice. 2018. Australia Risks Missing Out on China's One Belt One Road. *The Conversation*, May 16, 2016. http://theconversation.com/australia-risks-missing-out-on-chinas-one-belt-one-road-77704. Accessed 2 Aug 2018.

Kehoe, John 2018a. Navy 'Quad' Chiefs Slam Disruptive China. *The Australian Financial Review*, January 22.

———. 2018b. 'Quad' Naval Chiefs Take Aim at China. *The Australian Financial Review*, January 22.

———. 2018c. China Relationship on a 'Knife Edge'. *The Australian Financial Review*, March 6.

Kelly, Joe. 2017a. China Ties at 'Tipping Point'. *The Australian*, December 11.

Kelly, Paul. 2017b. One Belt, One Road: Australia Needs to Bide Its Time. *The Australian*, May 24.

Korporaal, Glenda. 2018. China Delivers Trade Warning Amid Strain on Ties. *The Australian*, April 19.

Ludlow, Mark. 2018. Pressure on NAIF to Splurge Before Election. *The Australian Financial Review*, September 10.

Macias, Amanda. 2018. China Quietly Installed Defensive Missile Systems on Strategic Spratly Islands in Hotly Contested South China Sea. *CNBC*, May 2. https://www.cnbc.com/2018/05/02/china-added-missile-systems-on-spratly-islands-in-south-china-sea.html. Accessed 2 Aug 2018.

Maley, Paul, and Nicola Berkovic. 2017. ASIO Flags Manchurian Candidates. *The Weekend Australian*, December 9–10.

Maley, Paul, and Primrose Riordan. 2018. PNGH Port Plan Stokes China Fears. *The Australian*, August 28.

McKenzie, Nick, James Massola, and Richard Baker. 2017. Dastyari's Failure to Explain. *The Australian Financial Review*, November 30.

McKenzie, Nick, Richard Baker, and Phillip Coorey. 2018. Explosive Tape Damns Dastyari. *The Australian Financial Review*, November 30.

Medcalf, Rory. 2017. An Indo-Pacific Quad Is the Right Response to Beijing. *The Australian Financial Review*, November 9.

———. 2018. India Moves to Lock in the Quad. *The Australian Financial Review*, January 25–28.

Ministry of Foreign Affairs of the People's Republic of China. 2017. Wang Yi and Foreign Minister Julie Bishop of Australia Jointly Meet the Press, February 9. http://www.fmprc.gov.cn/mfa_eng/zxxx_662805/t1437164.shtml. Accessed 2 Aug 2018.

Murray, Lisa. 2017. China Calls on 'Friends' Over Territory Issue. *The Australian Financial Review*, October 23.

———. 2018. Labor Backs the Quad in Indo-Pacific. *The Australian Financial Review*, March 16.

Murray, Lisa, and Angus Grigg. 2017. Japan Taps Australia for China Bulwark. *The Australian Financial Review*, October 27.

Needham, Kirsty. 2017a. New Silk Road: China Invites World Leaders to Hook Up to 'One Belt One Road'. *The Sydney Morning Herald*, May 12. https://www.smh.com.au/world/new-silk-road-china-invites-world-leaders-to-decipher-one-belt-one-road-20170512-gw3ge0.html. Accessed 2 Aug 2018.

———, 2017b. United Front, China's Important 'Magic Weapon'. *The Sydney Morning Herald*, November 29. https://www.smh.com.au/world/united-front-chinas-important-magic-weapon-20171129-gzv562.html. Accessed 2 Aug 2018.

Packham, Ben. 2018a. Bishop Urges UK to Up Its Role in Indo-Pacific. *The Australian*, February 20.

———. 2018b. China Gift Triggers More Aid for PNG. *The Australian*, March 8.

———. 2018c. China High on Macron Agenda. *The Australian*, April 30.

Reuters. 2017. China Conducting Extensive Espionage Against Australia: Defense Official, May 12. https://www.reuters.com/article/us-australia-china-idUSKBN1880ZB. Accessed 2 Aug 2018.

Riordan, Primrose. 2017a. Turnbull Look to Strengthen Security Ties with Asia. *The Australian*, November 7.

———. 2017b. Japan, Australia Mull Agreement on Closer Military Ties. *The Australian*, December 27.

———. 2018a. Japan Deal to Counter China Rise. *The Weekend Australian*, January 13–14.

———. 2018b. PM Deepens Japan Defence Ties. *The Australian*, January 19.

———. 2018c. Attack on China Over Pacific Aid. *The Australian*, January 10.

———. 2018d. Tokyo Eyes Our Help to Defy China. *The Australian*, January 25.

———. 2018e. Australia Beats China to Fiji Base. *The Australian*, September 7.

Riordan, Primrose, and Rachel Baxendale. 2018. DFAT Boss's China Trips Deferred. *The Australian*, March 2.

Riordan, Primrose, and Greg Brown 2017. Dastyari Under Pressure to Quit. *The Australian*, November 30.

Riordan, Primrose, and Rowan Callick. 2018a. Bishops Raps Minister for China Spray. *The Australian*, January 12.

———. 2018b. China's Push in Solomon Islands. *The Australian*, May 1.

Riordan, Primrose, and Glenda Korporall. 2018. Beijing Hits Out at 5G Ban on Huawei, *The Australian*, August 4.

Riordan, Primrose, Simon Benson, and Rowan Callick. 2017. China Fires Up Diplomatic Row. *The Australian*, December 7.

Saunokonoko, Mark, 2018. 'Bigoted' Australia Faces Trade War Over South China Sea, Paper Warns. *9News*, January 2.

Shanahan, Dennis. 2018a. Turnbull Welcomes Britain's Pacific Push. *The Australian*, April 21–22.

———, 2018b. Turnbull Trade Pitch to Counter Rise of China. *The Australian*, April 23.

Shanahan, Dennis, and Primrose Riordan. 2018. Cold War: China's Freeze on Ties. *The Australian*, March 1.

Sheridan, Greg. 2018a. Quad Dialogue Is Our Passage to India. *The Australian*, January 25.

———. 2018b. UK 'Will Draw Closer in Defence'. *The Australian*, May 7.

Smyth, Jamie. 2017. Australia Rejects China Push on Silk Road Strategy. *The Financial Times*, March 22. https://www.ft.com/content/e30f3122-0eae-11e7-b030-768954394623. Accessed 2 Aug 2018.

Stewart, Cameron. 2018. 'Beholden Unis Fear Offending Chinese'. *The Australian Financial Review*, April 27.

Stutchbury, Michael, and Angus Grigg. 2018. All the Way With Abe. *The Australian Financial Review*, January 20–21.

Thayer, Carlyle A. 2016. *Geopolitics and Maritime Security in the Straits of Malacca: Implications of China's Maritime Silk Road and Indonesia's Global Maritime Fulcrum*. Presentation to the 8th MIMA International Conference on the Straits of Malacca Resolving Regional Issues and Their Impact on the Straits of Malacca, Session 1, Paper 1, Malaysian Institute for Maritime Affairs, Istana Hotel, Kuala Lumpur, April 25. https://www.scribd.com/document/367339909/Thayer-Geopolitics-and-Maritime-Security-in-the-Straits-of-Malacca-Implications-of-China-s-Maritime-Silk-Road-and-Indonesia-s-Global-Maritime-Fulcr. Accessed 10 Sept 2018.

———. 2018. *Australia and China: Challenges Mitigate Opportunities for Cooperation*. Paper to China-Australia Cooperation Forum: Promoting Cooperation in the Asia Pacific Region, co-sponsored by the National Institute for Global Strategy, Chinese Academy of Social Sciences and Griffith Asia Institute, Griffith University, Fuzhou University, Fuzhou, People's Republic of China, May 11–12. https://www.scribd.com/document/379361115/Thayer-Australia-and-China-Challenges-Mitigate-Opportunities-for-Cooperation. Accessed 10 Sept 2018.

Tillett, Andrew. 2017. China Lashes Out at Foreign Crackdown. *The Australian Financial Review*, December 7.

———. 2018a. Turnbull's Japan Visit to Focus on Defence Deal. *The Australian Financial Review*, January 13–14.

———, 2018b. Aust-Japan Deal on Defence Likely to Anger China. *The Australian Financial Review*, January 15.

———. 2018c. Bishop Taps UK for Indo-Pacific Rules Oversight, *The Australian Financial Review*, February 20.

———, 2018d. Macron Vows 'Indo-Pacific Axis' with Australia. *The Australian Financial Review*, May 3.

Wen, Philip, and Ben Blanchard. 2017. China to Talk New Silk Road in Australia, No deal Expected Yet. *Reuters,* March 20. https://www.reuters.com/article/us-china-australia-idUSKBN16S0DX?il=0. Accessed 2 Aug 2018.

Wood, Richard. 2018. Turnbull Branded 'Anti-China Pioneer' by State Media. *9News*, February 27.

Wroe, David, 2018. China Eyes Vanuatu Military Base in Plan with Global Ramifications. *The Sydney Morning Herald*, April 9.

Xi, Jinping, 2018. Full Text of Chinese President Xi Jinping's Address to Australia's Parliament. *The Straits Times*, November 19. https://www.straitstimes.com/asia/australianz/full-text-of-chinese-president-xi-jinpings-address-to-australias-parliament. Accessed 2 Aug 2018.

Xinhua. 2016. China, Australia Seek to Make Bigger 'Cake' of Shared Interest, April 15. http://www.xinhuanet.com/english/2016-04/15/c_135283169.htm. Accessed 2 Aug 2018.

CHAPTER 9

Legal Challenges to the Belt and Road Initiative

Nguyen Thi Lan Anh and Mai Ngan Ha

INTRODUCTION

The Belt and Road Initiative (BRI, previously One Belt One Road) was first unveiled to the world during the speech of Chinese President Xi Jinping at the Nazarbayev University in Kazakhstan in 2013. The BRI is a multinational project designed to promote common development and prosperity all around the world. The focus of the Initiative is to promote the orderly and free flow of economics, which is realized by enhancement of connectivity between Asia, Europe, and Africa, and their adjacent seas via infrastructure development.

The views presented in this chapter belong to the authors only and do not reflect the views of the Diplomatic Academy of Vietnam.

N. T. L. Anh (✉)
Diplomatic Academy of Vietnam, Hanoi, Vietnam

M. N. Ha
Department of International Organizations, Ministry of Foreign Affairs, Hanoi, Vietnam

© The Author(s) 2020   159
A. Chong, Q. M. Pham (eds.), *Critical Reflections on China's Belt & Road Initiative*, https://doi.org/10.1007/978-981-13-2098-9_9

The BRI consists of the Silk Road Economic Belt and the twenty-first-Century Maritime Silk Road connecting China with nearly all parts of the globe via three landed and two maritime routes and will involve more than 60 countries in all continents. At the moment, about 1700 BRI-related projects are underway all around the world, funded by Chinese state-owned enterprises (SOEs), Chinese banks, and China-led financial institutions. Additionally, an announcement of nearly US$500 billion worth of projects was made at the beginning of 2016.

As lucrative as the Initiative may seem, there are prevalent issues that may affect the feasibility and success of BRI projects. In terms of legal problems alone, many aspects of the BRI are showing signs of inconsistency with the current international framework. Therefore, this chapter will discuss the legal challenges to the Initiative in relation to four branches of international law, namely (1) the current international legal framework on human rights in comparison with China's BRI practices, (2) the development of international environmental law and how China may be falling short of their obligations thereof, (3) China's perspective on the applicability of current dispute settlement mechanisms for BRI projects and China's proposal for a new means of dispute resolution hand-crafted for the Initiative, and (4) the issue of transparency of the BRI.

The Belt and Road Initiative (BRI) and International Human Rights Law

Labour has been one of the major concerns regarding the BRI since labour-related problems prevail in both field practice and financial institutions established under the Initiative. Chinese firms along the BRI have been facing growing claims arising from questionable labour practices. Studies on Chinese firms in Africa show problems concerning low wages, poor job security, and lack of work, health, and safety protections in manufacturing, construction, and mining sectors (Zou 2016). The trends of tense labour relations, hostile attitudes of Chinese managers towards trade unions, and lack of collective bargaining are more prevalent at Chinese firms than at other foreign multinational enterprises (Zou 2016). In terms of financial institutions, a Harvard study also found that the Asian Infrastructure Investment Bank (AIIB) Environmental and Social Framework (AIIB

Framework) does not incorporate many important labour standards established under the International Labour Organization (ILO) (Kim 2016). In particular, under the AIIB Framework, rights relating to freedom of association and collective bargaining are only protected to the extent of national law, without further consideration of the context where national law substantially restricts unions; provision against discrimination is only rendered consistent with relevant national law without any further explanation.

Under international human rights law, states have the obligations to respect, protect, and fulfil human rights. While states do not interfere with the enjoyment of human rights, states also have to be proactive to guarantee and facilitate effective enjoyment of such rights within their jurisdictions. Therefore, it would be useful to examine the duties of governments along the BRI under international human rights law to remedy this situation.

General discussions on states' obligations to human rights in the context of business activities within their territories have been abundant. The Guiding Principles on Business and Human Rights of the United Nations (i.e. UN Guiding Principles) provide that states have the duty to "protect against human rights abuse within their territory and/or jurisdiction by third parties, including business enterprises" (OCHR 2011). This duty was reiterated in the 2017 draft of the "General Comment on State Obligations under the International Covenant on Economic, Social, and Cultural Rights in the Context of Business Activities" that was later adopted in the 61st session of the Committee on Economic, Social and Cultural Rights (UN CESCR 2017). To be more specific, the draft lists certain acts of states that would constitute violations of the obligation to protect and fulfil human rights in relations to business activities, including, but not exhaustively, the failure to adopt and enforce legislation requiring business entities to exercise "human rights due diligence," the failure to take actions to intervene or provide victims of human rights abuses with access to effective remedies, and the failure to monitor the activities of business entities and their impacts on the enjoyment of economic, social, and cultural rights.

These developments in international human rights law may pose some challenges for the governments along the BRI. Some governments in Central Asia are already lagging in their obligations concerning human rights in relation to mega-infrastructure projects (Richardson and Williamson 2017). Most notably, nearly one-third of the BRI countries have not ratified the core ILO convention on freedom of association and the rights to collective bargaining (Zou 2016). This situation may be exacerbated by the economic dependence of these countries upon China's investments and grants, as the Chinese influence may undermine efforts to improve labour standards in host countries, therefore making host country governments hesitant in supporting trade union movements and collective bargaining against Chinese-invested firms (Zou 2016).

It is also worth noting that the obligations to protect and fulfil not only bind states within their own territory but also within their jurisdiction. The draft General Comment observes that while states are not directly responsible for violations of human rights caused by a private entity's conduct, they may be in breach of their duties for their failure to take reasonable measures to prevent such occurrences. Therefore, the draft suggests that states should pay heed to "any business entities over which [states] may exercise influence by regulatory means or by the use of incentives, including economic incentives, in accordance with [the UN Charter] and applicable international law"; such entities may include those being incorporated, having the seat of business or generating substantial revenues in a territory of states.

The extraterritoriality of human rights obligations of states implies that even the Chinese government may, to a certain extent, be held responsible for acts committed by its domiciliary companies, especially its SOEs, which may amount to abuses of human rights. As a matter of principle, acts of corporate entities are generally separated from the states, unless in special circumstances where the existence or operation of such entities is merely a vehicle for fraud (Barcelona Traction, Light and Power Company, Limited (Belgium v. Spain). 1970). Thus, it might be erroneous to say any violation of a Chinese-owned company amounts to a violation by China itself. However, traditionally, the Chinese government exercises substantial influence on the operations of Chinese firms abroad, especially in the energy and construction sectors (Zou 2016). In the narrative regarding geopolitical implications of the BRI, it is only logical to conclude that the companies under the BRI are subject to equal, if not, significantly stronger state influences in terms of organizing state capital and labour flow to host countries. Therefore, the proactive obligation of China to ensure observances of human rights of companies under their jurisdiction is ever more substantial, especially when labour practices in China have produced an observable effect in labour relations in Chinese firms abroad (Zou 2016).

A good example would be the case of labour disputes in a Chinese-owned coal mine company in Zambia, which involved "military style" labour discipline, incidents of deaths, and injuries of workers on strike. Shortly thereafter, this resulted in the revocation of the mine's licence by the Zambian government (Zou 2016).

In the light of this and similar other circumstances, China did attempt to curb Chinese companies' foreign activities in line with global labour practices. At the moment, the majority of China's attempts to deal with this issue are "soft law" instruments that are not legally binding—notably the 2008 Guidelines on the Implementation of Corporate Social Responsibility (CSR) for Central SOEs issued by the State-owned Assets Supervision and Administration Commission of the State Council to oblige Chinese SOEs to establish necessary CSR mechanisms (Zou 2016). However, given the evolution of international human rights laws, and the influence that the Chinese government exerts on its SOEs, China may need to be more proactive in regulating their businesses' conduct overseas to avoid labour challenges threatening the stability and legitimacy of its investments.

BRI and International Environmental Law

The environmental aspect of investment projects, especially major infrastructure projects, along the BRI should be taken into consideration. The fear that the BRI will allow Chinese firms, notorious for their environmental records, to take charge of construction and operations of infrastructure in ecologically fragile and sensitive areas is starting to become a reality. For example, in Laos the construction of hydropower plants on the Mekong River has led to the destruction of natural fora and the rise of temperature in the area (Zhang, et al. 2016). Another instance is the suspension of a dam and a copper mine in Myanmar, and a port in Sri Lanka due to environmental concerns (Gan and Mao 2016). Therefore, it is important to place the BRI within the framework of international environmental law in order to identify the problems with the current BRI mechanisms.

As a recently consolidated branch of international law, the current international environmental law is constantly evolving from the basic framework of the 1972 Stockholm Declaration of the UN Conference on the Human Environment and the 1992 Rio Declaration on Environment and Development. Two major legal principles concerning protection and preservation of the environment have emerged throughout this evolution—

the preventive principle and the precautionary principle (Crawford 2012, 356–360). The first principle requires states to take "all appropriate measures to prevent significant transboundary harm or at any event to minimize the risk thereof" (International Law Commission 2001), which arises due to the irreversible nature of environmental damage and the limitation of subsequent reparations (Crawford 2012. 356). Under the preventive principle, there exists an obligation of states to conduct environmental impact assessment for all planned activities likely to have an impact on the environment (Dupuy and Viñuales 2015). The customary ground of this obligation has been recorded by the International Court of Justice (ICJ) in the *Pulp Mills* case as follows:

> [the obligation to conduct an EIA] in recent years has gained so much acceptance among States that it may now be considered a requirement under general international law to undertake an environmental impact assessment where there is a risk that the proposed industrial activity may have a significant adverse impact in a transboundary context, in particular, on a shared resource. (Pulp Mills on the River Uruguay (Argentina v. Uruguay) 2010)

The second is the precautionary principle which says that measures to protect the environment shall be carried out even when there is a lack of evidence about a particular risk or when such risk is uncertain (Crawford 2012). Finally, as affirmed by the court in *Legality of the Threat or Use of Nuclear Weapons*, states must ensure that activity within their jurisdiction or control respects the environment of other states and of areas beyond national control (Crawford 2012). Therefore, states may be liable for damages to the environment caused by acts of non-state entities by virtue of due diligence obligations, or if they exercise jurisdiction and effective control over transnational corporations and benefit from such corporations' activity (Puvimanasinghe 2007).

It will be increasingly problematic for China to keep up with the prevention and precautionary principles because, at the moment, there is a clear lack of strong policies and regulations to deal with environmental issues. First, there has traditionally been an absence of environmental impact assessments in Chinese overseas investment projects (Tracy, et al. 2017). At the moment, there are rare, if any, occasions that this obligation is mentioned in the policy documents of the Chinese Government concerning the BRI. For instance, in 2015 the Chinese Government released the "Visions and Actions on Jointly Building the Silk Road Economic Belt and twenty-first Century Maritime Silk Road" document (Tracy et al. 2017). In discussions on the connection between the Silk Road Economic Belt and Russia's Eurasian Economic Union, China also adopted a "Roadmap on the Development of Cooperation between Russian Federation, the People's Republic of China and Mongolia for the Medium Term" (Tracy et al. 2017). Both documents spoke expansively and with details about the geographical scope and the scope of works for BRI's economic corridors, yet both were nearly silent about the impact of massive infrastructure projects on the environment and the ways to mitigate such impacts.

Second, there is also a lack of transparency in the planning of infrastructure projects along the BRI, which may make it difficult to avoid impacts on fragile ecologies (Tracy et al. 2017). Examples can be found in proposals for new transportation corridors, namely the two Primorsky corridors and the Louguhe—Pokrovka corridor, which will run through highly sensitive ecologies and critical habitats of many endangered species (Tracy et al. 2017).

Third, even financiers connected to the BRI such as the AIIB do not have strict environmental standards when compared to other similar institutions. While the AIIB will be an important source of finance for the BRI projects and can play an important part in pushing for effective standards amongst parties applying for these funds (Tracy et al. 2017), a study has found that the AIIB Framework is still lacking in details and may lead to arbitrary results (Kim 2016). For instance, the AIIB's evaluation of measures to mitigate adverse effects on the environment merely requires "measures acceptable to the Bank" (AIIB 2016), or its requirement for a cost benefit analysis for projects in natural habitats may be unclear in terms of methods. This may lead to the acceptance of projects that significantly destroy natural habitats with only slightly higher overall benefits (Kim 2016).

Nonetheless, China has begun to adopt environmental policies for its overseas investment activities. Most notably in 2013, the Chinese Ministry of Commerce and Ministry of Environment published the "Guidelines for Environmental Protection in Foreign Investment and Cooperation" in order to "direct enterprises in China to further regularize their environmental protection behaviours in foreign investment and cooperation" (PRC Ministry of Commerce 2013). The Guidelines provide some framework for the activities of Chinese firms prior to and during construction, as well as procedures for complaints should the local population desire to lodge. However, the Guidelines are only a suggestion and there will be no legal consequences for non-compliance. Moreover, it does not point out any specific authority to receive local complaints.

BRI AND THE PROSPECTS OF DISPUTE SETTLEMENT

Given its prioritization of the PPP model (i.e. public–private partnership cooperation), the BRI creates transactions in trade, services, and investment between the state of China, or Chinese SOEs, with enterprises of other countries. In cases of disputes, existing dispute settlement mechanisms like international commercial arbitration, investment arbitration under the International Centre for Settlement of Investment Disputes (ICSID), or the Dispute Settlement Understanding of the World Trade Organization (WTO) may be utilized. China has, however, argued that these dispute settlement mechanisms are improper for the BRI.

Firstly, China claims that the existing mechanisms contain significant flaws. The WTO dispute settlement mechanism is time-consuming and has low efficiency in terms of enforcement. Even when WTO member states obtain favourable reports from the panels and appellate bodies, they may still find it difficult to apply retaliatory measures. Lack of enforcement is also a problem for the ICSID. In addition, the relatively isolated operations of ICSID arbitrations may also create inconsistencies in treaty interpretation, which may affect the interests of both home and host states (Wang 2017).

Secondly, the BRI is a special grant project involving more than 60 countries, but with a single source of investment from China. Therefore, any dispute settlement mechanism that emerges from the BRI would take into account the interests of China. This is particularly important in the context that China has interests in interpreting certain concepts and provisions differently from other countries. For instance, contractual disputes between parties from China and the European Union (EU) may raise a number of legal issues. Under EU law, jurisdiction in civil and commercial matters and enforcement of the decisions of courts and arbitration of EU member states are regulated by the Brussels I Convention and the Lugano Convention. However, once non-member states are involved, these issues will be governed by national law. Chinese laws on these issues have a similar approach under Article 265 of the Civil Procedure Law in providing that:

the contract was executed or performed within the territory of the People's Republic of China, or the subject matter of the action is located within the territory of the People's Republic of China, or the defendant has distrainable property within the territory of the People's Republic of China, or the defendant maintains a representative office within the territory of the People's Republic of China, the action may come under the jurisdiction of the people's court of the place where the contract was executed, the place where the contract was performed, the place where the object of action is located, the place where the distrainable property is located, the place where the tort was committed or the place where the representative office is domiciled. (China International Commercial Court 2017)

Nevertheless, the EU and China's perceptions on the very notion of contract can be incompatible. Under EU perception, a contract is a formal document which has a binding force upon parties. Meanwhile, Chinese enterprises consider a contract only as the starting point in the transaction process that can be added alongside the implementation process. For them, negotiation instead of litigation should be used if disputes occur (Andersen 2016). The recognition of foreign arbitration awards under the New York Convention is another example. Under the New York Convention, member states shall give effect and recognize arbitration awards from other member states. Albeit being a member state, Chinese courts usually reject foreign arbitration awards if the disputing companies, although owned by foreigners, are registered in China (Zhou 2006).

Third, a number of bilateral treaties between China and other countries have already taken into account the specific approach of China on dispute settlement. For example, the model investment agreement on the draft of the Transatlantic Trade and Investment Partnership (TTIP) and the China-Australia Free Trade Agreement established an appeal system to meet the requirement of China (Wang 2017).

Given the expectation to establish a special dispute settlement mechanism for the BRI, in July 2015 the Chinese Supreme People's Court promulgated Opinion 7 providing guidance for dispute resolution for the Initiative. In Opinion 7, the court expressed its strong support for the use of international commercial and maritime arbitration for settling international disputes occurring in the process of BRI implementation. The Supreme Court also confirmed that Chinese courts should recognize and enforce arbitration awards from other states in accordance with Chinese law, international treaties, and practices. They further advocated for the conclusion of bilateral and multilateral legal assistance, particularly between countries participating in the BRI, in order to facilitate dispute settlement (Yuen 2016).

In addition to the general recognition of the role of arbitrations, the Chinese Supreme Court also published detailed guidance to lower courts for eight cases related to the BRI in 2015 and ten cases in 2017. These 18 cases covered a wide range of areas in international civil and commercial disputes and are related to company law, international contract law, maritime law, international air law, international trade and financial law, as well as recognition of arbitral awards and recognition of foreign judgements. The guidance tries to send a message that China acknowledges the existence of disputes concerning the BRI and is willing to treat foreign partners on an equal basis (King & Wood Mallesons 2016).

However, the insistence on the use of the Chinese International Economic and Trade Arbitration Commission in dispute settlement clauses in BRI contracts between Chinese banks and SOEs directly monopolizes the settlement measures in favour of Chinese arbitration. This will raise a number of issues regarding the due process such as problems of language, applicable law, or communication protocols. Nonetheless, it is considered a breakthrough in Chinese judicial procedure that China now allows the "normal" practice in litigation that foreign parties and media can participate in the trial process. This will increase overall transparency (Guo 2017).

In a more comprehensive attempt, the International Academy of the Belt and Road released a "Blue Book" on the dispute resolution mechanism for the BRI in October 2016. The Blue Book consists of a new set of rules and the scope of application of this mechanism will extend to three types of disputes, namely commercial, inter-state, and investor-State disputes. The dispute settlement means include conciliation, arbitration, and appeal procedures, in which conciliation is highlighted as a measure to reflect Asian values and ameliorate foreign entities' sensitivity to litigation from the Chinese approach. Conciliation, therefore, is proposed as a prerequisite to litigation. In addition, mediation is suggested as an initial step in arbitration procedures. However, mediators are not necessarily arbitrators in the later phase if mediation fails. Mediation procedures are strictly confidential, and mediators have to follow the mediators' code of conduct.

In case conciliation and mediation fail to succeed, arbitration will follow. In order to increase neutrality and reduce cultural differences, the Blue Book advocates for the appointment of at least one arbitrator who has specific qualification or expertise and/or understanding of local or regional culture and practices. If necessary, the arbitrator can appoint experts for a case after a consultation with the parties to such cases. Similar to mediation, arbitration procedure is also strictly confidential. In addition, the Blue Book also provides a fast-track arbitration procedure for disputes concerning an amount not exceeding US\$5 million, a matter of exceptional urgency, or involving perishable goods. The fast-track procedure may be invoked by any one party to the dispute before the establishment of the arbitration panel.

In a creative approach, upon the agreement of the parties, the mediation agreement can be converted to arbitration award and thus can be recognized and enforced by member states of the New York Convention.

The appeal procedures recommended in the Blue Book are learnt from the dispute settlement mechanism of the WTO and applied in all types of disputes, except those settled by commercial arbitration. The appeal procedure aims to correct the mistakes of arbitration and give the parties a second chance to present new evidence and arguments.

It can be said that the new measures and procedures provided by the Blue Book illustrate a serious attempt on the part of China in building a comprehensive dispute settlement for the BRI. Unfortunately, it still conforms very much to the Chinese style of dispute settlement. Based on the dispute settlement mechanism of the Blue Book, Chinese investors can easily bring claims against governments participating in the BRI for breach of investors' rights set out in bilateral investment treaties and ignore the host states' domestic legal system as well as other international dispute settlement mechanisms. Meanwhile, in terms of enforcement, China can still make use of the current dispute settlement mechanisms including ICSID and the New York Convention to force other parties to recognize and enforce arbitration awards under the Blue Book mechanism (King & Wood Mallesons 2016). Therefore, more attention should be given to such "exclusive" dispute settlement mechanisms under the BRI.

While this mechanism has yet to be finalized, all parties should carefully consider the settlement clauses with China upon entering into BRI contracts (Hayes 2017). Current practices prove that different regional arbitral institutions have their own advantages based on their expertise, list of arbitrators, neutrality, rules and procedures, venue, and administrative support. These mechanisms should offer a good selection of forums for the parties and advocate for the common prosperity goal of the BRI, rather than be overwhelmed by an "all roads lead to Beijing" approach under the mechanism proposed by the Blue Book (Hayes 2017).

BRI AND TRANSPARENCY

Since its introduction, much has been discussed about the contents of the BRI. The name of the grand project alone has been changed from "One Belt, One Road" to "Belt and Road Initiative" with the emphasis on more than one belt and one road. The map illustrating the geographical coverage of the project is also frequently updated. As of March 2019, 125 countries and 29 international organizations are part of the BRI (China Daily 2019). However, a broad and comprehensive picture on who will participate in the BRI Summits, what will be done, and how the BRI projects can be implemented are left for others to guess from scattered information available. The implementation still depends on the confidential and bilateral negotiations between China and each BRI member.

From the limited, publicly available material, China seems to prefer the implementation of BRI in the form of the PPP model which is popularly used in investment projects under strict conditions of transparency. For example, the OECD principles require PPP to establish a clear, predictable, and legitimate institutional framework supported by competent and well-resourced authorities, to be chosen on grounds of value for money, and to use budgetary process transparency to minimize fiscal risks and ensure the integrity of the procurement process (OECD 2012). The G20 also issues PPP Guidelines which emphasize the need for conducting environmental and social impact assessments to be included in the bidding process and the implementation of the PPP contracts (Aizawa 2018). Meanwhile, it is very difficult to assess risks posed by Chinese investments due to the uncertainties stemming from state control, state subsidies, and private companies acting as proxies for the Chinese government (Hemmings 2017).

Moreover, although China usually highlights the pure economic goals of the BRI, the security concerns are often perceived as an integral impact of the project. For example, a Chinese consortium, AVIC Trust, was allowed to obtain 49% of the stakes in Global Switch, a British-based cloud computing centre. Afterwards, it was discovered that AVIC Trust was subsidized by a Chinese defence industrial giant (Hemmings 2017). Another example is the successful deal where China gained control over Sri Lanka's Hambantota Port. This deal, a part of the Maritime Silk Route, aroused strong fears that the port will be used for Chinese naval vessels (Aneez 2017).

Moreover, it is hard to separate the "charm offensive" foreign policy of China from the BRI. It is coincidental that countries strongly supporting the BRI are also showing restraint in opposing China in international relations. The Philippines, for example, under the new administration of President Duterte, has pivoted to China to be part of the BRI and to receive huge investments from them in exchange for a softer position on South China Sea issues.

In addition, some commentators have expressed concerns on the potential of Chinese interference in the domestic affairs of other states through the BRI. By granting big investments, China may seek changes to many areas of domestic legislation in BRI countries, including laws governing trade, foreign investments, taxation, contracts, labour, environmental protection, intellectual property, physical property, law of obligations, land expropriation rules, and so forth (Zhang 2016). Li Ming, a prominent law professor at Peking University, advocated that "sufficient flexibility should be preserved in the application of the principle of non-intervention" in the context of the BRI (Seppänen 2018). Other Chinese scholars also suggest that limiting sovereign rights and reducing the role of "politics" in international relations will be helpful for promoting public welfare in the BRI regions (National Development and Reform Commission 2015). This tendency, to some extent, reveals a more ambitious plan to create new standards and systems to govern international trade and commerce as well as international order in those regions at least.

Therefore, the proactive involvement of BRI states in increasing the transparency of the Initiative is vital in building international standards for the BRI. In this context, the active participation of states within the AIIB can be seen as a good practice and applied to other areas of the BRI in the future.

CONCLUSION

Paul Kennedy in his 1987 book analysed the political and economic reasons for the rise and fall of great powers over the last five centuries (Kennedy 1987). From his arguments, it may be time for the rise of a new great power or the return of a past great power. This points at China, and the associated expectation that the BRI will play a critical role in that ascent to great power status. Addressing all the legal challenges of the BRI will no doubt contribute to the feasibility of the Initiative. For any such ascent, the world will face a competitive period when the old power has not yet fallen and the new has not firmly established its position. Such competition, historically, used to be resolved by conflicts and wars. However, the world has changed, and no great power can be established without support from others. Many countries, therefore, are given opportunities today to actively engage with and assist China to become a responsible great power through the BRI.

REFERENCES

AIIB. 2016. Environmental and Social Framework. https://www.aiib.org/en/policies-strategies/_download/environment-framework/20160226043633542.pdf.

Aizawa, Motoko. 2018. A Scoping Study of PPP Guidelines. *UN Department of Economic & Social Affairs Working Paper No. 154.* https://www.un.org/esa/desa/papers/2018/wp154_2018.pdf. Accessed 10 June 2018.

Andersen, Henrik. 2016. China's 'One Belt One Road' – Transnational and Multilevel Rule of Law Challenges from a European Perspective. *International Symposium of Foreign Law and Comparative Law: "Comparative Legal Systems and Legal Culture in the View of Globalization".* Beijing, China.

Aneez, Shihar. 2017. Exclusive: Sri Lanka's Cabinet 'Clears Port Deal' with China Firm After Concerns Addressed. *Reuters,* July 25. www.reuters.com/article/us-sri-lanka-china-port/exclusive-sri-lankas-cabinet-clears-port-deal-with-china-firm-after-concerns-addressed-idUSKBN1AA0PI. Accessed 3 Oct 2017.

CASES

Barcelona Traction, Light and Power Company, Limited (Belgium v. Spain). 1970. International Court of Justice, February 5. https://www.icj-cij.org/en/case/50.

China Daily. 2019. Belt and Road Projects: Past, Present, Future. April 22. http://www.chinadaily.com.cn/a/201904/22/WS5cbcf141a3104842260b7627.html. Accessed 11 June 2019.

China International Commercial Court. 2017. Civil Procedure Law of the People's Republic of China (Revised in 2017), June 27. http://cicc.court.gov.cn/html/1/219/199/200/644.html.

Crawford, James. 2012. *Brownlie's Principles of Public International Law.* 8th ed. Oxford: Oxford University Press.

Dupuy, Pierre-Marie, and Jorge E. Viñuales. 2015. *International Environmental Law.* New York: Cambridge University Press.

Gan, Junxian, and Yan Mao. 2016. China's New Silk Road: Where Does It Lead. *Asian Perspective* 40 (1): 105–130.

Guo, Shuai. 2017. Reflections on the Chinese "Belt and Road" Initiative. *Leiden Law Blog*, May 19. leidenlawblog.nl/articles/reflections-on-the-chinese-belt-and-road-initiative. Accessed 3 Oct 2017.

Hayes, Paul. 2017. The China Syndrome: Rethinking Arbitration on the 'One Belt, One Road'. *Kuala Lumpur International Arbitration Week*, May 15. Kuala Lumpur, Malaysia. https://1f2ca7mxjow42e65q49871m1-wpengine. netdna-ssl.com/wp-content/uploads/2017/05/2017-KLIAW-OBOR-Harmonisation-of-Arbitration-Rules-PJHayes-3rd.pdf. Accessed 3 Oct 2017.

Hemmings, John. 2017. Risky Business: Keeping an Eye on Chinese Investment. *Politico*, July 23. www.politico.eu/article/china-investment-europe-opinion-risky-business-keeping-an-eye/. Accessed 3 Oct 2017.

International Law Commission. 2001. Report of the International Law Commission on the Work of Its 53rd Session. http://legal.un.org/ilc/documentation/english/reports/a_56_10.pdf.

Kennedy, Paul. 1987. *The Rise and Fall of the Great Powers*. New York: Vintage.

Kim, Jisan. 2016. Regulating Economic Development: Environmental and Social Standards of the AIIB and the IFC. *Harvard International Law Journal*, April 19. http://www.harvardilj.org/2016/04/regulating-economic-development-environmental-and-social-standards-of-the-aiib-and-the-ifc/. Accessed 3 Oct 2017.

King & Wood Mallesons. 2016. *One Belt One Road: Protecting Your Investments on China's New Pan-Continental Superhighway*, May 10. www.kwm.com/en/knowledge/insights/one-belt-one-road-protecting-your-investment-on-chinas-new-pan-continental-superhighway-20160419. Accessed 3 Oct 2017.

National Development and Reform Commission of the PRC. 2015. Vision and Actions on Jointly Building Silk Road Economic Belt and 21st-Century Maritime Silk Road, March 28. en.ndrc.gov.cn/newsrelease/201503/t20150330_669367.html. Accessed 3 Oct 2017.

OCHR. 2011. *Guiding Principles on Business and Human Rights: Implementing the United Nations 'Protect, Respect and Remedy' Framework*. New York and Geneva: United Nations. http://www.ohchr.org/Documents/Publications/GuidingPrinciplesBusinessHR_EN.pdf.

OECD. 2012. *OECD Principles for Public Governance of Public-Private Partnerships*. www.oecd.org/governance/50254119.pdf. Accessed 3 Oct 2017.

PRC Ministry of Commerce. 2013. Notification of the Ministry of Commerce and the Ministry of Environmental Protection on Issuing the Guidelines for Environmental Protection in Foreign Investment and Cooperation, March 1. http://english.mofcom.gov.cn/article/policyrelease/bbb/201303/20130300043226.shtml. Accessed 3 Oct 2017.

Pulp Mills on the River Uruguay (Argentina v. Uruguay). 2010. International Court of Justice, April 20. https://www.icj-cij.org/en/case/135.

Puvimanasinghe, Shyami F. 2007. *Foreign Investment, Human Rights and the Environment: A Perspective from South Asia on the Role of Public International Law for Development*. Leiden and Boston: Martinus Nijhoff.

Richardson, Sophie, and Hugh Williamson. 2017. China: One Belt, One Road, Lots of Obligations. *Eurasianet*, May 12. www.eurasianet.org/node/83566. Accessed 3 Oct 2017.

Seppänen, Samuli. 2018. Performative Uses of Sovereignty in the Belt and Road Initiative. In *International Governance and the Rule of Law in China Under the Belt and Road Initiative*, ed. Yun Zhao, 32–56. Cambridge: Cambridge University Press.

Tracy, Elena F., Evgeny Shvarts, Eugene Simonov, and Mikhail Babenko. 2017. China's New Eurasian Ambitions: The Environmental Risks of the Silk Road Economic Belt. *Eurasian Geography and Economics*. 58 (1): 56–88.

Wang, Guiguo. 2017. The Belt and Road Initiative in Quest for a Dispute Resolution Mechanism. *Asia Pacific Law Review* 25 (1): 1–16.

Yuen, Rimsky. 2016. The Belt and Road Initiative: Impact on the Future of Dispute Resolution. *Asia Pacific ADR Conference (Session 1)*. Seoul, South Korea. www.doj.gov.hk/eng/public/pdf/2016/sj20161012e2.pdf. Accessed 3 Oct 2017.

Zhang, Yuejiao. 2016. Legal Considerations in the Implementation of the "One Belt, One Road" Strategy. In *International Law Perspective of the Belt and Road Initiative: Collected Papers from the 2015 Hong Kong International Forum on the "One Belt, One Road"*, ed. Guiguo Wang, 12–21. Hangzhou: Zhejiang University Press.

Zhang, Haibing, Xiaoyun Li, Taidong Zhou, Shixin Zhou, Lei Xue, and Yuzhu Wang. 2016. *Assessment and Prospect of China-Laos Development Cooperation*. Shanghai Institute for Internahtional Studies. http://www.siis.org.cn/UploadFiles/file/20170417/20170316_%E4%B8%AD%E5%9B%BD%E4%B8%8E%E8%80%81%E6%8C%9D%E5%8F%91%E5%B1%95%E5%90%88%E4%BD%9C_%E8%8B%B1%E6%96%87%E7%89%88.pdf. Accessed 3 Oct 2017.

Zhou, Jian. 2006. Judicial Intervention in International Arbitration: A Comparative Study of the Scope of the New York Convention in US and Chinese Courts. *Pacific Rim Law & Policy Journal* 15 (2): 403–455.

Zou, Mimi. 2016. Labor Standards Along "One Belt, One Road". In *Legal Dimensions of China's Belt and Road Initiative*, ed. Lutz-Christian Wolff, Chao Xi, and Jenny Chan, 357–392. Hong Kong: Wolters Kluwer.

CHAPTER 10

Is the Economic Hegemony Moving From the United States to China?: A Historical Perspective

Toshiaki Tamaki

INTRODUCTION

One of the most important issues in the contemporary world lies in the shift of the centre of economic power from the United States to Asia. Considering the growing population, the shift is unavoidable in the long run. Asia has two big states: China and India. Compared to India, China is in a more advantageous position to become a center of the world economy.

Chinese economic growth is very impressive, because its GDP surpassed Japan's in 2010. China is now the world's second-largest country by GDP after the United States. China is a very ambitious country in political, geopolitical, military as well as economic spheres, and it aims to expand its economy even more. It might become the most affluent country in the world in the future, but it is, needless to say, an extremely difficult task. What should China do in order to become the most advanced economic state? It is an important question we should ask for exploring its

T. Tamaki (✉)
Faculty of Economics, Kyoto Sangyo University, Kyoto, Japan
e-mail: tamaki@cc.kyoto-su.ac.jp

© The Author(s) 2020
A. Chong, Q. M. Pham (eds.), *Critical Reflections on China's Belt & Road Initiative*, https://doi.org/10.1007/978-981-13-2098-9_10

economic future globally. One of the ways to enhance Chinese economic presence is OBOR.

By this policy, China underwrites billions of dollars of infrastructure investment in countries along the old Silk Road connecting to Europe. China will spend about US$150 billion a year in the 68 countries that have signed up to the scheme. "Its ultimate aim is to make Eurasia (dominated by China) an economic and trading area to rival the transatlantic one (dominated by America)".[1]

Does Chinese policy really work? Some researchers may be skeptical towards the possibility of the realization of Xi's aim because it is a challenging enterprise. Can Eurasia really become an economic and trading zone similar to the Atlantic one in terms of the size and amount of money invested? Is economic hegemony moving from the United States to China? Can China overcome the issues of wage gap and environmental pollution while referring to OBOR? This chapter aims to discuss and reveal the meaning of OBOR from the perspective of economic history. First of all, however, I need to write about my methodology for the analysis, for though my approach is fundamentally based on economic history, it is a bit interdisciplinary-oriented.

METHODOLOGY

According to the theory of "Modern World System" by Immanuel Wallerstein (2011), the world-economy has had three hegemonic states—Netherlands in the mid-seventeenth century, Britain from the middle of the nineteenth century to 1914, and the United States from 1945 to the outbreak of the Vietnam War (Wallerstein 2011). The meaning of a "Hegemonic State," according to Wallerstein, is a state which dominates the world economy; that is, a state being the most powerful in the industrial, commercial and financial sectors at the same time. The period when a singular state is in the hegemonic stage is, by definition, short.

---

[1] *The Economist* (2017) blog. However, according to some (Riello 2013), since the nineteenth century, cotton trade has become truly global, connecting not just Afro-Eurasia but also the Atlantic and the Pacific. It is extremely difficult to distinguish the Eurasian and Atlantic economies in the contemporary global times. They are strongly related to each other.

Wallerstein's influence has declined in the past two decades. He had originally planned to write four volumes spanning the fifteenth to the twentieth centuries, dealing with the birth of the Modern World System and covering the entire world. However, he failed to do so, and that, according to me, revealed the limitation of his theory. His approach has been criticized by many researchers, but it still has a strong influence on economic historians.

The concept of hegemonic state is similar to Susan Strange's "Structural Power" to some extent. According to her, structural power is:

> the power to choose and to shape the structures of the global political economy within which other states, their political institutions, their economic enterprises, and (not least) their professional people have to operate. This means more than the power to set the agenda of discussion or to design (in American phraseology) the international "regime" of rules and customs. (Strange 1987, p. 565)

I think her definition is too complex for analyzing the real world. Nevertheless, structural power is still very useful for describing the real world of political economy if we can change her definition a bit. Her "structural power" can be changed to "the power to decide what is right in the real political economy." Moreover, the concept of Wallerstein's hegemonic state can conform to the same meaning too, because a hegemon has the strongest economic power, and without doubt can decide what is right in the real political economy. By using this definition, I argue and discuss the issue of hegemonic transition from the United States to China by OBOR.

What Is OBOR?

The concept of OBOR has been developing and changing for the past several years. However, it is clear that OBOR is an extremely ambitious attempt, but probably nobody knows whether this policy would be a success or not. We do not know exactly what the real aim of OBOR is. Premier Li Keqiang has not mentioned any military objectives, though it is probably related to the aim of shifting the military balance of power from the United States to China. It is, however, certain that the Chinese government considers some notion of a 'distribution system' as very important for controlling the global economy. Xi Jinping's ambitious initiative has three drivers: (1) energy, (2) security, and (3) markets. Like the silk strands on a loom, these drivers will weave together to create a fabric of interconnected transport corridors and port facilities that will boost trade, improve security, and aid strategic penetration (Fallon 2015, p. 140).

OBOR is different from the traditional Chinese trade policy—the "tributary system." China did not think the existing international distribution system was very important, because with the tributary system, the Chinese could expect to receive goods from abroad and via foreign ships. They did not have to develop their own shipping industry for several centuries. This led to the long-term decline of the Chinese shipping and economic power (Liang-lin 1974) as China accepted and allowed foreign countries to distribute Chinese and foreign commodities in maritime trade.

OBOR is a new system differing from that trend. Chinese economic growth was the most important factor for the change of the balance in East Asia (Oba 2013, p. 57). The policy can be considered to support and sustain this trend. Merchant networks who were self-organized entities in the early modern period established the Silk Road. On the other hand, Xi will utilize the Silk Road for state policy. The Chinese economy is still an export-led one. However, this system of economic growth, I suppose, is coming to an end, for the economy is too big to sustain by solely relying on exports to ASEAN, the United States, Japan and so on. Thanks to its huge population, 1.3 billion (officially, but it will in fact be more than that), China has a very large domestic market—the largest in the world. If the Chinese economy could utilize its domestic market so well, they could expect to grow even more. Despite the economic growth rate of China being very high, we are very skeptical about whether the reported figures are reliable or not. In any simple comparison, either online or offline, a map of all OBOR regions as of 2019, is similar to the seventh expedition undertaken by China's Admiral Zheng He at the beginning of the fifteenth century. His expedition was based on the maritime routes of Asia, mainly used by Islamic merchants. Some of the land-route overlapped the ones taken by Armenian merchants (Aslanian 2014).

Xi's policy, would therefore, be based upon independent early modern merchant networks. That is, he is planning to use Chinese governmental power to create a distribution system, and this would be made possible by huge investments of capital raised by the China-centered financial system—the Asian Infrastructure Investment Bank (AIIB). This will be a series of transportation, energy, and telecommunication infrastructure projects (Zimmerman 2015, p. 3). I suppose, however, the most important point with regard to this new, yet reborn, distribution system is that China can expect to control the distribution network in the Eurasian World. This already makes it different from the traditional and older Chinese policy of bygone dynasties of thriving on pluralism and difference in commercial cultures along the maritime and landed Silk Roads.

The Changing Role of Governments to Support and Promote Economic Growth

Historically, the Netherlands was the most advanced country and economy in Europe—the first hegemon (De Vries and Woude 1997). Two factors underpinned this achievement. Firstly, the Dutch hegemony depended on its extensive shipping industry in European waters and its cosmopolitan merchant networks. It was a decentralized country and not a state ('t Hart 1993, 1995). Secondly, the base of their prosperity lay not in the East Indies but in the Baltic trade because the latter constantly contributed to their wealth and so was called the "Mother of all trades" for the Dutch (Tielhof 2002). They gained money from their shipping industry and their economy developed because shipping was closely connected to the European trade networks. Amsterdam was the center of European trade and it could, potentially, become a trade hub of international settlements. Huge money was poured into Amsterdam as a financial center *automatically*.

Britain became a hegemonic state, after the Netherlands, as it won the wars against France after fighting for over a hundred years. The Industrial Revolution has been theoretically considered to be a phenomenon that was possible only in a free economic society. From the eighteenth to the nineteenth centuries, however, industrialization was realized by using the state's power. As we all know, the Industrial Revolution occurred in Britain in the latter half of the eighteenth century starting off in Manchester and was closely related to the slave trade. British industrialization started from cotton textiles, the product of *light* industries, that it imported from India. On the other hand, German and American industrialization in the nineteenth century is sometimes called the "second industrial revolution." In contrast to British industrialization, they started with the industrialization of the heavy chemical industry. The capital they needed, thus, was much higher than the British.

The manufacturers in Manchester did not borrow money from the banks in London. They procured capital from their relatives and banks in Manchester. Likewise, the money needed for industrialization on the rest of the Continent was raised basically within the states themselves. German enterprises used commercial banks, a fact that was revealed in Rudolf Hilferding's "Das Finanzkapital" (Hilferding 1985). The United States also established a monopoly capital. Despite the increasing size of enterprises in Germany and the United States, compared to the ones at the time of industrialization, they still made good use of their own states' financial intermediaries. The relations between enterprises and commercial banks were, however, closer in German and American industrialization.

THE AGE OF IMPERIALISM AND THE ROLE OF THE BRITISH FINANCIAL SYSTEM

The industrialization of Europe occurred at the time of imperialism. Continental (non-British) industrialization was closely connected to the rise of the British imperial system. European states imported raw materials from their colonies, processed them and exported the final goods back to their colonies who were their market and who could not yet develop their own factories. The British hegemony could also efficiently utilize the industrialization on the European Continent.

Britain had a formal and an informal empire and was the only one to do so. An informal empire means areas which were not British colonies but under the strict influence of the British political economy. In the age of imperialism, Britain started losing its status as the "workshop of the world," especially from the 1890s, but still possessed the largest commercial shipping fleets (Vries 2013, p. 32). They were carrying goods to and from all over the world. Steam ships voyaged all the way from Latin America to China. Without British shipping, world trade could not have been maintained (Qing 2015). One of the most important pillars of the British hegemony was, without a doubt, its shipping industry.

Another pillar was the telegraph. The telegraph was developed both in the United States and Britain, by various inventors. Although American inventor Samuel Morse is widely credited for the invention of the telegraphy system, its usage and popularity can be attributed to the British. Most of the telegraph lines worldwide were actually laid down by British companies.

And since Britain adopted the gold standard, many countries made the change too, especially in the 1870s when British telegraph lines had reached Japan and "united" most parts of the world except the Pacific. The telegraph was now being used for remitting money for the settlement of trade. London became the center of the settlement of international trade. Huge amounts of money earned from the commission for using the telegraph system was pouring into Britain.

The telegraph was, as Daniel Headrick says, "an invisible weapon" (Headrick 2012). It was being utilized for commercial as well as military purposes. As world trade grew and the global economy expanded, it corresponded to the increasing flow of commission the British got from the use of telegraphs (Ahvenainen 1981). It became the most important feature of the British hegemony or structural power. Britain needed to pay for the cost of maintenance and the proceeds from the telegraph system helped defray the expenses. Thus, Britain could maintain its hegemony.

It is true that in the age of imperialism, Europe acquired many colonies all over the world, but they would contribute part of their benefits to Britain as a form of "commission." This was the most typical feature of the British hegemony. Britain expected to get money *automatically* as a form of commission. Britain did not become a "hegemonic state" due to the Industrial Revolution, but built hegemonic foundations from steam ships and telegraphs. Britain successfully utilized other states' industrialization[2].

THE FEATURES OF AMERICAN HEGEMONY AND INCREASING ECONOMIC COMPETITION

Most of the international institutions were established after World War II—the United Nations (UN), International Monetary Fund (IMF), General Agreement on Tariffs and Trade (GATT), and so on. These institutions appeared to be neutral in their management, but in fact, were and are established for the benefit of the United States. The hegemony of the United States has been partially based on this fact, leading to the emergence of a new pattern of hegemonic state.

The United States, moreover, adopted the gold standard—completely severing it only in 1971. Many parts of international payments were

[2] On this point, this chapter's aim is similar to "Gentlemanly Capitalism" (Cain and Hopkins 2003).

carried out in New York. A regularly high volume of commission was pouring into New York and the United States. Almost all currencies, except for those of socialist countries, were connected by this system. The increase in world trade meant the strengthening of the economic power of the United States. By using this system, the United States could expect to obtain benefits *automatically*.

In the contemporary world, the number of economic communities such as the European Union (EU) and ASEAN Economic Community (AEC) have been increasing. The capital needed for investment has become larger and larger in the course of the century. Although international institutions were established for the benefit of the United States, the number of non-United States-oriented international institutions has been rapidly increasing, partly because of the decline of the United States' power.

After World War II, the unit for economic competition gradually became regional economies. The birth of the European Coal and Steel Community (ECSC) was one of the first signs of this trend. It was established by the Western European states to compete against the socialist states of Eastern Europe. The economic and political threat of socialism to Western Europe was so strong that Western economies had to form a united area to efficiently compete with socialist states. The money required for investing in economic growth has continued to increase, making it almost impossible for one country to gather such a huge amount. This is a feature of the global economy in the contemporary world. The birth of the EU, AEC, and the more recent Comprehensive and Progressive Agreement for Trans-Pacific Partnership (CPTPP) should be studied from this perspective.

From Economic Backwardness to Economically Advanced Country

China's GDP is the second largest next to the United States in the world, and its GDP per capita was 73rd globally in 2016. China is, therefore, a semi-developed country. It is absurd to give too much attention to figures such as GDP for estimating its real economic power, but, it can be a good baseline for comparison.

China will fall into the "middle income trap" if the government does not do anything to remedy the situation. It can also lose its competitive advantage over time (Onishi 2017, p. 1). Understandably, the Chinese government has been investing heavily in technology, making some Japanese afraid of the Chinese potential to catch up with, and surpass, the Japanese preeminence in technology. Remarkably, Chinese FDI for countries that are part of OBOR has also been increasing for the past decade, from 2005 (Onishi 2017, p. 9).

China could, potentially, utilize OBOR for enhancing its technological innovations. However, they do not seem interested in that, and they are far more concerned about the transformation of logistics fit for the Chinese economy. They have been actively concluding Preferential Trade Agreements (PTA) with the countries that are part of OBOR (Gokuryo 2017).

China has an extensive energy requirement for its continuous economic growth, but it has to import that. The countries along OBOR have 46.1 billion tonnes of oil and 108 trillion cubic meters of natural gas reserves. The ratio, when compared to global reserves, is 20% and 56% respectively (Ri 2017, p. 55). China expects to make use of this for OBOR. However, considering Chinese dependence on energy sources, it may either waste or overuse energy. The OBOR participating countries should consider this possibility.

The Chinese economy is a typical case of industrialization in "economic backwardness" (Gerschenkron 1952). China utilizes advanced countries' technology to develop its economy rapidly and under state supervision. Gerschenkron also stressed on the importance of leadership for industrialization of such backward countries. Xi could be that leader due to his advocacy of OBOR. He has the strategy to increase economic growth, yet he appears more interested in logistics, which he thinks, will be beneficial for the Chinese government—but not the Chinese people.

Economists tend to consider the world of "Kuznets curve" normal, in the sense that they think that as an economy develops, market forces will first increase income inequality and then eventually decrease it (Kuznets 1955). However, Thomas Piketty proved this curve does not exist today and inequality has actually risen over the past several decades (2017a). We are, without a doubt, moving into an increasingly unequal global society. I suppose one of the reasons for this is the failure to form a middle class in most countries.

The middle class would purchase consumer goods in order to raise their standard of living. If the proportion of the middle class continues to increase, I suppose the Kuznets curve will still operate. Or the Kuznets curve can be used as a model for the convergence of income. Kuznets based his theory on the experience of the United States, for example, the boom the country experienced in the 1920s which saw an increasing consumption of consumer goods such as automobiles.

In the case of Japanese economic history, the purchasing of durable consumer goods—TV, washing machine, refrigerator, automobile, air conditioners—increased and created a middle class. They succeeded in the making of a stable society. We should not ignore the importance of consumer goods as an engine for economic growth and a stable society and for the explanation of the existence of the Kuznets curve.

All of us know that the income inequality in China is huge. The inequality exists between maritime and inland zones. As Piketty writes in his blog:

> The problem is that the growth in income of the poorest 50% of the Chinese population has only been half the average. According to our estimates, which must be considered as lower bound levels of inequality in China, the share of the poorest 50% in the national income in China fell from 28% to 15% between 1978 and 2015, while the income of the 10% richest rose from 26% to 41%. The extent of the phenomenon is impressive: the levels of inequality in China are clearly higher than in Europe and are rapidly approaching those observed in the United States. (Piketty 2017b)

Without looking too deeply into the accuracy of these figures, it is certain that the Chinese government should reduce this wage gap. Can the gap, however, be decreased? Will the Chinese gap overtake the one in the United States? The increasing wage gap is a tendency seen all over the world and supported by Piketty's 2017 book which denied the Kuznets curve. Can China become a hegemon after the United States (2017a)?

The most important task for China is therefore to find the source of the rising income inequality. Some leads can be sought in a 2012 OECD report. It reads, "China has moved towards a market-oriented economy. Such a transformation initially entailed a marked rise in inequality, which was an inevitable consequence of the transformation of the economy that has delivered a higher and more sustained growth in incomes than observed in any other major economy" (Goglio et al. 2012, p. 16). If the Chinese government does not change their policy, the inequality will continue. The government would end up losing the trust of their people (Molander 2016, p. 174).

The income difference between rural and urban areas in China also used to be particularly high. By 2009, the ratio of consumption between urban and rural households had reached 3.3, which is much higher than in other emerging economies, such as India, where it was just under 2 in 2009. Since then, the Chinese gap had been decreasing and by 2011 had dropped back to 2003 levels. Indeed, the reliability of the reported decreasing gap is still doubtful, but current estimations put it at around 3.1 (Molander 2016, pp. 18–19).

We have to accept the existence of an income gap in all states, but as Per Molander explains (2016, p. xi):

> The appropriate question is not "Why are all societies characterized by equality?" but rather "Why have certain societies managed to keep inequality within reasonable bounds?"

What should China do to reduce the wage gap? I do not have an answer, but I have to say that they can make good use of the OBOR to achieve this goal.

CONCLUSION

With OBOR, China aims to make itself more prosperous with money from foreign countries. This should see a transformation of the Chinese economy from being export-led to domestic-demand led economy. China should use OBOR to ensure this process takes place either without causing environmental pollution, or by drastically decreasing pollution.

OBOR has the potential to support economic growth based on investment in infrastructure and flow of money. It will also, possibly, lead to job creation for the people in Central Asia as well as China. At the same time, however, it could spread environmental pollution. In case of the AIIB, it will support and help the development of infrastructure at first (Ou Shikei 2017). Indeed, AIIB does refer to the importance of environmental pollution, but I do not suppose that the bank considers it as an extremely important prerequisite. What is worse, is that China's inefficient use of oil and natural gas would cause much more serious damage globally than any other state.

Environmental pollution has been an ever-present phenomenon—historically caused by mankind. Our economic activities have been, and continue to, cause environmental pollution. It has been exacerbated by industrialization since the late eighteenth century. The China-led OBOR might have a harmful effect in Eurasia if we do not consider this problem sincerely and do not act against environmental pollution. This is a lesson we need to learn from history.

Many states have shown an interest in OBOR, and they may invest in the project. They should bear the responsibility and cost for protecting the environment from pollution and not make the situation worse. Are they willing to do so? If they do not want to, they should be severely criticized for not being sensitive towards the after-effects of their investment in OBOR. Many statesmen and moneyed interests might feel responsible for the return on their investment, but they do need to settle environmental pollution issues too.

In addition to providing solutions to environmental problems, we also have to pay attention to the job creation effects of OBOR and the reduction of the wage gap within China. On the domestic front for China, the continued degradation of their arable land and increased soil pollution have driven China to become a major food importer, especially for grains. China's grain self-sufficiency declined from 93% in 2008 to 86% in 2014, despite the fact that the number of annual new births was largely stable during the same period (He et al. 2015). Moreover, the standard of living in rural China is still too low; if the government fails to ameliorate it, China itself might face economic collapse in the end. The Chinese government possibly does not think that OBOR is extremely important for the purpose of raising their domestic standards of living.

Is the economic hegemony moving from the United States to China if the United States' power is declining? I do not think so. The Chinese are still not inventing a new system through which huge money can *automatically* be poured into the hegemonic state. The Chinese policy continues to follow the tried-and-tested system established by the United States and Europe. Thus, there is no push on their part to create a new system. Therefore, China is currently beset by too many problems to become a hegemon. Do they have the possibility or potential if they could solve the issues? Yes, I think so. But it would not be realized by OBOR. China is a long way from becoming a hegemonic state.

REFERENCES

Ahvenainen, Jorma. 1981. *The Far Eastern Telegraphs: The History of Telegraphic Communications Between the Far East, Europe and America Before the First World War.* Helsinki: Suomalainen Tiedeakatemia.

Aslanian, Sebouh D. 2014. *From the Indian Ocean to the Mediterranean: The Global Trade Networks of Armenian Merchants from New Julfa*. Berkeley: University of California Press.

Cain, Peter J., and Anthony G. Hopkins. 2003. *British Imperialism 1688–2000*. 2nd ed. London: Longman.

de Vries, Jan, and Ad van der Woude. 1997. *The First Modern Economy: Success, Failure, and Perseverance of the Dutch Economy, 1500–1815*. Cambridge: Cambridge University Press.

Economist, The. 2017, May 15. The Economist Explains: What Is China's Belt and Road Initiative? https://www.economist.com/the-economist-explains/2017/05/14/what-is-chinas-belt-and-road-initiative.

Fallon, Theresa. 2015. The New Silk Road: Xi Jinping's Grand Strategy for Eurasia. *American Foreign Policy Interests* 37 (3): 140–147.

Gerschenkron, Alexander. 1952. Economic Backwardness in Historical Perspective. In *The Progress of Underdeveloped Area*, ed. Bert F. Hoselitz, 3–29. Cambridge, MA: MIT Press.

Goglio, Alessandro, Richard Herd, and Theodora Xenogiani. 2012. Inequality: Recent Trends in China and Experience in the OECD Area. In OECD, *China in Focus: Lessons and Challenges*, pp. 16–34. http://www.oecd.org/global-relations/keypartners/50146214.pdf.

Gokuryo, Houu S. 2017. 'Ittai Ichiro' Koso to sono Ensen no Tokkeibouekikyotei ni Kansuru Kenkyu. In *'Ittai Ichiro' Koso to sono Chyugoku Keizai he no Eikyo Hyoka*, eds. Institute of Developing Economies and Shanghai Academy of Social Sciences, pp. 13–29. Tokyo.

't Hart, Marjolein C. 1993. *The Making of a Bourgeois State: War, Politics, and Finance During the Dutch Revolt*. Manchester: Manchester University Press.

———. 1995. "De nieuwe economische geschiedenis van Nederland" (*The New Economic History of the Netherlands*). *Tijdschrift voor Sociale Geschiedenis (Journal of Social History)* 21 (3): 260–272.

He, Christina, Claire Wang, Yan Yan, and Julian Zhu. 2015, July 13. China's Environment: Big Issues, Accelerating Effort, Ample Opportunities. pp. 8–9, Goldman Sachs Equity Research. https://www.goldmansachs.com/insights/pages/interconnected-markets-folder/chinas-environment/report.pdf.

Headrick, Daniel R. 2012. *The Invisible Weapon: Telecommunications and International Politics, 1851–1945*. Oxford: Oxford University Press.

Hilferding, Rudolf. 1985. *Das Finanzkapital (Finance Capital: A Study of the Latest Phase of Capitalist Development)*. London and Boston: Routledge and Kegan Paul.

Kuznets, Simon. 1955. Economic Growth and Income Inequality. *American Economic Review* 45 (1): 1–28.

Liang-lin, Hsiao. 1974. *China's Foreign Trade Statistics, 1864–1949*. Cambridge, MA: MIT Press.

Molander, Per. 2016. *The Anatomy of Inequality: Its Social and Economic Origins and Solutions*. Brooklyn and London: Melville House.

Oba, Mie. 2013. The New Japan-ASEAN Partnership: Challenges in the Transformation of the Regional Context in East Asia. In *ASEAN-Japan Relations*, ed. Takaaki Kojima and Takashi Shiraishi, 55–72. Singapore: ISEAS-Yusof Ishak Institute.

Onishi, Yasuo. 2017. "'Ittai Ichiro' no Koso no Genjo to Kadai" *('OBOR' Initiative; Current Situation and Prospects)*. In *'Ittai Ichiro' Koso to sono Chyugoku Keizai he no Eikyo Hyoka*, eds. Institute of Developing Economies and Shanghai Academy of Social Sciences, pp. 1–12. Tokyo.

Ou, Shikei. 2017. "AIIB no Unei to 'Ittai Ichiro' Koso no Kenkyu" *(A Study on the Management of AIIB and the Concept of OBOR)*. *Keiei to Keizai (Journal of Business and Economics)* 47 (1/2): 35–50.

Piketty, Thomas. 2017a. *Capital in the Twenty-First Century*. Cambridge, MA: Belknap Press of Harvard University Press.

———. 2017b, Feb 14. On Inequality in China. Le Monde.fr. http://piketty.blog.lemonde.fr/2017/02/14/on-inequality-in-china/. Accessed Mar 17 2018.

Qing, Han. 2015. Western Steamship Companies and Chinese Seaborne Trade during the Late Qing Dynasty, 1840–1911. *International Journal of Maritime History* 27 (3): 537–559.

Ri, Ritushan. 2017. 'Ittai Ichiro Koso' wo Haikei Toshita Chugoku to Chio Ajia no Enerugii Kyoryoku *(Cooperation in Energy Between China and Central Asia based on OBOR.)*. In *'Ittai Ichiro' Koso to sono Chyugoku Keizai he no Eikyo Hyoka*, eds. Institute of Developing Economies and Shanghai Academy of Social Sciences. Tokyo.

Riello, Giorgio. 2013. *Cotton: The Fabric That Made the Modern World*. Cambridge: Cambridge University Press.

Strange, Susan. 1987. The Persistent Myth of Lost Hegemony. *International Organization* 41 (4): 551–574.

van Tielhof, Milja. 2002. *The Mother of All Trades: The Baltic Grain Trade in Amsterdam from the Late 16th to the Early 19th Century*. Leiden: Brill Publisher.

Vries, Peer. 2013. *Escaping Poverty: The Origins of Modern Economic Growth*. Vienna: V&R Unipress GmbH.

Wallerstein, Immanuel. 2011. *The Modern World System*. Berkeley: University of California Press.

Zimmerman, Thomas. 2015. The New Silk Roads: China, the U.S., and the Future of Central Asia, pp. 1–21. *New York University Center on International Cooperation*. https://cic.nyu.edu/sites/default/files/zimmerman_new_silk_road_final_2.pdf.

CHAPTER 11

China's Belt and Road Initiative: China's Motivations and Its Impacts On Developing Countries

Nguyen Thi Thuy Trang

INTRODUCTION

The "Belt and the Road" Initiative (BRI) was launched in 2013 by Chinese President Xi Jinping under the initial title of "One Belt One Road" (OBOR). OBOR encompasses a land-based Silk Road and a maritime Silk Road connecting China and countries in Asia, Africa and Europe. From the beginning, China has sought to involve assorted countries and regions in the BRI. Most of the countries involved in the initiative are developing countries. Chinese leaders argue that the BRI presents an opportunity to deepen economic ties, enhance free trade, and undertake infrastructure development. However, many countries in the initiative have so far adopted a cautious attitude with regards to the potential impacts of

N. T. T. Trang
University of Social Sciences and Humanities, Vietnam National University, Hanoi, Vietnam

© The Author(s) 2020   189
A. Chong, Q. M. Pham (eds.), *Critical Reflections on China's Belt & Road Initiative*, https://doi.org/10.1007/978-981-13-2098-9_11

BRI. This is reflected in the 2017 Belt and Road Forum, which saw the participation of 100 countries and international organizations. However only 29 countries sent their heads of state or government. Although the second forum in 2019 witnessed 150 countries represented by their Heads of State or lower level officials, many attendees complained of the thinness of the substance of the BRI. (Lee and Elmer 2019).

Due to the BRI's wide scope and potential impacts, it is imperative for the developing countries involved to have a clear sense of what China wants from the project and what their participation would mean. Therefore, what were the motivations of China when they launched this initiative, and how would the BRI impact developing countries participating in the initiative? Using a multi-level analysis, this chapter argues that China has strategic, economic, and political calculations and motivations behind their leaders' rhetoric. In the case of the participating developing countries, besides the benefits they could potentially receive, they would also face economic, political, and security risks.

The BRI and China's Motivations

China views the BRI as a new way of fostering global development. Inspired by the ancient Silk Road, this strategy aims to expand connectivity with Asian, African and European countries with hundreds of billions of dollars poured into infrastructure. China's ambitious initiative will provide funds for building highways, railways, pipelines, seaports, and power plants which are essential for developing countries. The project also encourages Chinese businesses to boost investment in seaports and rail systems across the continents. The essence of this initiative is infrastructure projects aimed at linking participating countries with China. It is divided into two main sections, the land-based Silk Road Economic Belt and the Maritime Silk Road. The land-based belt has a three-pronged route: a branch from China through Central Asia and Russia to the Baltic region of Europe; a branch from China through Central Asia, West Asia to the Persian Gulf and Mediterranean; and a branch from China to Southeast Asia, South Asia and the Indian Ocean. The Belt aims to provide a link between Europe and Asia and to develop China's economic corridors with Mongolia, Russia, Central Asia, and Southeast Asia. The twenty first Century Maritime Silk Road runs from China's eastern coast through the South China Sea to Europe, Oceania and the South Pacific. This route not only creates a perimeter of ocean traffic, but will also construct economic corridors across the Indian Ocean, linking China with South Asia, the Middle East, Africa, and the Mediterranean.

The vast majority of the countries within the BRI are in great need of resources for investment, as they have less-developed economies or suffer from chronic instability. Hence, the resources for those countries who are empowered to carry out projects are derived mainly from China, which provides a substantial amount of credit. In its 13th Five-Year Socio-Economic Development Plan, China has identified three multilateral financial institutions to be involved in this effort: the Asian Infrastructure Investment Bank (AIIB), the Silk Road Fund (SRF), and the New Development Bank (NDB).

In 2013, the AIIB was proposed, and 57 countries registered to become its founding members by March 2015. Of these 57 countries, 37 countries are in Asia and Oceania, while the rest are in Europe, Africa and Latin America. The Bank officially began operations on January 16, 2016 (Chin 2016, p. 3). With an initial capital of US$50 billion (later raised to US$100 billion), the AIIB would play a role in financing infrastructure projects in the Asia-Pacific region and Africa. The Silk Road Fund was established in 2014 with a starting capital of US$40 million (Ha Thu 2015), with a focus on providing loans to build railways, and oil and gas pipelines along the Silk Road.

Along with the financial institutions established after the launch of the BRI, other major Chinese banks, such as the China Development Bank (CDB) and the China Export-Import Bank (CEIB), also had a significant role. China's loans to other countries since 2013 have made a sharp shift as two-thirds of CDB and CEIB loans, which are estimated at nearly US$50 billion at an interest rate of 4 to 4.5% per annum, are to BRI-related countries. During the period from 2014 to 2016, Chinese enterprises signed US$305 billion worth of projects in the countries included in the Initiative. A significant portion of them are long-term projects. (Minh Son 2017).

On March 28, 2015, at the Boao Forum for Asia, China's National Development and Reform Commission together with the Ministry of Foreign Affairs and the Ministry of Commerce announced an action plan entitled a "Vision and Actions on Jointly Building the Silk Road Economic Belt and twenty first Century Maritime Silk Road." It is stated in the action plan that, "It [the BRI] is aimed at promoting orderly and free flow of economic factors, highly efficient allocation of resources and deep integration of markets; encouraging the countries along the Belt and Road to achieve economic policy coordination and carrying out broader and more in-depth regional cooperation with higher standards; and jointly creating an open, inclusive and balanced regional economic cooperation architecture that benefits all. Jointly building the Belt and Road is in the interests of the world community. Reflecting the common ideals and pursuit of human societies, it is a positive endeavour to seek new models of international cooperation and global governance, and will inject a new positive impetus for world peace and development." (China's NDRC 2015) If the objectives set out in the action plan are really what China is aims for the BRI, this is a desirable programme, especially for less-developed countries.

However, based on China's own considerations and the international context when President Xi Jinping launched the OBOR and the implementation of related projects, China's motivations in the BRI could be interpreted as follows:

Firstly, for economic benefit, the BRI can bring both profit and serve Xi's Chinese economic restructuring plan. In the context of excess production in heavy industry, especially steel and cement, Chinese construction firms will benefit from infrastructure projects in developing countries. In the process of economic restructuring, they can also export older technologies and manual labour to other countries. And as China's manufacturing industries move to less accessible provinces, improved infrastructure links to international markets will help to open up alternative markets for Chinese goods and meet Beijing's development needs. Xi hopes that infrastructure investment will bring more returns on China's huge foreign reserves, which are mostly used to buy low-yield bonds from the US government (J.P. 2017). However, the construction of transport infrastructure and oil pipelines in the BRI will help energy-hungry China bolster its energy security, proactively ensuring supplies, while reducing costs.

Secondly, since becoming the world's second largest economy, China wants to assert its role in building a regional and inter-regional economic order, as well as strengthen its influence in the global economic order. Eventually, China aims to be the leader and determine the rules of the game for other players. In recent events, such as the World Economic Forum in Davos in January 2017 or the International Belt and Road Forum in May 2017 and again in April 2019, Xi announced that China wants to engage actively and constructively in global governance and play the role of a global leader. The BRI is thus a powerful tool to help China realize that desire.

Thirdly, it is obvious that it is China's strategic intention in countering American influence in different regions, especially in the Asia-Pacific. As previously mentioned, the idea of OBOR was announced in 2013 and it was also the first year of US President Barack Obama's second term. It was also the time when the United States was stepping up its re-pivot to Asia while accelerating negotiations for the Trans-Pacific Partnership (TPP). At that time, one of Beijing's objectives for OBOR was to strengthen relations with Asian countries and balance the influence of the United States. For example, China boosted relations with Malaysia through massive investments during that period. In 2017, when Donald Trump succeeded Obama as president and promoted an "America First" policy, which in part, meant opposing trade liberalization, the BRI would become a tool for China to gradually counter America's global leadership role. Through this initiative, Xi wanted to show to the world China's willingness to champion globalization and be the main driving force behind trade liberalization.

Fourthly, China's incentive to intervene and influence the countries receiving investment and loans within the BRI framework cannot be ruled out. Many developing countries involved in the BRI are strategically and geographically important for China's political and security interests. It is clear that pouring hundreds of billions of dollars into infrastructure projects in these countries is not just for short-term gain. Infrastructure projects in many countries are long-term and it is difficult to determine whether they can be profitable. China's investment in developing countries is not just for philanthropic purposes. Many countries in the BRI are poor countries which are in dire need for investments and loans, but they are also unable to repay them in the short-term. This suggests that China is using its funds in the BRI to promote its political and security interests.

Drawing from the analysis of China's major motivations in initiating and implementing the BRI, it can be seen that China's aim is not simply to build infrastructure, help poor countries, and promote free trade. Rather, Beijing has other political and strategic goals.

THE BRI AND ITS IMPACT ON DEVELOPING COUNTRIES

In his speech at the International Belt and Road Forum, Xi claimed that the BRI would be open to all, arguing that in an increasingly interdependent world, no country can tackle global challenges and solve international problems on its own. (Khanh Lynh 2017). As shown in the following table, according to a report by the China International Trade Institute, there are 65 countries participating in the BRI (Table 11.1).

Table 11.1   The 65 Countries in the Belt and Road Initiative

Region	Country
East Asia	China, Mongolia
Southeast Asia	Brunei, Cambodia, Indonesia, Laos, Malaysia, Myanmar, Philippines, Singapore, Thailand, Timor-Leste, Vietnam
Central Asia	Kazakhstan, Kyrgyzstan, Tajikistan, Turkmenistan, Uzbekistan
Middle East and North Africa	Bahrain, Egypt, Iran, Iraq, Israel, Jordan, Kuwait, Lebanon, Oman, Qatar, Saudi Arabia, Palestine, Syria, United Arab Emirates, Yemen
South Asia	Afghanistan, Bangladesh, Bhutan, India, Maldives, Nepal, Pakistan, Sri Lanka
Europe	Albania, Armenia, Azerbaijan, Belarus, Bosnia and Herzegovina, Bulgaria, Croatia, Czech Republic, Estonia, Georgia, Hungary, Latvia, Lithuania, Macedonia, Moldova, Montenegro, Poland, Romania, Russia, Serbia, Slovakia, Slovenia, Turkey, Ukraine

Based on the list, the vast majority of BRI member states are developing countries. These 65 countries, including China, have a combined population of 623 million worldwide, but only account for 30% of global GDP (Chin 2016, p. 2). The need for development, especially in terms of infrastructure, in these countries is enormous. The BRI will strengthen the development prospects of many of these countries through the construction of transport and other related physical infrastructure. With the Chinese government's financial commitment, the BRI will provide alternative sources of funding besides having to rely on traditional public financing. Strong investment flows in the construction sector will also bring greater technical capacity to less-developed countries such as improved transport infrastructure standards and liberalized cross-border trade. Due to these perspectives, the initiative was welcomed in most countries when it was first initiated and implemented. However, there are also concerns about the possible risks that the BRI can bring to developing countries. The chapter will now highlight both benefits and risks in the next two sections.

Benefits for Developing Countries

Firstly, many countries along the BRI need to improve their infrastructure as the poor state of their infrastructure is hindering their economic growth. Moreover, pressures from a rising population, urbanization, and industrialization also require financial resources to support the development of physical infrastructure. However, many governments along the BRI lack the public financial capacity to develop infrastructure while the private sector is also unable meet this demand. For example, according to a report by the Asian Development Bank, Southeast Asian countries will require US$2.759 billion for infrastructure investment between 2016 and 2030 (Le 2017). The substantial funds stemming from the BRI will help developing countries meet their infrastructure funding needs.

Secondly, the initiative will boost trade and investment as trade between China and other countries along the BRI accounts for about a quarter of Beijing's external trade. Continuous investment in infrastructure will encourage trade flows, not only from China to countries along the route, but also boost exports from developing countries to other markets. Improved infrastructure, including highways, airports, seaports, and railways, will also create the conditions for trade and tourism to be expanded amongst the countries along the BRI.

Thirdly, the BRI will contribute to better integrate private sector involvement in the construction sector, rather than relying solely on state-owned enterprises (SOEs). The BRI funding model is that loans from Chinese banks will be paid to Chinese contractors to undertake infrastructure development projects in developing countries. This can bring some benefits, such as reducing the financial burden on governments, increase productivity and improve the quality of public services, facilitate the transfer of knowledge, and the sharing of experience. The growth of the private sector in many developing countries along the BRI is relatively recent and many enterprises lack the capacity, or resources, to carry out major construction projects. Reliance on SOEs clearly limits private sector involvement. However, when engaging Chinese companies, countries can take advantage of their surplus capacity and technology. However, by implementing this mixed model, states need take into account several conditions. These include whether funding is distributed transparently, whether a balance between public and private funding can achieved, the presence of strong management systems to function across borders, and ensuring that these companies adhere to market principles. Without meeting these conditions, engaging Chinese companies might end up having negative impacts for developing countries as explained earlier.

Risks from the Belt and Road Initiative for Developing Countries

Firstly, there are financial risks associated with funding mechanisms and investment patterns in the BRI. The system of Chinese bank loans being redirected to Chinese contractors to implement infrastructure development projects in developing countries will not only provide China with financial gain, Beijing also stands to benefit from the infrastructure once they are completed. However, the receiving countries are exposed to financial risks. This comes from one of the BRI's hidden objectives, which aims to promote China's economic interests abroad, as analyzed above. The risks for developing countries include: foreign exchange volatility, the risk of recession, price instability, excessive private sector investment, regulatory and non-regulatory issues, corruption and the lack of transparency. For example, in countries like Vietnam, infrastructure projects financed by Chinese loans and carried out by Chinese contractors have suffered from various problems such as construction delays, cost overruns, poor construction quality, and high maintenance costs after completion.

Secondly, the use of Chinese contractors can also lead to other dangers to developing countries such as becoming technology dumping grounds for outdated Chinese technology while local workers would risk losing their jobs in their home market. Beijing will also bind the projects under certain conditions as their contractor has the right to choose technology, use their equipment and employ Chinese labourers. Among developing countries within the BRI, a few countries, such as India and Indonesia, have demonstrated relatively strong project management experiences. This is because Beijing is unable to assume full control of the projects as these countries were not keen to accept large numbers of Chinese workers. Other BRI countries, such as Cambodia and Pakistan, have weaker governance. In such cases, China could be in a better position to set the conditions and impose more risky projects on these countries.

Thirdly, developing countries face the risk of owing substantial amounts of debt to China. This is the infamous 'debt trap' argument. Chinese banks provide BRI countries with large loans with interest rates between 4% to 4.5%. However, most of the projects that have been funded are long-term ones with their profitability in doubt. This combined with China's ability to set loan conditions and impose financial risks, as outlined above, cannot guarantee the success and effectiveness of all projects. In the event a project is stalled or scrapped for some reason, these countries still have to foot the bill and accrue more debt owed to China.

Fourthly, developing countries receiving loans from China may become 'economic vassals' of Beijing (Phillips 2017). The analyses of Chinese motives in the above section show that China initiated the BRI not only for economic gain. Although the BRI may bring benefits to the Chinese economy, trade and international cooperation, the main driver behind the initiative is China's domestic ambitions, and its political and strategic calculations. Thus, when receiving grants or loans from China, developing countries are exposed to risks that could weaken their national sovereignty. Some countries like India had doubts over this initiative and suspect that the BRI could be used as a smokescreen for Beijing to capture and assert control over the Indian Ocean. (Phillips 2017) In Southeast Asia, some experts are concerned that receiving Chinese financing will divide ASEAN, weakening its role, and making it difficult to come to a consensus on issues related to China, such as the South China Sea dispute. Countries in the region which receive major BRI investments might only respond to disputes in a highly moderated manner out of gratitude to Beijing (Le 2017).

In addition, developing countries also need to take into account the human and environmental risks posed by BRI projects. China's goal of investing in other countries is motivated by Beijing's own interests over than the interests of the local people in countries where they invest in. Therefore, economic gains will overshadow the safety and welfare of the local population. One example was the case of China National Offshore Oil Corporation's construction of a refinery at the end of the 1200-kilometer-long oil pipeline in Myanmar. The pipeline was built to avoid transshipment of oil to Yunnan via the Malacca Straits. On its end, Myanmar would receive US$13.81 million worth of commissions and the cost of transferring the oil was fixed at US$1 per ton. However, in 2013, local residents claimed that the refinery plant would produce paraxylene, the substance used to make plastic and polyester bottles. It is also considered to be very toxic to the human body if inhaled or swallowed. Although there is still no concrete evidence whether the plant would produce paraxylene or not, it was nevertheless completed and became operational in May 2017. (An Nhien 2017) This example shows that initiatives that link economic development are of great significance to many poor developing countries. However, when these initiatives do not respect the local community and the environment, they pose long-term negative implications for not only the stakeholders mentioned above, but also the sovereignty of the recipient country.

198 N. T. T. TRANG

Conclusion

In his opening remarks at the inaugural 2017 Belt and Road Forum, Xi said, "China will endeavor to build mutually beneficial relations with States participating in the Belt and Road Initiative." (Phillips 2017) Indeed, the perception of developing countries regarding the BRI is still positive on the whole. However, the analysis provided in this chapter shows that China's motivations in the BRI are not just to "build mutually beneficial relations" as Xi claimed. Developing countries need to understand the motivations of China behind the BRI projects, the potential impact on their country in order to determine the extent and scope of their participation in the BRI. They also need to adopt certain positions and principles in the process of joining the BRI in order to protect their sovereignty and interests while minimizing potential risks.

References

An Nhien. 2017. Những dự ánVành đaivà Con đường Trung Quốc muốn giấu (BRI Projects China wants to hide). Bao Dat Viet. http://baodatviet.vn/the-gioi/tin-tuc-24h/nhung-du-an-vanh-dai-va-con-duong-trung-quoc-muon-giau-3341028/.
Chin Helen. 2016. *The Belt and Road Initiative: 65 Countries and Beyond.* Global Sourcing, Fung Business Intelligence Centre, 3.
China's National Development and Reform Commission (NDRC). 2015. *Vision and Actions on Jointly Building Silk Road Economic Belt and 21st Century Maritime Silk Road.* http://en.ndrc.gov.cn/newsrelease/201503/t20150330_669367.html.
Ha Thu. 2015. Ngân hàng AIIB chính thức thành lập (AIIB is formally established). https://kinhdoanh.vnexpress.net/tin-tuc/quoc-te/ngan-hang-aiib-chinh-thuc-thanh-lap-3334005.html.
J.P. 2017, May 15. What Is China's Belt and Road Initiative? *The Economist.* https://www.economist.com/blogs/economist-explains/2017/05/economist-explains-11.
Khanh Lynh. Ông Tập kêu gọi APEC tham gia sáng kiến Vành đai và Con đường (Xi called for APEC to join the Belt and Road initiative). https://vnexpress.net/tin-tuc/the-gioi/ong-tap-keu-goi-apec-tham-gia-sang-kien-vanh-dai-va-con-duong-3585032.html.
Le, Hong Hiep. 2017. Belt and Road Initiative: Southeast Asia's Boon or Bane? *The Strategist.* https://www.aspistrategist.org.au/belt-road-initiative-southeast-asias-boon-bane/.

Lee, J-H., and Keegan Elmer. 2019, April 27. Can China Do Soft Power? Poorly Organised Yet Tightly Controlled Forum Raises Questions. *South China Morning Post*. https://www.scmp.com/news/china/diplomacy/article/3007953/can-china-do-soft-power-poorly-organised-yet-tightly.

Minh Son. 2017. Vành đaivà Con đường' – Toàn cầu hóa kiểu Trung Quốc (Belt and Road – Chinese styled-Globalization). https://vnexpress.net/projects/vanh-dai-va-con-duong-toan-cau-hoa-kieu-trung-quoc-3589083/index.html.

Pham, S.T. 2017. *Một vành đai, một con đường (OBOR): Chiến lược của Trung Quốc và hàm ý chính sách đối với Việt Nam (One Belt, One Road: China's Strategy and Policy Implications for Vietnam)*. Hanoi: Thegioi Publishing House.

Phillips, Tom. 2017. The $900 bn Question: What Is the Belt and Road Initiative? *The Guardian May 12th, 2017*. https://www.theguardian.com/world/2017/may/12/the-900bn-question-what-is-the-belt-and-road-initiative.

PART IV

Critical National Perspectives

CHAPTER 12

US Attitudes and Reactions Towards China's "Belt and Road" Initiative

Nguyen Thi Thanh Thuy

China's Belt and Road Initiative (BRI) is a colossal plan, with an estimated investment of a trillion US dollars in various infrastructure projects across Asia, Africa and Europe. Dozens of countries have agreed to join the BRI, to different extents. However, many other countries, including the United States, have suspected China's political, economic and military ambitions in implementing this initiative. In this chapter, the author focuses on analyzing the attitudes and reactions from the US, including the federal and state governments, as well as the business and scholarly communities, towards China's BRI. An analysis will also be done to help identify how they could potentially affect American interests as well as international affairs.

N. T. T. Thuy (✉)
Faculty of International Studies, University of Social Sciences and Humanities, Vietnam National University, Hanoi, Vietnam

© The Author(s) 2020
A. Chong, Q. M. Pham (eds.), *Critical Reflections on China's Belt & Road Initiative*, https://doi.org/10.1007/978-981-13-2098-9_12

ABOUT THE BELT AND ROAD INITIATIVE

In the last decade of the twentieth century, China achieved great economic success which was marked with consecutive high growth rates
annually. By the second decade of the twenty-first century, China has
become the second largest economy in the world. Thanks to its rapid economic development, China is able carry out massive projects across different fields in order to realize the Chinese Dream of national rejuvenation
and restoring China's status as a pre-eminent global power (Liu 2011).
One such enormous project would be the "One Belt, One Road Initiative",
or informally known as the New Silk Road, which references the ancient
Silk Road. It was initiated by President Xi Jinping in September 2013 and
was later renamed the "Belt and Road Initiative" (BRI) in May 2017.
(New Delhi Times Bureau 2017)[1]

The BRI is a mammoth undertaking, with the bulk of investments
coming from China. The investments are mainly in infrastructure projects located in dozens of countries in Asia, Africa, and Europe. It aims to
connect China with countries in the three continents along the so-called
"New Silk Road". The road consists of two major parts. The first part is
called the "Silk Road Economic Belt" (also known as the Land Silk
Road), connecting China's west and northwest regions with Central
Asia, Russia, Iran, Turkey, and Europe. The second part is named the
"Maritime Silk Road of the 21th Century", departing from China's ports
on its eastern coast to the South China Sea, the Indian Ocean, the Red
Sea, and to the Mediterranean Sea, creating a transport sea route con-
necting China with Southeast Asia, South Asia, Middle East, and Africa.
(Vo 2015; MinhSon 2017).

So far, China has implemented many mega projects along the BRI. On
the "Land Silk Road", China is building a high-speed road running from
China's Xinjiang autonomous region to Kyrgyzstan, Uzbekistan,
Tajikistan, Turkmenistan, Iran, and Turkey. Additionally, another road is
also built to connect China with Kazakhstan, Russia, and Europe.

As for the "Maritime Silk Road" in Southeast Asia, China has completed the construction of a 2400 kilometer-long pipeline from Myanmar
to China's Kunming province, reducing the time of oil transportation and

---

[1] According to observers, the word "One" is dropped from the original name of the program "One Belt, One Road" because "China is trying to avoid the impression that it wants
to control the increasingly international program, and make it a consultative process" (New
Delhi Times Bureau 2017).

avoiding a risky passage through the Malacca Straits. China is also interested in building the 102 kilometer-long Kra Canal in Thailand, which will connect the South China Sea to the Indian Ocean. The project is estimated to cost US$28 billion and will help to shorten the 1200-kilometre-long route by avoiding passage through the Malacca Straits. In South Asia, China sponsored the construction of a strategic port of Gwadar in Pakistan and a deep water port in Sri Lanka. When these two ports are in operation, they will be maritime hubs to receive Chinese exports and provide fuel for Chinese naval vessels.

In Africa, China is negotiating with the Northeast African state of Djibouti about constructing a naval base. In addition, Beijing has largely sponsored a US$4 billion project which has been carried out by Chinese companies to build a 466 mile-long electric train route running from Djibouti to the Ethiopian capital of Addis Ababa. China also helps to upgrade a train route between Mombasa and Nairobi in Kenya in order to facilitate the logistics flow of Chinese goods in the East African state. (Perlez and Yufan 2017).

Thus, projects under the BRI aim to build a powerful network of transport and communications infrastructure, creating favorable conditions to connect the inner provinces of China with the outside world, and help to narrow the development gap between the coastal regions and western China's remote interior. At the same time, the maritime transport system facilitates China's transportation of imported raw materials and petrol from the Middle East and Africa, while also making it easier for China to transport its exports. Moreover, the overseas infrastructure projects help open investment markets for China's US$3 trillion worth of idle capital, which accounted for 30 percent of the world's foreign reserves in February 2017, (MinhSon 2017), while bringing about other benefits in the diplomatic, security, and military fields for China.

To support the implementation of the BRI, China created a US$40 billion "Silk Road Fund" in November 2014. At the same time, China and more than 50 other countries jointly set up the Asian Infrastructure Investment Bank (AIIB) to sponsor the BRI's projects. On 29 June 2015, 50 out of 57 AIIB founding countries signed the AIIB Charter in Beijing with an initial capital of US$100 billion. With a 30 percent share, China was the largest contributor, essentially giving it a veto on the bank's activities. China was also the largest donor in the New Development Bank (NDB) of the BRICS group, comprising Brazil, Russia, India, China, and South Africa, in order to take advantage of this new financial institution for its BRI projects (Jiang 2017; Vo 2015; MinhSon 2017). Since the launch of the BRI, China has invested hundreds of billions of dollars in numerous infrastructure projects in BRI countries coupled with the participation of thousands of Chinese enterprises. By 2016, with the support of the Chinese Ministry of Commerce, 77 projects have been implemented in 36 countries and territories with a total investment value of US$24.19 billion. These projects will eventually add more than US$70 billion in value. In addition, the BRI projects also receive financial support from other Chinese financial institutions. For example, the Export-Import Bank of China financed 1279 projects with the loan balance exceeding CNY671.4 billion. Meanwhile, the total investment of projects supported by the Silk Road Fund has topped US$80 billion (Jiang 2017). These projects are implemented mainly in developing countries in Asia and Africa, which have great demand for infrastructure construction, but lack the capital to do so.

On Chinese media as well as through international forums, China has made efforts to propagate the benefits of the BRI for the common good of the international community (Xinhua 2017c, d). As a result, many countries have joined the BRI. Meanwhile, a number of Western developed countries, including the United States, are suspicious and concerned about the economic efficiency of the BRI as well as China's diplomatic and strategic security motives of implementing this plan. For example, some argue that the Chinese BRI can be equated with the American Marshall Plan implemented in Europe after World War II, while at the same time being filled with political motives and impose various conditions on BRI participants (Washington Post 2017; Perlez and Yufan 2017, Xinhua 2017a). Others say that the BRI indicates China's ambitions for global leadership, thus challenging the US-led order even though China's power still lags behind the United States (White 2017; Sputniknews 2017). Some experts also note that rail and seaport projects under China's BRI can be potentially used to benefit Beijing's military besides their oft-cited economic benefits. Hence the BRI will in the long term help China to realize its ambitions of increasing its economic power and influence in the world (Johnson et al. 2017).

In order to dispel international skepticism and to attract more countries to join the BRI, China hosted the Beijing International Cooperation for the Belt and Road Forum (BRF) in May 2017. According to the Xinhua News Agency, the BRF attracted the participation of delegates from 130 countries and regions, and leaders from 29 countries, representing more than two thirds of the world's population and 90 percent of total global GDP (Xinhua 2017d). At the forum, Chinese President Xi Jinping praised the enormous significance of the BRI, calling it the project of the century which contributes to the building of a new type of international relations in which all parties can enjoy win-win cooperation. President Xi also affirmed that the Chinese "have no intention to interfere in other countries' internal affairs, export our own social system and model of development, or impose our own will on others...[and] have no intention to form a small group that would dismantle stability but we hope to create a big family of harmonious coexistence" (Xinhua 2017c; Sputniknews 2017; Hillman 2017).[2] According to China, the BRF is a historic international event which saw successes in the areas of policy, infrastructure, trade, finance, and people-to-people connectivity. At the same time, the forum "sent a positive signal for all parties to work together to build a community of shared future, which would be extremely important for China and the world" (Xinhua 2017d). Following the success of the inaugural BRF, China convened a second BRF in 2019 to consolidate commitments to the BRI.

Thus, since the inception of the BRI, China has made tremendous financial investment alongside diplomatic and propaganda efforts to carry out this enormous project. Initial economic results can be observed, but it is still too early to fully assess the impact of the projects that China has undertaken in many countries around the world. In fact, countries around the world have had different attitudes and responses to China's BRI which stem from their respective calculations and national interests (White 2017). Differences in attitudes and responses to China's initiative are also evident in different political circles and communities in the United States.

DIFFERENCES IN US ATTITUDES AND RESPONSES TO THE BRI

There have been a huge variety in attitudes and responses made by the American government both at the federal and state levels, the business community, as well as American academics and scholars. Among them, some suggest that the US get involved in the BRI for specific economic

[2] Observers are skeptical about who will be the head of the "big family" that President Xi has talked about. This is considered to be one of the most ambiguous and confusing aspects of the BRI (Sputniknews 2017).

interests. There are, however, disagreements over the economic viability of the proposed projects, and some even hold suspicions of China's political, security and military motives in implementing the BRI.

Attitudes and Reactions of the US Federal Government

Diplomatically, President Trump's administration officially expressed support for China's BRI. After the first session of the US-China Comprehensive Economic Dialogue on 11 May 2017, US Treasury Secretary Steven T. Mnuchin, US Commerce Secretary Wilbur Ross, and Chinese Deputy Prime Minister Wang Yang, reached a consensus on the initial commitments under the 100-day plan and objectives for next steps between the two countries. The initial actions of the U.S.-China Economic Cooperation 100-Day Plan consists of ten commitments, and the last issue of the Plan spells that "The United States recognizes the importance of China's One Belt and One Road initiative and is to send delegates to attend the Belt and Road Forum in Beijing May 14–15" (Office of Public Affairs 2017). At a White House Press Conference on 5 May 2017, White House spokesman Sean Spicer said that the US government was considering further cooperation with China under the BRI as it is a "major trade initiative" and "obviously, trade is a major issue for us [the United States]" (Office of the Press Secretary 2017). Later, at a White House meeting between President Trump and China's top diplomat, State Councilor Yang Jiechi, on 22 June 2017, Trump said "the US hopes to cooperate with China in projects related to the Belt and Road Initiative" (China Daily 2017).

In practice, however, the actions of the Trump administration in response to the BRI have vacillated from their statements. This can be clearly seen in two specific cases. The first case is that the United States does not participate in the AIIB, which was initiated by China. Just before the bank went into operation, the US government officially expressed its views. In a hearing focused on the state of the international financial system before the House Financial Services Committee in March 2015, then-US Treasury Secretary Jacob J. Lew raised concerns about the AIIB. He said that "There are obviously vast needs in Asia and many parts of the world for infrastructure investment. Our concern has always [not been] is there going to be an investment institution, but will it adhere to the kinds of high standards that the international financial institutions have developed? Will it protect the rights of workers, the environment, deal with corruption issues appropriately? Our point all along has been that anyone joining needs to ask those questions at the outset. And I hope before the final commitments are made, anyone who lends their name to this organization will make sure that the governance is appropriate" (Latortue 2015). In addition, Lew stated that, "for the United Sates, we will continue to engage directly with China and to coordinate with the rest of our international partners to provide concrete suggestions on how the AIIB can best adopt and implement high quality standards" (Latortue 2015). In this regard, Lew's testimony has shown that the United States is suspicious of the AIIB's international financial standards, and the United States only offers advice on how the bank should operate in accordance with international financial standards of the established international financial institutions such as the World Bank or the International Monetary Fund, in which America plays a leading role.

Therefore, if America joined the AIIB, it means that America would accept the standards set by China and would recognize China's leading role in this international financial institution. According to experts, the AIIB is a financial instrument that helps China increase its national interests in the financial sector, especially to accelerate the internationalization of the Renminbi, compete with the established international financial institutions, and make China an Asian financial hub (BaoLinh 2015). In the context of China's rising power and its aims to compete for global leadership, the Trump administration is unlikely to concede to Beijing's ambitions. Hence, should the US join the AIIB, it would in fact help China to fulfill its ambition at Washington's expense.

The second case is the US delegation's attendance of China's BRI Forum in May 2017. The forum attracted the participation of 29 heads of state from all over the world, including Russian President Vladimir Putin and Italian Prime Minister Paolo Gentiloni, among others. Breaking with decorum, the US government sent Matt Pottinger, who was the Special Assistant to the President and a Senior Director of the National Security Council for Asia, as the head of the US delegation to the BRI Forum. That showed that the Trump administration does not appreciate the importance of the BRI Forum. Disappointed Chinese officials said that Washington's action was a "sharp contrast" from the Trump administration's previous attitude of "recognizing the importance of the BRI" (Liu 2017). In addition, Pottinger urged China to ensure transparency in government procurement before implementing any BRI project during the forum. He also said that "transparency will ensure that privately-owned companies can bid in a fair process, and that the cost of participating in tenders will be worth the investment" (Perlez and Bradsher 2017). In this aspect, Mr. Pottinger's remarks showed US concerns about transparency regarding the effectiveness of these Chinese-initiated projects. It was also an indirect demonstration of concern towards the BRI. Thus, American concerns about the international financial standards of the AIIB and the transparency of the BRI can partly explain why the US federal government does not want to join China's BRI.

Attitudes and Reactions of Individual US Officials

When discussing China's BRI, both incumbent and former US federal government officials have expressed different opinions. Some of them share the Trump administration's views in questioning China's motives for launching the BRI. For example, at a Senate hearing on global threats on 11 May 2017, U.S. national intelligence director Dan Coats said that the BRI was "aggressive" and that the initiative had "a strategy", implying it as a threat to the interests of the United States. Coats's comments were rebutted by Chinese media which claimed that he had exaggerated "fears raised in some countries and [chosen] to highlight the difficulties some projects have encountered" (Xinhua 2017b). Other US federal government officials also shared Coats's view. For example, Paul Haenle, a former director of the China section of the US National Security Council, commented that "China needs to realize that the way it sees BRI is unlikely to be the same as other countries do", and that countries like the United States "cannot fail to see [the BRI] through [the] geopolitical lens to assume that China is trying to expand its influence" (MinhSon 2017). In another view, Max Baucus, a former US ambassador to China, said China's BRI has "if not frightened, then at least concerned, a lot of countries along the way" (Griffiths et al. 2017).

However, some other former officials of the US federal government thought otherwise, and called on the US to cooperate more with China on the economy and trade, including participating in the BRI. For example, in a November 2016 opinion piece in the South China Morning Post, former CIA Director James Woolsey, who at the time served as a senior advisor to U.S. President-elect Donald Trump on national security and intelligence, said that the United States made a "strategic mistake" by not joining the AIIB. He also encouraged the Trump administration to cooperate with China in joining the BRI (Stone 2017a). Another former US federal government official, Marc Grossman, holds a similar view. Marc Grossman is a former US diplomat and served as US ambassador to Turkey, special representative for Afghanistan and Pakistan, Assistant Secretary of State for European affairs, and Undersecretary of State for Political Affairs. In an April 2017 interview with China's Xinhua News Agency in New York, Grossman said that "China's message has to be clear that the Belt and Road Initiative is a joint project on a voluntary basis", and "not some effort by China to control a lot of other countries." He also said that the BRI has "positive things, so I'm sure there are lots of reasons to be interested in the Belt and Road Initiative, but for me, it's the question of economic growth" (Yang and Zhang 2017). In yet another interesting interview with *The People's Daily*, Stapleton Roy, a senior State Department diplomat and a former US ambassador to China in the 1990s, said that "the United States and China should show respect to each other, expand shared interests, and manage disagreements between the two countries". At the same time, Roy urged US businesses to engage in BRI projects with the belief that it would benefit US businesses (Zhang 2017).

Thus, the attitudes and reactions of US officials are divided into two groups which respectively support and oppose China's BRI. Their opinions, regardless of which group they belong to, stem from their personal reasons. These reasons could either be showing support or expressing disagreement with the Trump administration, or it could also be due to their understanding of Sino-American relations in general and of China itself. Whatever the reasons may be, the differences in views among these officials have divided public opinion in the US with regards to Sino-American relations in general and the issue of America's participation in the BRI.

Attitudes and Reactions of State Governments and the American Business Community

As the United States comprises of 50 states, it is not possible to analyze the views of all 50 states within this chapter. However, states which support the BRI share similarities such as geographical locations which favor trade with the Chinese, or have direct and lasting economic relations with them. Two typical cases come from the states of Oregon and California. Both states are located on the American Pacific Coast, and possess large ports that favour trade with China, which is located on the other side of the Pacific.

In the case of Oregon (Wikipedia 2017b),[3] it is a state that has extensive relations with China ranging from commerce, culture, and education. China is Oregon's largest trading partner, with exports to China reaching $5.8 billion in 2016 while enjoying a trade surplus of $3.7 billion. Oregon exports agricultural products, semiconductor devices, and other products to China. In addition, more than 20,000 jobs in the state depend on trade with China. Compared to other US states, Chinese tourists make up the largest proportion of tourist revenue in Oregon (Xinhua 2017f). Notably, Oregon is one of eight US states that enjoy trade surpluses with China. This is very significant as the US perennially suffers from trade deficits with China (Morrison 2017).[4] The tremendous economic and commercial benefits are the main drivers for the Oregon state government to strengthen its economic and trade links with China. In July 2017, the Oregon state legislature passed a resolution on strengthening economic and trade relations with China, becoming the first state in the US to legalize economic and trade relations with China. It is in this context that the Oregon state government supports the BRI. Oregon governor Kate Brown affirmed the importance of economic and trade relations with China in a 2017 interview with Xinhua, and stated that she saw many opportunities for Oregon to participate in the BRI (Xinhua 2017f).

In the case of California (Wikipedia 2017a),[5] it is an economic juggernaut among the 50 states and also boasts a significant range of longstanding economic and trade relations with China. California's Port of Los Angeles is the largest in the US. It accounted for 43 percent of total US imports and received 90 percent of total goods coming from Asia, of which two thirds were from China (People's Daily Online 2017a). California is also famous for its Silicon Valley, where many high-tech electronics and semiconductor companies are based. Many corporations have longstanding business ties with their Chinese partners. For example, the Apple company had 346 equipment suppliers from China, which was almost half of its 766 global equipment suppliers. Apple's iPhones are

[3] This is the 9th largest state in the United States with an area of 254,806 km² with a population of 4 million, and total GDP of more than $200 billion, (Wikipedia 2017b).

[4] According to data from the US International Trade Commission (USITC), between 2012 and 2016, US trade with China continued to suffer deficit at over $300 billion per year (2015, $367 billion, 2016: $347 billion) (Morrison 2017, p. 3).

[5] It is the most populous state in the United States with a population of 39 million, the third largest state in the United States with an area of 423,970 square kilometers, and the largest state in the United States with total GDP of $2603 billion (2016) (Wikipedia 2017a).

predominantly assembled in China, where labor costs are low, and thus contributed to Apple's high competitiveness and enormous profits (Morrison 2017, pp. 14–15). The enormous benefits resulting from trade and economic relations with Asian countries across the Pacific, particularly with China, have become a major reason for Californian leaders to support the BRI. According to Jim MacLellan, the Director of Trade Development for the Port of Los Angeles, "China's Belt and Road Initiative is a valuable opportunity for the United States...(the) Port of Los Angeles can be America's maritime outpost to integrate into the plan...(and) can become a key maritime hub for "Belt and Road" projects in the Pacific, even making inroads beyond the coasts of North America and South America" (People's Daily Online 2017a). California governor Jerry Brown was also an enthusiastic supporter of the BRI. According to Brown, California was willing to join the BRI and looked forward to a stronger cooperative relationship with China in trade, investment, clean technology and environmental protection. Brown also wanted China to invest in two major transportation projects in California, including putting four to five million electric cars on its roads by 2030 and build a high-speed rail line from San Francisco to Los Angeles (People's Daily Online 2017b).

Similarly, the American business community has been enthusiastically supporting the BRI. They argue that they have many opportunities to invest and provide equipment for BRI projects. Their support for the BRI is due to one fundamental reason—China has been one of America's leading economic partners for years. In fact, many big American companies have been profiting from doing business with their Chinese counterparts, especially Apple as mentioned above.

In the case of General Motors (GE), it signed a contract in 2014 to supply $400 billion worth of equipment to Chinese engineering and construction companies for their overseas projects. In 2016, GE received a total of US$2.3 billion worth of orders from Chinese companies and planned to bid for an additional US$7 billion in orders for natural gas turbines and other power equipment in the next 18 months. Rachel Duan, the chief executive of GE China, spoke optimistically about the BRI projects, suggesting that, "when the roads are built, when the ports are built, when the power plants are built, I think the other opportunities will come" (Bradsher and Tang 2017). Jacob Frenkel, chairman of JPMorgan Chase International, also commented positively on the BRI. He thought that it would very beneficial as it would connect hundreds of millions of peoples and markets. Hence, people should not worry about it. (MinhSon 2017).

Michael Bloomberg, the founder of Bloomberg and former mayor of New York, said that "China-US cooperation is of vital importance for the current global challenges...China's growth has spurred [the] US economy, and the country's policy to further open its market for international investors is also inspiring" (Zhang et al. 2017).

For the American business community, the attractiveness of the BRI lies in its economic benefits and the Chinese are fully aware of this. Hence they have been actively reaching out to the American business community in order to bypass the US government (Stone 2017b). In fact, China has held many business conferences and forums in both the United States and in China to discuss the BRI. These publicity efforts have attracted many major American companies. The positive responses given by the American business community during these conferences clearly show their support for the BRI. (Xinhua 2017c, e; Gao and Jin 2017).

Attitudes and Reactions of American Political Observers and Scholars

American experts on China and Sino-American relations argue that the BRI's motives and impacts are concentrated in the economic and political-security fields, and both carry significant risks. From an economic point of view, opinions have been quite diverse, and point out the motives and economic benefits of China's implementation of the BRI. According to Nick Marro, an analyst with the Economist Intelligence Unit (EIU) and former US Department of Commerce official, Beijing aims to use BRI as a platform to create overseas demand for its domestic overproduction. In Marro's view, Beijing's previous overseas investments had earned a bad reputation for not uplifting local economies. One very salient example would be its investments in Africa, where large state-owned enterprises ship in Chinese workers instead of hiring local labor, and re-export the mined raw materials back home (Griffiths and Stout 2017). Similarly, Christopher Balding, Professor of Political Economy at the University of California, and concurrently a lecturer at Beijing University, doubts the effectiveness of the BRI projects. He argues that Beijing has a negative track record of their overseas investments, pointing to widespread problems, such as in Myanmar, Sri Lanka, and Venezuela, all of whom serviced China's loans intended for investment in Chinese-backed infrastructure projects (Griffiths and Stout 2017). Other US experts posit that such countries need to enjoy trade surpluses with China in order to repay their debts with Beijing. However, this is not possible as China always has a trade surplus with those countries. According to data from Tom Orlik, a Bloomberg Intelligence economist, China had a trade surplus of US$250 billion in 2016 with BRI countries. For example, Sri Lanka and Pakistan have respective trade deficits with China worth US$2 billion and US$9 billion respectively (Balding 2017). In addition, Clyde Prestowitz, president of the Washington-based Economic Strategy Institute, said that the BRI is a "brilliant strategic move" by Beijing, but faces serious risks of countries defaulting on their debts. In the case of Venezuela, Prestowitz argues that Caracas would not repay its debt, and foresees similar developments in the future (Mascarenhas 2017).

In the field of security and politics, US experts and scholars point out that China's motive is to expand its global influence by taking a leading role in a new form of globalization manifested in the BRI. According to Professor David M. Lampton, director of the Johns Hopkins University's School of Advanced International Studies (SAIS), China can easily impose its rules and easily shape the economic belts and communities along the BRI, as it is the key player in this initiative. (MinhSon 2017). Sharing Lampton's views, Balding holds that the BRI project comes across as more of a diplomatic effort to increase its global influence than one which is purely economic. If successful, the BRI could see China overtake the US as the world's preeminent superpower (Griffiths and Stout 2017). Senior experts of the Centre for Strategic and International Studies (CSIS) in Washington D.C. commented on the BRI's elasticity in terms of its scope and scale, "but all signs point to an ambitious and consequential endeavor: a future where all roads lead to Beijing". They also contended that "strategically, the United States has an interest in ensuring that no single entity dominates the Eurasian landmass, where a majority of the world's people and economic power resides" (Johnson et al. 2017). Similarly, analysts at the American Stratfor Strategic Research Center expressed concerns about China's motives for implementing the BRI. They argued that the BRI "is not just a combination of infrastructure projects but also a carefully designed strategy to pursue China's geopolitical goals in Europe and Asia...[; tries] to make China's economy stronger, [and] prevent the United States from imposing embargo against China from a distance" (Bao Linh 2015). American experts also warned that Chinese projects in each of the BRI countries have been carefully calculated to bring strategic benefits for Beijing (Perlez and Yufan 2017).

Overall, although the opinions of American academics and think-tank specialists were expressed in different ways, they were all negative towards the BRI and question China's economic and security-political motives for implementing the initiative. As they are specialists in their field of research and possess profound knowledge of China and Sino-American relations, their opinions and warnings should be heeded.

Concluding Remarks

Studying the attitudes and reactions of different political circles and communities in the United States show that despite support from some quarters, the US government is firm about its position to avoid participating in the BRI. Overtly, Washington argues that the BRI does not meet international financial standards and transparency. However, the main reason for staying outside the BRI is strategic. This is because the BRI is perceived as a tool for China to implement the so-called Chinese Dream of restoring China's global stature. In this sense, China could potentially unseat America as the most powerful nation in the world and challenge the US-led world order. Hence, participating in the BRI means that Washington would be indirectly helping China pursue its ambitions at the expense of the United States.

At this point, two questions should be raised: Could the implementation of the BRI be hindered by the absence of the United States? What are possible impacts of the BRI on the US should it be successfully implemented? Regarding the first question, the reality is that China enjoys many advantages to continue the BRI at present. In terms of finance, it has the world's largest foreign reserves of nearly US$3 trillion, making it easy to invest in key projects of the BRI. In terms of its domestic politics, the fifth generation of Chinese leaders exercise more power compared to their predecessors and embrace a long-term strategic vision. According to Vietnamese experts, the current Chinese leadership has made "initial changes that have profound effects on the global power balance, the political life of all nations, and political and economic institutions, especially those in the Asia-Pacific" (Nguyen 2015).

Moreover, the activities of the Chinese government are supported by the following factors—the generally stable domestic political situation, abundant financial resources, the support of many Chinese billionaires living inside and outside of China, and the strong support of a rapidly modernizing military. In terms of external relations, the BRI's infrastructure projects meet the investment needs of many developing countries in Asia and Africa, and even some in Europe. Therefore, it was easy to attract fairly broad-based political support for the projects in these countries. In spite of the risks in joining BRI projects, many countries willingly accept Chinese investment. With so many advantages, China enjoys opportunities to continue with the BRI even without American participation in order to fulfill its Chinese Dream.

On the second question, the Trump administration's pursuit of an "America First" policy is creating a void in international affairs, leaving a political and economic vacuum for China to play a leading role in the international political arena. The BRI is one of China's methods to expand its strategic and political influence throughout the globe at America's expense. According to warnings from American experts, Washington is unable to stifle China's global ambitions as the BRI puts China in the driving seat. They also suggested that if the United States and its allies are determined to counter China's challenges to the current US-led global order, the Trump administration would need a powerful and ambitious global economic vision equal to that of China (White 2017; Griffiths et al. 2017).

Although the United States remains the world's number one power in many ways, its position is beset with a number of difficulties, such as budget and trade deficits, a huge partisan and societal divide, as well as decreasing trust and confidence in America's global leadership and governance. This has to a certain extent limited the capacity of the United States to respond to profound changes in the international arena. In fact, since his inauguration in January 2017, President Trump has struggled to make good on his domestic and foreign policy goals as a result of internal divisions. Meanwhile, the Chinese view the current situation in the United States as a failure of the American model and they are optimistic that "the Chinese model is not destined to fail simply because it does not look like the American model of democracy". They also say that a "malfunctioning" U.S. leadership is making China "great again" (Stones and Chengliang 2017; CNBC 2017).

At this point, based on President Trump's campaign promise to "Make America Great Again", coupled with China's belief and determination to attain national rejuvenation, three additional new questions need to be raised. First, will the Trump administration credibly restore American prestige and power at home and abroad? Second, is it possible for China to return to its former glory with the success of the BRI? Lastly, will it be possible for both of the two powers to be in the global spotlight at the same time in the foreseeable future? At present, there are no concrete answers for all three questions. However, if any of these questions become reality, they will certainly have a great impact on regional and global affairs. To this end, all other countries should prepare themselves for enormous changes that lie ahead for the global order.

References

Balding, Christopher. 2017. *Can China afford its Belt and Road?* https://www.bloomberg.com/view/articles/2017-05-17/can-china-afford-its-belt-and-road. Accessed 17 May 2017.

Bao Linh. 2015. *Tham vong thuc su sau "Mot con duong, Mot vanh dai" cua Trung Quoc* [China's real ambition behind the "One Belt, One Road"]. http://www.tinmoi.vn/tham-vong-thuc-su-sau-mot-con-duong-mot-vanh-dai-cua-trung-quoc-011365382.html. Accessed 30 June 2015.

Bradsher, Keith, and Ailin Tang. 2017, May 15. As China Builds, U.S. Firms Want In. *New York Times*, p. B1.

China Daily. 2017. *Progress in ties showing benefits, Yang tells Trump.* http://en.people.cn/n3/2017/0624/c90000-9232644.html.   Accessed   24 June 2017.

CNBC. 2017. *"Making China Great Again": Beijing-run Media Crows as US Stumbles.* http://www.cnbc.com/2017/07/19/making-china-great-again-beijing-run-media-crows-as-us-stumbles.html. Accessed 19 July 2017.

Gao, Pan, and Minmin Jin. 2017. *Chinese, U.S. Entrepreneurs Pledge to Boost Bilateral Trade, Investment.* http://en.people.cn/business/n3/2017/0719/c90778-9243823.html. Accessed 19 July 2017.

Griffiths, James, and Kristie Lu Stout. 2017. *Just What Is This One Belt, One Road Thing Anyway?* http://edition.cnn.com/2017/05/11/asia/china-one-belt-one-road-explainer/index.html. Accessed 12 May 2017.

Griffiths, James, Kristie Lu Stout, David McKenzie, and Serena Dong. 2017. *China's New World Order: Xi, Putin and Others Meet for Belt and Road Forum.* http://edition.cnn.com/2017/05/13/asia/china-belt-and-road-forum-xi-putin-erdogan. Accessed 14 May 2017.

Hillman, Jonathan. 2017. *China's "Belt and Road" Initiative Must Become a Strategy.* https://www.csis.org/analysis/chinas-belt-road-initiative-must-become-strategy. Accessed 12 May 2017.

Jiang, Jie. 2017. *China to Pour Trillions into Belt and Road Projects.* http://en.people.cn/n3/2017/0713/c90000-9241409.html. Accessed 13 July 2017.

Johnson, Christopher K., Matthew P. Goodman, and Jonathan E. Hillman. 2017. *President Xi Jinping's "Belt and Road" Forum.* https://www.csis.org/analysis/president-xi-jinpings-belt-and-road-forum. Accessed 9 May 2017.

Latortue, Alexia. 2015. *Secretary Lew's Hearing on the International Financial System.* https://www.treasury.gov/connect/blog/Pages/Secretary-Lew%E2%80%99s-Hearing-on-the-International-Financial-System.aspx. Accessed 19 Mar 2015.

Liu, Minh Phuc. 2011. *Giac mo Trung Quoc: Tu duy nuoc lon va dinh vi chien luoc trong thoi dai hau My,* Nha xuat ban Thoi dai, Ha Noi 2011. [Liu, Ming Fu, *China's dream: Great power's thinking and strategic positioning in the post-American times,* Times Publishers, Hanoi 2011].

Liu, Jianxi. 2017. (People's Daily). *B&R Can Open Opportunities for China-US Cooperation.* http://en.people.cn/n3/2017/0515/c90000-9215874.html. Accessed 15 May 2017.

Mascarenhas, Bianca. 2017. *Here's why China's 'Belt and Road' Initiative Is Risky – Think Tanker.* https://www.cnbc.com/2017/07/18/heres-why-chinas-belt-and-road-initiative-is-risky-think-tanker-says.html. Accessed 18 July 2017.

MinhSon. 2017. *'Vanh dai va Con duong' – Toan cau hoa kieu Trung Quoc* ["Belt and Road" – Chinese Globalization]. http://vnexpress.net/projects/vanh-dai-va-con-duong-toan-cau-hoa-kieu-trung-quoc-3589083/index.html. Accessed 24 May 2017.

Morrison, Wayne M. 2017, April 24. *China-U.S. Trade Issues.* Congressional Research Service, 7-5700, www.crs.gov, RL33536, p. 3.

New Delhi Times Bureau. 2017. *Few from West Drawn by China's One Belt, One Road conference.* https://www.newdelhitimes.com/few-from-west-drawn-by-chinas-one-belt-one-road-conference123. Accessed 19 April 2017.

Nguyen, Thai Yen Huong (ed). 2015. *The he lanh dao thu nam cua Trung Quoc: Nhung dieu chinh chinh sach voi My va cac tac dong toi khu vuc Chau A – Thai Binh Duong* [The fifth generation of Chinese leaders: Policy changes toward the United States and their implications on the Asia – Pacific]. National Political Publishing House, Hanoi 2015, p. 9.

Office of Public Affairs. (The White House). 2017. *JOINT RELEASE: Initial results of the 100-Day Action Plan of the U.S. – China Comprehensive Economic Dialogue.* https://www.commerce.gov/news/press-releases/2017/05/joint-release-initial-results-100-day-action-plan-us-china-comprehensive. Accessed 11 May 2017.

Office of the Press Secretary. (The White House). 2017. *Press briefing by Press Secretary Sean Spicer, 5/12/2017, #47.* https://www.whitehouse.gov/the-press-office/2017/05/12/press-briefing-press-secretary-sean-spicer-5122017-47. Accessed 12 May 2017.

People's Daily Online. 2017a. *Los Angeles Port Would Bring US into Belt and Road Initiative: US Executive.* http://en.people.cn/n3/2017/0519/c90000-9218042.html. Accessed 19 May 2017.

———. 2017b. *Visiting California Governor Looks to China for High-speed Rail Inspiration.* http://en.people.cn/n3/2017/0608/c90000-9225976.html. Accessed 8 June 2017.

Perlez, Jane, and Keith Bradsher. 2017. Xi Jinping Positions China at Center of New Economic Order. *New York Times*. https://www.nytimes. com/2017/05/14/world/asia/xi-jinping-one-belt-one-road-china. html?mabReward=ACTM_MP1&recp=0&moduleDetail=recommendations-0&action=click&contentCollection=Business%20Day&region=Footer&modu le=WhatsNext&version=WhatsNext&contentID=WhatsNext&src=recg&pgt ype=article.

Perlez, Jane, and Huang Yufan. 2017. Behind China's $1 trillion plan to shake up the economic order. *New York Times*, https://www.nytimes. com/2017/05/13/business/china-railway-one-belt-one-road-1-trillion-plan. html?action=click&contentCollection=Asia%20Pacific&module=RelatedCover age&region=EndOfArticle&pgtype=article. Accessed 13 May 2017.

Sputniknews. 2017. *New Silk Road Indicates China's Ambition for Global Leadership*. https://sputniknews.com/world/201705161053654539-china-silk-road-leadership. Accessed 16 May 2017.

Stone, Curtis. 2017a. (People's Daily Online). *U.S. Is Welcome to Join 'Symphony' of the Belt and Road Initiative*. http://en.people.cn/n3/2017/0428/c90000-9209096.html. Accessed 28 April 2017.

———. 2017b. People's Daily Online. *Op-Ed: Deepening Engagement with U.S. Business Community Is the Best Bet for China*. http://en.people.cn/n3/2017/0519/c90000-9217957.html. Accessed 19 May 2017.

Stone, Curtis, and Wu Chengliang. (People's Daily Online). 2017. *Op-Ed: The Malfunctioning of the US System Is Making China "Great Again."* http://en.people.cn/n3/2017/0718/c90000-9243062.html. Accessed 19 July 2017.

Vo, Anh Tuan. 2015. *Mot vanh dai mot con duong* [One Belt, One Road]. http://baoquocte.vn/mot-vanh-dai-mot-con-duong-15933.html. Accessed 2 Aug 2015.

Washington Post (Editorial Board of the). 2017. China Has a Plan to Become a Global Superpower. It Probably Won't Work. *The Washington Post*, https://www.washingtonpost.com/opinions/global-opinions/china-has-a-plan-to-become-a-global-superpower-it-probably-wont-work/2017/05/15/02f22e7 2-3998-11e7-8854-21f359183e8c_story.html?utm_term=.42905e7027a5. Accessed 15 May 2017.

White, Hugh. 2017. *China's One Belt, One Road to Challenge US-led Order*. http://www.straitstimes.com/opinion/chinas-one-belt-one-road-to-chal-lenge-us-led-order. Accessed 25 April 2017.

Wikipedia. 2017a. *California*. https://en.wikipedia.org/wiki/California. Accessed 27 Aug 2017.

———. 2017b. *Oregon*. https://en.wikipedia.org/wiki/Oregon. Accessed 27 Aug 2017.

Xinhua. 2017a. *Can We Equate Marshall Plan with Belt and Road Initiative?* http://en.people.cn/n3/2017/0513/c90000-9214847.html. Accessed 13 May 2017.

———. 2017b. *Commentary: Is China's B&R Initiative Just Hegemony in Disguise?* http://en.people.cn/n3/2017/0514/c90000-9214963.html. Accessed 14 May 2017.

———. 2017c. *Full Text of President Xi's Speech at Opening of Belt and Road Forum.* http://en.people.cn/n3/2017/0515/c90000-9215493.html. Accessed 15 May 2017.

———. 2017d. *Belt and Road Forum Points Clear Way for Future Cooperation: Chinese State Councilor.* http://en.people.cn/n3/2017/0518/c90000-9217031.html. Accessed 18 May 2017.

———. 2017e. *China, U.S. Businesses Call for Two-way Openness in Trade, Investment.* http://en.people.cn/n3/2017/0621/c90000-9231523.html. Accessed 21 June 2017.

———. 2017f. *Interview: Oregon Governor Calls Relationship with China "Critically Important" for Local Economy.* http://en.people.cn/n3/2017/0709/c90000-9239091.html. Accessed 9 July 2017.

Yang, Shilong, and Zhihuan Zhang. (Xinhua). 2017. Interview: Belt and Road Initiative to Boost Sustainable Economic Development – Former U.S. Diplomat. http://en.people.cn/n3/2017/0428/c90000-9208952.html. Accessed 28 April 2017.

Zhang, Penghui. (People's Daily Online). 2017. *Chinese, US Leaders to Work for Positive Outcomes from Bilateral Ties.* http://en.people.cn/n3/2017/0403/c90000-9198564.html. Accessed 3 April 2017.

Zhang, Niansheng, Miao Yin, and Bingxin Li. (People's Daily Online). 2017. *Chinese, US Think Tanks Discuss Mutually Beneficial Cooperation.* http://en.people.cn/n3/2017/0627/c90000-9233912.html. Accessed 27 June 2017.

CHAPTER 13

China's Belt and Road Initiative (BRI): Challenges and Opportunities for Vietnam

Pham Thi Thu Huyen and Ngo Tuan Thang

Overview of the BRI

The Silk Road was formed in the second-century BC and was named after the most popularly traded product along the path—Chinese silk. This transcontinental trading route continued between the main East and West corridors for centuries. The relations emerging on this path were an important element in developing the civilizations in China, India, Persia, Europe and Eastern Africa. Trade generated political and economic commingling among the nations. Besides silk, there were other important ideas being exchanged too, including those on religion, philosophy and technology.

The Belt and Road Initiative (BRI), as proposed by Chinese President Xi Jinping in 2013, is meant to restore the historic Silk Road Economic Belt and the Maritime Silk Road. This initiative includes five interconnected sectors: policy, infrastructure, trade, finance and manpower. In particular, the

P. T. T. Huyen • N. T. Thang (✉)
University of Social Sciences and Humanities, Vietnam National University, Hanoi, Vietnam

© The Author(s) 2020
A. Chong, Q. M. Pham (eds.), *Critical Reflections on China's Belt & Road Initiative*, https://doi.org/10.1007/978-981-13-2098-9_13

implementation of this initiative includes the measures to promote trade and investment; developing the infrastructure of railways, highways, freeways, seaports, telecommunications, energy pipelines and warehouses; cooperation between industrial and sub-regional economies; cooperation in finance; and promoting people-to-people exchanges.

The BRI connects East and Central Asia, the Middle East, North Africa and Europe. The Maritime Silk Road connects China to Europe via the South China Sea and the Indian Ocean, and stretches across to the South Pacific also via the South China Sea. In December 2014, President Xi announced that China pledged US$40 billion to establish the Silk Road Fund (Trong 2017). This showcased that the BRI is a trade initiative and a large scale economic connectivity strategy that is meant to promote the cooperation among countries and regions not only in economics but also socio-culturally.

Vietnam, a member of ASEAN, holds an essential position in the BRI. It has the intention to cooperate in the Initiative framework in order to efficiently exploit the potentials and advantages that they would receive across the geographical reach of the BRI. In the context of the growing relationship between Vietnam and China, the cooperation has created opportunities for the two parties to work together to promote international cooperation and mutual development. At the same time, Sino-Vietnamese cooperation will also be accompanied by serious challenges.

VIETNAM'S PERSPECTIVE

Since the normalization of relations in 1991, Sino-Vietnam relations in general have rapidly developed. In 2008, the two countries established a comprehensive strategic cooperative partnership. High-level meetings are maintained in various forms, which help in increasing political trust, promoting cooperation and creating conditions to gradually resolve disputes and differences. A number of agreements and cooperation documents have been signed to set up the legal basis for a long-term partnership.

The cooperation between the two states has also been strengthened by the exchange of delegations and Party committees, and the organization of seminars on Party theories. A mechanism of cooperation has been established.

In late 2006, the Steering Committee for the Vietnam-China Bilateral Cooperation (SCBC) was established. The committee meets annually and this has helped in increasing the interaction between key sectors such as diplomacy, security and defense. Cooperation agreements were also implemented between the two Ministries of Foreign Affairs (2002), the Ministries of Public Security (2003) and the Ministries of Defense (2003).

Sino-Vietnam relations are enhanced in many forms under the following mechanisms: the Joint Working Commission of four Vietnamese provinces—Cao Bang, Lang Son, Quang Ninh and Ha Giang—and the bordering Guangxi Zhuang Autonomous Region in China; the Joint Working Groups from the Vietnamese border provinces of Dien Bien, Lai Chau, Lao Cai, Ha Giang and the Chinese province of Yunnan; the Conference to review the cooperation between ministries, sectors and localities in Vietnam and China's Guangdong province; and the Conference on Economic Corridor Cooperation of Vietnam's cities in the provinces of Lao Cai, Hanoi, Hai Phong, Quang Ninh and the city of Kunming in China's Yunnan province. By sheer volume, there is a great deal of linkages going on.

The development of bilateral relations between Vietnam and China, and the signing of the documents by both parties has had an important role in creating a peaceful and stable environment in the region. The late Vietnamese President Tran Dai Quang, speaking at the Leaders' Roundtable Summit at the BRI Forum for International Cooperation in 2017, said that the world was at a turning point. All countries and regions were seeking new and creative approaches to maximize their potential and advantage to exploit scientific and technological achievements while ensuring a peaceful, secure and stable environment for sustainable development. Accordingly, Quang stated that Vietnam welcomed all initiatives of economic integration and regional connection in general and with the BRI in particular. It was willing to cooperate with other countries to study, develop and implement projects for mutual benefit and to meet sustainable development goals. The President emphasized that the cooperation in the BRI framework should be linked to the agenda of the United Nations on sustainable development and the existing regional and global cooperation frameworks. He wanted the BRI to meet the criteria of sustainability, effectiveness and coverage, and to provide a framework to prioritize the practical BRI projects stemming from the development needs of the countries and regions. He emphasized that the BRI should adhere to the Five Principles of Peaceful Coexistence—mutual respect for each other's territorial integrity and sovereignty, mutual non-aggression, mutual non-interference in each other's internal affairs, equality and cooperation for mutual benefit and peaceful coexistence (Trung 2017b).

Regarding the BRI projects in Vietnam, Quang asserted that the country is ready to receive the flow of new investment from high technology projects that already serve as symbols of Chinese expertise. These investments must meet the needs of Vietnam in fields such as infrastructure, mechanics, electronics, pharmaceuticals, supporting industries and high-tech agriculture, among others. Within the scope of long-term cooperation, Vietnam expects Chinese enterprises and investors to pay special attention to environmental protection, employee interests and more active participation in the social aspects of the security of Vietnam (Trung 2017a).

In order to have a long-term vision of planning and developing the synchronous transportation systems under the BRI, international institutions should serve as consultants and play the role of providing the overall assessment to identify the key areas that would attract investments and develop collaborative projects connecting different regions. The cooperation proposals under the framework of the BRI have been continuously accumulated since 2013. For example, in his October 2013 visit to Vietnam, Chinese Prime Minister Li Keqiang agreed to set up three bilateral working groups to promote the cooperation in finance, maritime issues and infrastructure development. Then in 2015, when the General Secretary of the Communist Party of Vietnam Nguyen Phu Trong paid a visit to China, they announced the establishment of the above-mentioned groups. In November 2015, Vietnam's Ministry of Industry and Trade and China's National Development and Reform Commission signed a memorandum on cooperation boosting the production capacity between the two countries.

As such, Vietnam recognized that the BRI needs to be based on the principles of consensus, equality, voluntariness, transparency, openness, mutual respect and mutual benefit. Vietnam defined the motto of cooperation as 'possibility and activeness', intending to promote socio-economic development, protect national sovereignty and interests, and contribute to the general development and stability of the region (Ministry of Foreign Affairs of Vietnam 2012).

Opportunities for Vietnam

Vietnam is an important destination located on the main path of BRI. Along with the development of the comprehensive strategic cooperative partnership, Vietnam and China are now having a discussion on the framework of the BRI. In accordance, Vietnam faces a few opportunities and challenges.

Firstly, Vietnam enjoys the opportunity to develop its trade and invest-ment. Following the BRI, Chinese enterprises and investors in finance, consulting, architecture, energy, water and waste processing, engineering, construction, law, accounting and transportation have actively entered Vietnam to invest in many sectors and to implement the BRI projects. Vietnam, while ensuring its own sustainable development, welcomed the investment flow and created favorable conditions for Chinese enterprises to efficiently and stably do business.

As a result, since 2016, China has been Vietnam's biggest trading part-ner. The number of Chinese people in Vietnam is increasing. Accordingly, Vietnamese and Chinese enterprises have developed economic and trade cooperation zones in An Duong in Hai Phong province and Long Giang in Tien Giang province. They jointly constructed the Bac Luan Bridge connecting Mong Cai in northern Vietnam, to the city of Dongxing in China. They also deployed projects on building cross-border economic cooperation zones in Mong Cai-Dongxing, Dong Dang-Pingxiang, Lao Cai-Hekou and Tra Linh-Longbang. This development is meant to attract investors from both countries to these zones.

In addition to this, Vietnam has actively upgraded, modernized and promoted the construction of important seaports such as Cai Lan, Lach Huyen and Vung Ang, and improved airports such as Noi Bai in Hanoi and Cat Bi in Hai Phong. Major Chinese-investment backed projects are underway, including ones by Texhong Textile Group and Trina Solar. Projects such as the power plant Vinh Tan 1 and Cat Linh-Ha Dong Urban Railway Project rapid transit system in Hanoi are in progress. The development of the border areas and the infrastructure upgrades not only promote Vietnam's participation in the BRI but also help it to connect more effectively with other ASEAN countries.

Secondly, Vietnam can take advantage of the capital sources for infra-structure projects from China's Infrastructure Investment Fund, Silk Road Fund and from banks such as the Export-Import Bank of China and the China Development Bank. Vietnam has developed the Transport Development Strategy in key northern economic areas where most of the traffic routes are linked with the Nanning-Singapore Economic Corridor. Some of the declared projects are:

- Upgrade and expand sections of National Highway 1 into 4 lanes; build new sections of the North-South Highway, the highways in the Vietnam-China "Two Corridors and One Economic Circle" plan, and centripetally oriented highways and belts of Hanoi; upgrade the remaining national highways to the newest technical specifications; connect and upgrade the national highways in the northern belt system; and complete the border patrol road system according to the approved planning schemes.

- Construct the East-West Economic Corridor, and the routes connecting the coast with the Central Highlands and the ports of Vietnam with neighboring countries such as Laos, Thailand and Cambodia.
- Construct highways linking Ho Chi Minh City with important gateways and traffic hubs.
- Upgrade and modernize sections of the North-South railway; explore the construction of new express railways in the "Two Corridors and One Economic Circle" plan and linking the railways to seaports and big economic zones.
- Study the investment for a new 1435-mile railway linking Ho Chi Minh City with Vung Tau and Ho Chi Minh City with Can Tho; study the possibility of restoring the Di An-Loc Ninh railway to connect with the Trans-Asian Railway. (Ministry of Transport 2013, 2–4)

By developing the transport infrastructure, Vietnam will meet its society's increased demands and create the premise for socio-economic development, and defense and security maintenance—resulting in the industrialization and modernization of the state. In fact, after the connecting highways from Hekou to Kunming and from Lao Cai to Hanoi were launched, the total trade between China and Vietnam through these two gateways soared. This shows that the prospects of transport development in Vietnam strongly increase trade cooperation between the two countries and complement the initiative to build the cross-border economic cooperation zone.

Thirdly, Vietnam can attract more Chinese tourists. China has been promoting the opening of its border cities of Pingxiang, Dongxing and Chongzuo in the Guangxi economic zone. Meanwhile, Vietnam has also constructed expressways connecting Hanoi-Lao Cai and Hanoi-Hai Phong. In Lang Son province, the Huu Nghi border gate has been upgraded and expanded. The highways linking Lang Son to Mong Cai and Hanoi have also been completed to facilitate the entrance of people coming in from land routes through China.

In recent years, the number of Chinese tourists traveling to Vietnam has been increasing. Specifically, in the first four months of 2017, there were 4.2 million international visitors of which 1.2 million were Chinese. On average, 3.5 out of 10 tourists were Chinese, 1.7 times higher than Korean tourists who were the second largest group. The year also set the record where the share of Chinese tourists increased by up to 61.1% over the same period when compared to 2016 (Ha 2017).

As for the modes of transportation, air travel remained the most popular with more than 3.5 million people flying into the country—a record increase of 32.6% over the same period in 2016. The number of passengers traveling by sea and land grew by 11% (Ha 2017). Most Chinese visitors entering Vietnam do so through the railway and roads from Mong Cai and Lao Cai border gates (Ha 2017). Besides Hanoi and Ho Chi Minh City, they also fly into the airports in Da Nang and Nha Trang. According to the Vietnam National Administration of Tourism, since the Vietnamese government allowed passenger cars with less than nine seats from China to enter Quang Ninh province, the number of Chinese tourists crossing the Mong Cai border gate has increased sharply (Ha 2017).

Historically, China has always been the main tourist market for Vietnam. There are multiple reasons for the increase of Chinese visitors coming to Vietnam including the growing appeal of Vietnam; the positive outcomes from cooperation among the markets, airlines and locales; and the development of better Sino-Vietnamese ties. All of these factors have given Vietnam an advantage in the tourism sector.

CHALLENGES FOR VIETNAM

However, the strong Chinese push on BRI projects has also posed some challenges and difficulties for Vietnam.

Firstly, the BRI has divided ASEAN, which impacts Vietnam in resolving the disputes in the South China Sea. Regarding the territorial issues in the South China Sea, Vietnam and China penned an Agreement on Basic Principles Guiding the Settlement of Sea-Related Issues between the two parties in 2011, as a fundamental step toward eventually solving the dispute. Accordingly, they both agreed to peacefully settle the issue on the basis of international law, the United Nations Convention on the Law of the Sea 1982 and the Declaration on Conduct of the Parties in the South China Sea (DOC). They set up a specialist-level negotiation mechanism for the area off the mouth of the Gulf of Tonkin and another negotiation mechanism for cooperation in less-sensitive maritime areas. In addition, Vietnam, as a member of ASEAN, is expected to take advantage of this diplomatic channel to promote negotiations with China on the development of the Code of Conduct in the South China Sea.

However, China is also a factor that fragments ASEAN countries. China enhances its influence in ASEAN countries through economic cooperation and the BRI framework—making participating states more dependent on China. Since 2013, China has accelerated the implementation of the BRI in the ASEAN region. Accordingly, China together with the Asian Development Bank has actively consulted ASEAN on adjusting the content of the cooperation, strengthening the mechanism of economic cooperation, and by holding Sino-ASEAN summits to discuss these issues. The China-Indochina Peninsula Economic Corridor envisions connecting Nanjing-Hanoi-Vientiane-Ho Chi Minh-Phnom Penh-Bangkok-Kuala Lumpur-Singapore into a 3000-km-long network made up of a system of railways and highways. The rail network theoretically integrates the trans-Asia railway connecting Singapore, Malaysia, Thailand, Cambodia, Vietnam and China. Likewise, the projected Kunming-Singapore railway also traverses parts of continental ASEAN.

In addition, China proposed and then set up the Asian Infrastructure Investment Bank (AIIB) with the participation of many countries in 2014. ASEAN member states such as Laos, Cambodia, Thailand and Malaysia have actively cooperated with China in infrastructure projects, especially those on transportation. In 2013, China became ASEAN's largest trading partner, making up 14% of total ASEAN trade (Foreign Investment Agency 2015). However, the dependence of ASEAN countries on China for export and import markets varies. While the richer countries, such as Brunei and Singapore, tend to diversify their trading partners, the poorer countries depend heavily on China, particularly in terms of import. The share of Vietnam's imports and exports to China has increased rapidly over the past few years while Singapore's share has declined in comparison to the whole bloc.

This shows that China wants to use this framework to promote bilateral economic cooperation with individual ASEAN countries while increasing its orbit of influence. By the time China became an important investor in Cambodia, the latter's stance on the South China Sea issue had turned in China's favor. Countries such as Laos and Thailand remain neutral by neither supporting China nor becoming a claimant ASEAN state. In recent years, it has become difficult for ASEAN to reach any consensus in making a joint statement regarding the South China Sea issue. This stems from the individual states' concerns about affecting their bilateral ties with the much more powerful China. This negatively impacts any attempt by Vietnam to mobilize the support of the ASEAN community to pressure China on the South China Sea issue.

Secondly, China's request to the UNESCO to recognize the Silk Road as a heritage site is an obstacle to Vietnam. Although the Silk Road has not been used as an official route for centuries, China is still campaigning for its World Heritage status. In 2008, China identified 48 points along the Silk Road as important landmarks (BBC 2015). Reports from China confirmed that their heritage agencies had conducted archaeological investigations in the Paracel Islands and expanded comparable efforts to the south at the Spratly Islands. This raises the concerns that China might use the Maritime Silk Road as a way of reaffirming its presence in the region like before, and allowing it to enhance its presence and claims in the South China Sea. While Chinese policymakers rush to develop a detailed plan for the Maritime Silk Road, it may be more helpful for them to address the concerns of the region rather than continue avoiding the latter issue.

The restoration of the Maritime Silk Road should be perceived through the overall strategies of covering the South China Sea with Chinese sovereignty and extending China's influence. Shortly after the end of the Gulf of Tonkin negotiations with Vietnam in 2000, China called for the establishment of the Tonkin Gulf Economic Belt as part of the cooperation program on 'two corridors, one economic belt'. The scope of this belt consists of three cities of Guangxi province (Beihai, Qinzhou, Fangchenggang), one city of Guangdong Province (Zhanjiang), Hainan Island of China and ten provinces and cities of Vietnam (Quang Ninh, Hai Phong, Thai Binh, Nam Dinh, Ninh Binh, Thanh Hoa, Nghe An, Ha Tinh, Quang Binh and Quang Tri). The contents of cooperation include trade, investment, maritime economics, tourism and environmental protection. Obviously, the idea of this Maritime Silk Road is not just about the registration of a world heritage site. It is, instead, aimed at creating a new economic belt on the west coast of the Pacific to rival America's now-stalled initiative of Trans-Pacific Partnership (TPP) and its strategy of rotating the Asian axis.

In an extended strategic imagination, the BRI is the performance of Chinese soft power rather than a purely instrumental initiative of economic linking and integration. Accordingly, China's powers of economics and connectivity push the other countries in the world to revolve around its axis and create the circulation of goods, services and trade around a Chinese pole. The initiative of superimposing the Silk Road design on the

South China Sea is shrewdly a push to codify Beijing's controversial 'nine dash line' maritime claims in the various national documents and registering it at various international organizations and international forums. The maritime Silk Road must thus be viewed as an adjunct to China's assorted activities of harassment and exploration along the 'nine dash line' boundary to impose its ownership and management over the South China Sea.

Conclusion

In summary, the promotion of the BRI is a systematic program that adheres, on the surface, to the principles of mutual discussion, mutual development and mutual benefit, in tandem with the developmental strategies of the countries along the BRI. As it continues to develop, the ancient Silk Road should be designed as the means of helping the countries of Asia, Europe and Africa to become more closely connected for their mutual benefit—the herald of a new historical period. However, Vietnam will continue to harbor some reservations about Chinese intentions the longer the South China Sea dispute is not resolved and Beijing is suspected of adopting the BRI as a cover for eroding rival claims over the contested islands.

References

BBC. 2015. Xi'an Through the Senses. http://www.bbc.com/travel/bespoke/specials/xian-through-the-senses/silk-road.html.

Foreign Investment Agency. 2015. Một số đặc điểm về đầu tư thương mại giữa Trung Quốc và các nước ASEAN *(Some Characteristics of Investment and Trade Between China and ASEAN Countries)*, July 22. http://fia.mpi.gov.vn/tinbai/3547/Mot-so-dac-diem-ve-dau-tu-thuong-mai-giua-Trung-Quoc-va-cac-nuoc-ASEAN.

Ha, Trang. 2017. Khách Trung Quốc đến Việt Nam du lịch tăng kỷ lục *(Chinese Tourists Visit Vietnam in Record-Breaking Numbers)*. Dulich.dantri.com.vn, April 27. http://dulich.dantri.com.vn/du-lich/khach-trung-quoc-den-viet-nam-du-lich-tang-ky-luc-20170427133435803.htm.

Ministry of Foreign Affairs of Vietnam. 2012. Báo cáo tình hình triển khai tham gia của Việt Nam trong khuôn khổ sáng kiến 'Một trục, hai cánh' *(Report on Vietnam's Participation in the Framework of 'One Axis, Two Wings' Initiative)*. Documents for internal usage.

Ministry of Transport. 2013. Quyết định số 355/QĐ-TTg Về việc phê duyệt điều chỉnh Chiến lược phát triển giao thông vận tải Việt Nam đến năm

2020, tầm nhìn đến năm 2030 *(Decision no. 355/QD-TTg by Ratifying the Approval of Transport Development Strategy of Vietnam by 2020, with a Vision Towards 2030)*, February 25. http://mt.gov.vn/vn/Pages/ChiTietVanBan. aspx?vID=24040&TypeVB=1.

Trong, Nghia. 2017. Vành đai và Con đường – tham vọng dần thành hiện thực của Trung Quốc *(BRI – China's Ambition Becomes a Reality)*. *Vnexpress.net*, May 15. https://vnexpress.net/tin-tuc/the-gioi/phan-tich/vanh-dai-va-con-duong-tham-vong-dan-thanh-hien-thuc-cua-trung-quoc-3584243.html.

Trung, Quynh. 2017a. Chủ tịch nước: Việt Nam hoanh nghênh dòng đầu tư mới từ Trung Quốc *(President: Vietnam Welcomes New Investment Flows from China)*. *tuoitre.vn*, May 12. http://tuoitre.vn/chu-tich-nuoc-viet-nam-hoan-nghenh-dong-dau-tu-moi-tu-trung-quoc-1313124.htm.

———. 2017b. Diễn đàn Vành đai và Con đường: hợp tác để cùng thắng *(BRI Forum: Cooperation for Mutual Winning)*. *tuoitre.vn*, May 16. https://tuoitre. vn/dien-dan-vanh-dai-va-con-duong-hop-tac-de-cung-thang-1315008.htm.

CHAPTER 14

Conclusion

Alan Chong

In many ways, critical analysis of China's proposition of the Belt and Road Initiative (BRI) (or in its earlier moniker, OBOR) brings a sense of déjà vu from China's incipient inroads into the Third World during the Cold War. In the 1960s, Beijing had for instance developed a detailed Africa strategy that preached an all-encompassing solidarity amongst the non-white populations of the world (Cooley 1965, pp. 3–7). This was directed at goading all formerly colonial territories towards adopting a communist Chinese view that the future was destined to be revolutionary, socialist and anti-western. With the BRI (or OBOR), China's new pan-global vision has lost its anti-western, revolutionary and socialist stridency even if Beijing intends to challenge the western centrism of the current Liberal world order in economics and politics. Back in the 1960s, the competition to aid many developing states operated much in their favour as this excerpt from John Cooley's Cold War-Era study shows in explaining the reactions from the great powers triggered by the Somali foreign minister's claim that he accepted Soviet military aid simply because it was more generous than the western offers and that he practised 'strict non-alignment', circa 1964–5:

A. Chong (✉)
Centre for Multilateralism Studies, S. Rajaratnam School of International Studies, Nanyang Technological University, Singapore, Singapore
e-mail: iscschong@ntu.edu.sg

© The Author(s) 2020
A. Chong, Q. M. Pham (eds.), *Critical Reflections on China's Belt & Road Initiative*, https://doi.org/10.1007/978-981-13-2098-9_14

This launched the aid race in earnest. The United States offered to build fishing boats, donated three DC-3s to the infant Somali airline, and provided teacher training and construction work at the port of Chisimaio. Italy supplied an airline staff, and price supports for Somali bananas. Russia sent doctors, agricultural machinery and small industrial and food processing plants. Red China, after [Somali Prime Minister] Dr Shirmarke's trip, promised another US$17 million for future development projects. Rice is an increasingly popular crop and food among the Somalis, and after experiments at Merca in growing the same kind of rice that has been successfully grown in Tanganyika, the government decided to build a new series of state farms, using army help. One of them was a large rice farm about twenty-five miles from Mogadishu, run along the lines taught the Somalis by the Chinese. To compete with this, the United States aid mission gave some advice on techniques of bread making, grain cultivation and soil conservation. United States and Italian oilmen investigated promising petroleum possibilities near Merca. The West Germans built a road, and the European Economic Community financed another. And so the competition went on. The Somali economy profited and showed real progress by 1965. (Cooley 1965, p. 33)

In the era of the BRI, China is no longer the underdog. Its vision of large-scale infrastructure projects and the construction of transportation facilities connecting diverse locations along the path of the ancient landed and maritime Silk Roads promises qualitative development to the non-West. This is moreover occurring at a moment when the western power centres in Washington, DC, London, Paris, Berlin and Rome are either inward-oriented in their politics or experiencing significant economic disenchantment caused by misguided welfare and fiscal policies. These traditional aid donors are also recalibrating their policies following their decades of inability to stem the migration of people from the Global South to their shores in search of sustainable economic livelihood and physical safety from crime, political persecution and genocide. In many ways, 'aided' development according to western norms seems unproductive, and in Africa's case, economic improvement has not materialized fast enough for much of its population. Along with the turmoil unleashed by the aftermath of the Arab Spring in the Middle East, the stymied condition of African development has indubitably fed into the refugee exodus across the Mediterranean into Europe. Amidst this rumination on the déjà vu of Chinese developmental policies, we have refracted their salient issues upon themes such as 'empire', discussion of what development means, and the idea of intra-Global South discussions about how 'solidarity' can be achieved between the Middle East, Africa and Asia. By extrapolation from the point about solidarity, it is also plausible to speculate that the BRI opens up dialogical possibilities between Asia and the Middle East, and just as importantly, between China and the rest of Asia, and *between the subregions* of Asia.

This volume has not been the most perfect critique of China's BRI. Understandably, being the product of a workshop assembled with some funding urgency, some chapters were converted from policy-oriented papers, others from empirical readings of trends in China's influence in other states' domestic political economy—for instance in Iran, Saudi Arabia and Australia—as well as the socio-economic implications of railway developments along the landed Silk Road. A few chapters were written from the start with a normative angle to ponder how the vision of the BRI is an open invitation for Asian intellectuals to revisit the idea of harmony and inter-religious, intercultural dialogue across Asia, within Asia and reviving the accommodative spirit of traders and missionaries along the ancient Silk Roads. A number of chapters have also raised the spectre of China's own colonial enterprise under the banner of the BRI by making reference to Chinese imperial history and its often difficult relations with its neighbours and economic partners. Given such diversity, this book is more of an appetizer in the inevitably long train of books to come about the twenty-first-century revival of the ancient Silk Road. It has been critical insofar as it has treated the BRI as a notion that transcends simple ideas of development and the currently tiresome charge of China's colonial feats in the name of great power aspirations. In closing, it is possible to highlight three themes that the assorted chapters in this book have alluded to for further research and debate.

EMPIRE

Several of the chapters, especially the one by Trinh van Dinh, highlighted the possibilities of a new Chinese empire arising under the guise of BRI/OBOR. The original name, One Belt, One Road, signalled the holistic territoriality and ideological domination one might expect from empires in the nineteenth and early twentieth centuries. These empires assumed their shape and longevity by controlling the physical assets of land, labour and capital, and in this era of information technology, even the mastery of digital formats if the current collision course between Beijing and

Washington over '5G' telecommunications is anything to go by. The Belt and Road infrastructure building frenzy fits this narrative almost completely. Frequent reports in the world's major newspapers painted the picture of a rising, populous Chinese superpower exporting its own workers and technical know-how in a self-serving manner in the name of building bigger and better for foreign countries. Moreover, many of these overseas Chinese workers scarcely ventured beyond their social and urban enclaves beyond Chinese shores. They worked tirelessly, shopped mostly at stores operated by, or were affiliated to, their compatriots, and dined on Chinese cuisine delivered by chefs from their homeland. Moreover, there were widespread complaints that the locals were hardly involved in skill transfers through sponsored education or on-the-job training. It seemed as though Beijing had merely followed the template of the nineteenth-century European empires in recycling underused national capital in distant Global South economies to earn incomes for imported Chinese workers (Mayer 2018; Maçães 2019). All this was purportedly done to solve Beijing's domestic mismatch between rising expectations and the failure to sustain job creation. This reprise of empire is summarized in the colourful description of a *New York Times* report in 2017:

> The Chinese migrants who have gone out into the world, the risk-takers who have found spots in Asia, Latin America and Africa, are as diverse as China itself: young and middle-aged, unschooled and highly educated, working for private companies and state-owned enterprises—and even for themselves. They are not a monolith. And yet, in these far-off places, they are connected to one another in a way that they never could be back home in a land of 1.4 billion people. It's not just the shared food, culture or language—or the solidarity that comes from being thrown together in a harsh environment. What binds these individuals together is an abiding belief that their presence overseas is making China better and stronger. This shared conviction, as much as the state that has nurtured it, is what makes China a colossus, a nation that can be seen by others, in the same instant, as a blessing and a curse. (Larmer 2017)

Indeed, one has to ponder how much of the BRI is a blessing for the future on the Global South, or little more than a reprise of imperial history from several centuries ago.

DEVELOPMENT

In many ways, China's BRI vision of building bigger and better is not new. Its parallel promises to deliver education, jobs and technology to the less developed is a tried and tested formula exhibited in the 'tiger economies' of East Asia and some modern economies in Latin America. There is the assumption that if Beijing builds infrastructure, businesses will come and the locals will prosper. To the extent that Chinese state-owned enterprises can jumpstart the promise of the special export zones beside Sri Lanka's brand new Hambantota port, the standard complaint against the 'debt trap' diplomacy of Beijing will evaporate eventually. Likewise, the massive construction of dry ports, seaports, roads and railways in Central Asia, the China-Pakistan Economic Corridor and Cambodia will be much anticipated to provide some kind of economic boost to the local economies through a multiplier effect via investments in manufacturing and export industries. However, what remains reassuring and worrying at the same time is China's politically flexible attitude towards making loans to the Global South partners under the BRI rubric. Between 2018 and 2019, Malaysian premier Mahathir Mohamad successfully renegotiated several railway and housing projects funded by Chinese capital following the downfall of his predecessor due to 'corrupt' deals he struck with assorted foreign investors. Likewise, both Bangkok and Jakarta have driven tough bargains with Beijing over the funding of their high-speed railway projects and have decided to parcel out some projects to their Japanese rivals to maintain a semblance of political and economic 'balance' (Wu and Chong 2018). In the same spirit, Mongolia is striving to attract foreign investment from all directions while praising China for being willing to accommodate their concerns over loan repayment terms. The jury on the Chinese path of development under the BRI remains out as far as this volume can discern. But it is quite clear from most of the chapters in political economy and the national perspectives that Beijing continually faces a legitimacy test in the BRI's development 'model': is it willing to empathize with local concerns and concede some control of projects to the local partner? (Breslin 2013)

INTRA-ASIAN DIALOGUE ON INTERNATIONAL
AND INTERSOCIETAL RELATIONS

Finally, unlike many other scholarly works on the BRI to date, this volume ponders the rich possibilities afforded for intra-Asian philosophical and cultural dialogues by the idea of the revival of the ancient landed and maritime Silk Roads. The unusual chapters by Ling and Chong speak of this. Ling, in particular, draws attention to the underlying meanings behind the Chinese rhetoric behind the BRI—mutual gain, harmonious relations and the spirit of 'prosper thy neighbour'. This is not to be regarded as insincere propaganda if one takes political philosophizing seriously. Ling has highlighted that the problem of polarizing values and attitudes will always plague grand projects like the Belt and Road. But in the ancient Silk Roads, the travellers, missionaries and kingdoms resorted to assorted syncretic religions and philosophies to cope with difference. Ling, in particular, drew on the Buddhist-Daoist approach of embracing the spirit of non-duality with duality. In short, to mitigate the gulf of difference over values and points of interests, one has to water down the Westphalian dogma of treating national interests as zero-sum conceptions; the 'Silk Road spirit' has to embrace inclusiveness and some degree of give and take. Theoretically, half the chapters in this volume do not agree with this approach, but such disagreement is also productive of debate about power and its relationship with the respect for identity and difference along the revived Silk Roads.

In his reading of premodern and early modern travellers' accounts of the landed Silk Roads, Chong, in turn, identifies what he terms a culture of 'mercantile harmony'. This concept captures the idea of harmony between peoples and individual elite rulers rather than states. Moreover, this is a harmony based on empathy and the happenstance of spiritual revelation. On a third level, this harmony is 'mercantile', or trade-like and merchant-like, in the sense that interlocutors exchange ideas and admiration on the basis of perceived relative advantages. In a fourth sense, mercantile harmony is the solidarity forged amongst fellow travellers on the road. They could be pilgrims, traders, religious persons, owners of hospitality premises, itinerant workers or diplomats. To varying degrees of distinctions, all travellers need to brave the capricious weather, the prospect of drought, shortage of food, attacks by wild animals and bandits, and the possibility of being treated as belligerents amidst warring conditions. Enlightened travellers develop a healthy reciprocal relationship with the political authorities controlling cities, towns, monasteries and agricultural lands straddling the Silk Roads. Surely, between Ling and Chong's chapters, there are some tangible contributions to the growing enterprise of building non-western, Asian international theory drawn from ancient philosophies on the ground. In sum, the critical reflections on the Belt and Road must continue through many more scholarly sequels to this volume. It manifests the revival of the Silk Roads, with modern mind-sets, developmental aspirations, communitarian ideas and technologies added to the mix. This is a matter of urgency for one is essentially also trying to understand the complexity of new ways of forging global relations amongst states and ordinary human beings.

References

Breslin, S. 2013. China and the South: Objectives, Actors and Interactions. *Development and Change* 44 (6): 1273–1294.

Cooley, J.K. 1965. *East Wind over Africa: Red China's African Offensive*. New York: Walker and Company.

Larmer, B. 2017. Is China the World's New Colonial Power? *New York Times International Edition*, May 2.

Maçães, B. 2019. *Belt and Road: A Chinese World Order*. Oxford: Oxford University Press.

Mayer, M. 2018. China's Rise as Eurasian Power: The Revival of the Silk Road and Its Consequences. In *Rethinking the Silk Road: China's Belt and Road Initiative and Emerging Eurasian Relations*, ed. M. Mayer, 1–42. Singapore: Palgrave Macmillan.

Wu, S.-s., and A. Chong. 2018. Developmental Railpolitics: The Political Economy of China's High-Speed Rail Projects in Thailand and Indonesia. *Contemporary Southeast Asia* 40 (3): 503–526.

INDEX[1]

---

[1] Note: Page numbers followed by 'n' refer to notes.

© The Author(s) 2020
A. Chong, Q. M. Pham (eds.), *Critical Reflections on China's Belt & Road Initiative*, https://doi.org/10.1007/978-981-13-2098-9